DAVID P.

STIRRED
BY THE
Almighty

MODERN-DAY PSALMS
for the
HUNGRY HEART

Copyright © 2015 David P. Wasmundt

The moral right of the author has been asserted.

All rights reserved.

No part of this publication may be reproduced, stored in a retrieval system, or transmitted, in any form or by any means, without the prior permission in writing of the publisher, nor be otherwise circulated in any form of binding or cover other than that in which it is published and without a similar condition including this condition being imposed on the subsequent purchaser.

Published by Exalted Worship Publishing
Dallas, OR 97338
exaltedworship.com

Printed by Gorham Printing
Centralia, WA 98531

Cover design by Adazing.com

Library of Congress Control Number: 2015901910

ISBN: 978-0-9864072-0-8

Typesetting services by BOOKOW.COM

Stirred By The Almighty

The Goff family,

Let the blessings of the Almighty flow through you.

David P. Wasmundt

Acknowledgments

When a work of any magnitude is put into words, one should always acknowledge its source of input and outflow, inspiration, and urgings.

Recently I read a short story from a book titled "The One Year Christian History" authored by E. Michael and Sharon Rusten. It briefly told the life story of Richard Baxter – a passionate Puritan preacher and a prolific author. As he lay there in his final hours he praised and blessed God for His peace. *"When his friends reminded him of the encouragement and comfort his books [more than 160] had been to others, he replied with humility, 'I was but a pen in the hand of God. What praise is due a pen?'"* It is with this statement I find much kinship for I have always credited the Holy Spirit as the author, and I am merely the scribe. He has allowed me to speak His words through my persona.

My loving and faithful wife Barbara deserves accolades for always having been available throughout this project – whenever a need has arisen she has served not only as a sounding board but has been a continual source of encouragement and prayer. I have depended greatly upon her for moral support and also as proofreader extraordinaire.

Milton Tuck (my brother in the Lord) was certainly a catalyst and instigator for these writings, besides being a godly mentor and faithful supporter and encourager. When this project began it was two friends encouraging each other and was never intended for publishing. Then it morphed into an outpouring of a heart desperately in love with Jesus. Thank you Milton for your ardent support and the sharing of your vision.

One of my biggest supporters and non-stop allies is Wilma Barker who has never failed to have a smile and kind words. She is a huge prayer warrior, and God has special rewards for these saints.

A great big pat on the back for those who were my test subjects or more commonly known as guinea pigs. They received weekly emails of 5 Psalms for the number of weeks it took to complete the Psalms in this book. My gratitude goes to the following for their support, feedback, and counsel: Clarence & Wilma B., Carol G., Cynthia B., Dewayne T., Don & Helen W., Jeff A., John & Cleo J., Kirk B., Lonelle A., Jeff R., Pat W., Roy D., Sharon B., Ted G., & Theresa F. This core group consisted of true friends and boosters who became my cohorts. Thank you all!

I could not neglect to extend my deepest thanks to my editor Donna Ferrier for her excellence and hours of feedback. Whether by phone or email she was always available for questions, corrections, or advice. Thank you Donna, for being ready, willing, and able to go the second mile. Anyone needing a first class editor should check out www.donnaferrier.com.

A hearty debt of gratitude goes to Steve Passiouras, owner & typesetter of bookow – painless print & e-book formatting. Thanks for having the patience of Job and the excellency of your work: it truly speaks for itself. Check out his work at www.bookow.com.

Introduction

Does the Lord still speak to hungry hearts, or has His voice grown silent with the culmination of scripture?

Allow this book to be an inspiration to your searching heart and the Spirit of the Almighty will give you a definitive answer to this question.

As the breeze refreshes all in its path, so the Lord stirs all who seek after Him. Amos 4:13 (NLT) so aptly states we are recipients of His thoughts:

> "For the LORD is the one who shaped the mountains,
> stirs up the winds, and reveals his thoughts to mankind.
> He turns the light of dawn into darkness
> and treads on the heights of the earth.
> The LORD God of Heaven's Armies is his name!"

This book was born out of a desire to pursue God with total abandonment. In it you will learn to face your struggles as your soul is swept clean and you emerge triumphant. Its words are inspired from on high and not from human wisdom – it will speak truth to your innermost parts if you so allow.

The 222 psalms contained in this book are original, fresh, and speak to present-day areas of all walks of life. Although this volume is in no way an overnight read, you can sit and read it daily as you drink your coffee or tea and enjoy edifying and uplifting moments throughout the year.

Has the elusiveness of knowing Him in deeper ways plagued you? Then travel with me on this journey and you will be stirred by the Almighty and see glimpses of His glory. You will excitedly explore each and every psalm to hear what the Spirit is saying. And what He says to you will be totally different than what He says to your neighbor.

Contents

1. Searching for You 1
2. Sharing the Joy of Your Light 2
3. You Saved Me From Myself 3
4. I Bring You All of Me 4
5. Your Strength Gives Me Courage 5
6. Your Salvation Overflows All Around Me 7
7. You Cause Sweet Melodies To Flow From Me 8
8. The Bitter Cup 11
9. You Saturate Me With Honor 12
10. You Order The Steps Of My Journey 13
11. You Keep My Heart Clean 15
12. You Are Rich Beyond Measure 17
13. You Quiet My Yearning Soul 18
14. The Lord Our Provider And Salvation 19
15. Chosen, Favored, and Blessed 20
16. Cherish Your Time With Him 22
17. He is Still God When the Brook Dries Up! 25
18. O Great America – How You Have Fallen! 26
19. You Purchased My Healing 28
20. Listen Earnestly for His Voice 29
21. Your Amazing Strength Covers My Weaknesses 31
22. You Breathe In Me Wisdom And Power 32
23. You Set Me Free When I Abandon All 33
24. The Joy Of Knowing You Brings Peace and Quiet Assurance 34
25. Worship In The House Of The Lord 35
26. Praise For Your Unfailing Love 37
27. I Sing Your Praises For Another Day 39
28. You Are A Safe Haven For My Thoughts 40
29. You Are The Commander In Chief 42

30. A Plea For This Land I Love 43
31. You Are Always Listening For My Call 46
32. My Heart Beats Strong For You 47
33. Laid Bare, I Will Praise You 48
34. Rising In Humility, I Run To You 50
35. Saints Of All The Ages Will Praise You 52
36. Your Word Is The Lifeblood Of My Spirit 53
37. Your Spirit And Mine Unite 56
38. Open The Eyes Of America 59
39. In The Presence Of The King 60
40. You Give Joy To My Daily Life 61
41. Shaped Into His Image 64
42. I Need To Know You Intimately 66
43. You Fill Me Up 67
44. You Fill Me With Pleasures Unending 69
45. Your Presence Is My Home 71
46. You Created Everything From Nothing 72
47. You Establish Your House Upon The Prayers Of The Saints 74
48. He Chooses My Path And I Follow 75
49. He Speaks Peace To My Turbulence 77
50. Your Sleep Rejuvenates Me 79
51. Your Word Intervenes In My Heart 80
52. I Have Eagerly Answered Your Call 82
53. You Breathe New Life Into Me 84
54. Your Creation Is Immense 85
55. Your Seal Of Approval Is On My Heart 87
56. Your New Life Is Contagious Joy 89
57. My Sacrifice of Love To You 91
58. Your Word Purifies The Heart 92
59. You Replace Sin With Celebration 94
60. Your Spirit Is As Fresh As The Early Morning Sunrise . . . 96
61. The Mantle Of Your Voice Gives Me Guidance 98

62. You Give Me Strength And Success 100
63. Will His Mission Be Yours? 101
64. I Am Life and Everlasting Glory 103
65. The Love Of God – How Incredible 105
66. I Trust You No Matter What 106
67. Your Light Shines Brightly Through Me 108
68. You Join Us All Together .109
69. You Have Given Me Your Gifts 111
70. His Love Revealed 114
71. For Mom & Dad 117
72. His Mercies Refresh The Weary 118
73. I Am That Drifter.... 120
74. Your Greatness Overwhelms Me 122
75. Swallowed By His Purpose 123
76. Thoughts Of You Are All I Desire 124
77. Exposed Weakness = Judgment 126
78. Your Word Exists For All 127
79. You Fill Godly Hearts 129
80. God's Word Answers All 130
81. You Are My Secret Place 132
82. I Will Go All-Out For You 134
83. Your Righteous Ones Are Light To The World 136
84. Each Day You Are My Praise 137
85. When The Heart Of God Invades A Man... 140
86. A Life Destined To Glorify His Greatness 141
87. He Lives For You And Me 142
88. A psalm for Anna 144
89. Your Face Is All I Need To See 145
90. Made In Your Image 147
91. Stir Me Until I Am Changed 149
92. In The Secret Place – He Is There 151
93. His Ways Are Mysterious 153

94. Surrender Your Worship 155
95. You Bring Forth A Song Of Praise 157
96. Your Praises Dance! 158
97. A Martyr's Testimony 160
98. Worship All His Fullness 161
99. Yes, Lord, I Am Yours 163
100. Your Justice Upon America…Foretold 167
101. My Soul Is Covered By Your Glory 169
102. My Afflictions – For Your Glory 171
103. I Have Beheld Your Love 174
104. I Will Praise You All Of My Days 176
105. Let Praises Ring Out For Our King! 177
106. His Favor Rests Upon Those Who Praise 180
107. Your Wisdom Gives Life To Those Who Listen 180
108. He Supports My Life 182
109. He Is The God Of All Tomorrows 185
110. Walk The Path Of Righteousness For His Glory 187
111. He Awaits Your Praise! 188
112. No One Knows The Day Or The Hour… 190
113. You Give Grace To The Humble 191
114. The Depths Of My Soul Are Stirred 192
115. My Desire = Your Good Pleasure 194
116. My Soul Sings You A Love Song 196
117. How Big Do You Believe I Am? 197
118. My Judgment Upon The Nations 198
119. All Creation Sees And Hears His Majesty 199
120. Down That Road Of Unending Praise 202
121. My Heart Gladly Welcomes You 204
122. Test Me…And I Will Come Forth In Shining Splendor . .205
123. Who Can Behold The Light Of His Glory? 206
124. Salvation Comes To Those Who Seek You 208
125. You Bring The Hidden Ones Into The Light 209

126. His Blessings Are New Every Morning 210
127. The Godly Will Shine 212
128. You Deserve Our Very Best 214
129. Your Love Surrounds Me 216
130. A Passionate Heart Is Above All 217
131. Take Charge Of My Thoughts, O God 219
132. I Will Glory In Your Power 220
133. Hope For Our Helplessness 222
134. You Guide Our Days 'Til Eternity 223
135. He Is Pleased With A Sincere Offering 225
136. You Speak Boldly In The Quietness Of My Soul 226
137. You Have Written Your Love Upon My Heart 228
138. His Continual Presence Becomes My Pledge 230
139. If I Should Die Before I Wake... 232
140. The Tenets Of Godly Wisdom 232
141. You Fill My Temple With Glory 235
142. The Heavenlies Testify To Your Truth 237
143. My Soul Worships You In The Safety Of Your Arms 239
144. You Are My Father 241
145. Thank You For My Sufferings 242
146. Remind Us Of Your Awesome Power, O God 243
147. Your Light In Our Hearts Shines Through Our Worship .244
148. Follow Me Into Life Everlasting 246
149. You Honor The Prayers Of A Sincere Heart 248
150. Walking The Highways Of God 250
151. The Nearness Of His Presence 251
152. The Voice Of God Made Plain – Can You Hear It? 252
153. The Lord's Presence Fills My Home 254
154. His Glory Lights The Way 255
155. Unseen Victories Are Yet To Come 256
156. Praise Him With Your Measure Of Life 257
157. We Are His Light To The Nations 259

158. A psalm for Dot & Jerry 260
159. Call Upon Him And Receive His Favor 261
160. Usher Me Into Your Holy Presence 262
161. Your Faithfulness Is Witness Of Your Perfection 264
162. A psalm for Mary M .265
163. I'm Giving You My All 267
164. I Praise You For Who You Are 267
165. You Even Change The Thoughts Of The Heart 269
166. My Soul Is Complete Under Your Rest 271
167. Each Life Has A Story To Tell 272
168. He Surrounds Me With High Walls So I Am Safe 275
169. His Abiding Presence Covers All 276
170. Your Light Brings Beauty To My Soul 278
171. Your Love Shows Us The Pathway Of Peace 279
172. Wherever I Am, You Are There 281
173. You Are Fully Attentive To Our Worship 282
174. As For Me – I Will Praise Him 284
175. His Wisdom Comes To Those Who Seek Her 286
176. The Breath Of God Sustains Me 287
177. Build Our Cities On Your Salvation 288
178. Catch Sight Of His Form And Be Blessed 290
179. Your Love Covers All Mankind 293
180. Unending Praise For His Majesty 295
181. Trust In The Lord Brings Peace 297
182. Let His Love Set You Free 298
183. Physical Strength Is For A Season – His Power Is Forever .299
184. He Will Set Your Heart Free 301
185. He Has Bid Me Come Closer – How Can I Do Less? 303
186. You Are So Worthy Of My Praise 304
187. Entertain The Glory Of The Lord Daily 306
188. You Are The Keeper Of My Heart 308
189. I Will Follow Your Voice Down The Narrow Path 310

190. You Do Your Will Through Thankful Hearts 311
191. Fresh Praises Prevail Against A Faded Mind 313
192. A Faithful Walk Brings His Rewards 314
193. I Will Praise You While Looking Mortality In The Eye. . .316
194. Your Majesty Is Inescapable 317
195. I Will Bring Forth Your Beauty In Due Season 319
196. Cradled In His Holy Hush 321
197. Behold, I Come Quickly… 322
198. What Is Too Great A Sacrifice? 323
199. See Him For Who He Is 324
200. He Is My Story 326
201. He Takes The Barren To New Heights 327
202. The Earnest And Sincere Heart Will See God 328
203. His Grace Can Heal Any Disease 329
204. Bow Before Him Today Like There Is No Tomorrow . . .330
205. He Reveals Himself To The Passionate Soul 332
206. The Word Of Our God Stands Forever 333
207. Peace In The Midst Of Despair 335
208. You Are The Desire Of My Heart 336
209. The Yielded Spirit Stands Triumphant Before God 338
210. Every Day Is A New Day With Him 339
211. For Lonnie & Linda .341
212. Sacrifices Of Praise Draw Us Closer To Him 342
213. There Awaits Your Heart's Desire 344
214. Let His Wisdom Forge New Paths 345
215. He Dwells In The Secret Place 347
216. Intimacy Brings Almighty Blessing 349
217. Rejoice In The Mile Markers He Places Along The Way . .351
218. The Marvels Of His Glory 353
219. True Worship Knows No Bounds 354
220. Your Mercies Exceed My Needs 356
221. I Will Praise You Beyond The Final Amen 357
222. His Breath – Is Life .359

Psalm 1

Searching for You

¹I have searched for You, but at times it is merely like trying to see the wind or to grasp a greased pig—a seemingly unattainable prospect.

²As hard as I may try, I am unable to see You with these eyes—yet You allow me to catch microscopic glimpses of Your limitless glory each time I view the rising or setting of the sun.

³My eyes looked to the heavens and I cried—"Where are You, my God?"—I only see the work of Your hands—but You I cannot see.

⁴I look for Your form but it eludes me—O that You might open the eyes of my inner man that I may gaze upon Your beauty.

⁵Since You know my intimate longings and desires, then surely it is no secret to You that what my earthly eyes cannot see—in my heart I will still believe.

⁶What You desire is that I use the eyes of my spirit to guide my steps because when I use the eyes of my flesh, I only fall flat on my face.

⁷I am in awe when I see the works of Your creation praise You—I have witnessed the brook racing downstream—babbling its songs to our God.

⁸When I see the trees waving their arms in praise to You, it stirs a song of joy in my spirit and makes me want to join with them in praise to Your majesty.

⁹I am breathless the moment I gaze upon the vastness of Your universe—I marvel that it was all created by Your spoken word.

¹⁰My mind is crippled whenever I attempt to account for Your might and power and majesty—if I try for more than a moment to reason out Your greatness.

¹¹When I lay down to sleep—I know I have the full assurance and backing of Your promises that You will keep me safe.

¹²Who is it that tucks all the stars and planets into bed—who pulls the covers over them?

¹³It is He who lovingly sings me a lullaby—His angels are ever present watching over me—they are eager to do His bidding—they stand watch while I sleep and cover me with blessings.

¹⁴My life is in Your hands—yet in confidence I know that when I awake I will be with You.

Psalm 2

Sharing the Joy of Your Light

¹When I awoke this morning I said, "Lord!—perhaps You will allow me to share Your light and mercies with a fellow traveler."

²Every day brings a new song of joy with which to bless and praise Your name—the freshness of each melody serves to herald the fulfillment of Your Word.

³O hasten that long-awaited day—when Your Word shall stand complete—when sin and mourning will be rolled away unto everlasting destruction.

⁴Let all His saints rejoice in their redemption—salvation will be their reward.

⁵I give You praise for another opportunity to serve my King—You are my song and my delight—Your praises pour forth from my innermost being.

⁶As water cascades over a falls—so Your praises cascade over my heart—may You be pleased with a heart that is seeking Your favor.

⁷As I concentrate on You it becomes clear—in the same way one would bring a lens into focus—that my delight in You would turn out to be the melody of my song.

⁸I can sing of Your love only as long as You give me breath—my joy does somersaults every time I think of the goodness You show me.

⁹O Lord! I will praise You even in my silence—knowing that You are a beacon of light that shines forth through me, Your vessel.

¹⁰Your Word is nourishment to my soul—how I long to be fed by it—it sustains me in seasons of drought.

¹¹Your Word produces in my heart the same effect as a blacksmith who hones a razor-sharp edge to the chisel he owns.

¹²When a person treasures a valuable, he puts it in a safety deposit box—my heart is that lockbox for Your Word, O God, for I treasure it as my life.

¹³My mind has become shackled like the man being led by a prison guard; O Lord that You would break those restraints so I might be free to worship You.

¹⁴Because of Your joy, even my complaints are turned into songs of praise.

¹⁵O Mighty One—You light my way as the sun brightens the earth at noontime—Your light is more powerful than a match's light in the blackness of a cave.

¹⁶When I stumble as a blind man without his cane—then Your Word becomes my eyes so that I might see truth.

¹⁷I look for You to be there no matter what comes my way—You guide each footstep I take.

¹⁸When the wind howls and the storm rages on, I take shelter under the roof of the Almighty—His Word speaks peace to my heart and calms the storm in me.

Psalm 3

You Saved Me From Myself

¹In despair I saw myself as an item someone had turned in to a lost and found department—I sat on a shelf for quite some time—waiting for my owner to reclaim me.

²I became covered in dust and stained with dirt from the objects nearby—as even more items were placed in front of me—eventually I was shoved to the back.

³Forlorn and with little hope of being discovered—I petitioned the Lord as one might do with a judge—He heard my cry, O praise His name.

⁴The same day my Lord came in and asked for me by name—how that caused my heart to skip a beat.

⁵As the shop owner started digging to the back of the shelf—I felt my pulse beat wildly as he found me in a dark corner.

⁶Slowly he held me up to the light as he dusted me off—"Is this what you were looking for?" he inquired.

⁷You replied, "Yes, he is mine," and I was ecstatic—You took me into Your loving hands, held me close, and caringly embraced me.

⁸You negotiated the redemption price and paid it without batting an eye—the owner was astounded that You would pay so much for such a useless trinket.

⁹Your patience astounds me—You never gave up on me—You were just waiting for me to cry out to You—Your love has made me glad once again.

¹⁰Now I sing with delight—I once was lost but now I'm found—You rescued me from my bondage and pointed me in the way of freedom.

¹¹In You, my Lord, I have put my trust—I shall never be distraught or saddened.

Psalm 4

I Bring You All of Me

¹What do I have to bring You except what You have already blessed me with—is there anything more to offer You but all of me?

²O that You would find a wholesome heart and a desirable spirit residing within me—one that You might be pleased with.

³Lord—I bring everything to You and ask You to take all of me—I simply lay my life with all of its hopes at your feet—all of my dreams and ambitions are Yours, too.

⁴My one desire is You and You alone—there is no other besides You—I leave no room in this heart of mine for any other.

⁵You heard my plea and rolled all my prior failures and disappointments into the farthest parts of the cosmos.

⁶You washed my past clean with Your forgiveness—for that I am eternally indebted to You.

⁷Grant me the ability to set my mind free from its domination to my past—otherwise I will go to my grave with guilt as my covering.

⁸My heart seeks to know You in personal and private fellowship—O that there would be no secret place where I would try to hide from Your view.

⁹Here's my heart—take it now—look inside and see—all I'm longing for is more of You and less of me.

¹⁰A sacrifice is not required but just a heart that's pure—here's my heart, take it Lord, I'm Yours.

¹¹Now I am well aware that You know my thoughts before even one of them comes to mind—so

I humbly ask for Your guidance—then my thinking will be innocent and clean before You.

[12]Consume me Jehovah, with the fire of Your Spirit—in the same manner as when an ember ignites and flames burn an entire forest to the ground.

[13]All that remains in me is praise to my God from whom every blessing flows—I give glory to Your name with a heart of thanksgiving—praise be to the Lord.

[14]The breath of heaven has brought a certain sweetness to my soul—its manna is more luscious than nectar—its taste is divine.

Psalm 5

Your Strength Gives Me Courage

[1]Whenever I am afraid—I look to You and find strength—You cause my fear to subside in a hurry and dissolve my anxieties faster than an antacid tablet dissolves in a glass of water.

[2]Even before I cry out, You hear me because my mind is fixed on You—You tune your ear to my plea.

[3]In my despair I know You are there—You are never far from me—You make my anguish slip away as easily as night fades into early morning.

[4]During the quietness of the dawn You are there—even when darkness wraps her arms around me—You are still there.

[5]My soul waits for You like a lion cub waits impatiently for food from his mother—O how he is filled with excitement at the sight of her from afar.

[6]Encourage my soul, O Most High, and I will find boldness to travel on—You have replaced my timidity with courage.

[7]I invite You to come in—not as one would invite a guest or a stranger—but as a man might invite his close friend or family member.

[8]I find power for my inner man anytime I converse with You—You fill me with potential as Your Word satisfies me.

[9]I listen intently for Your voice—even straining to hear You speak

Psalm 5 - Your Strength Gives Me Courage

to me.

¹⁰Your Spirit washes over me like the waves of the ocean over the seashore and I find refreshing cleansing for the days ahead—blessed be the name of the Lord.

¹¹Encourage my soul for I am weak but You are strong—while I am dismal and wretched, You are a mighty force to contend with—You make me glad that You are my strength.

¹²When I need focus of mind and determination, I just ask myself—who is more stirring than the oceans with their mighty waves and billowing depths?

¹³Who is greater than the mountains that stand so tall and majestic—those stately peaks that tower in the distance—their vastness that causes all to marvel?

¹⁴Who is stronger than the fearsome tornado that sweeps the land with devastation—a windstorm with the power to ravage and wreak havoc on all that comes in its path?

¹⁵Who is more powerful than the great planets that circle our earth—those celestial bodies that make earth look like the period at the end of a sentence?

¹⁶Who is equal to the awesome quaking of the earth as it creaks and groans in agony—as it trembles with holy fear?

¹⁷Who is above the earsplitting and deafening thunder of the storm—who can stand the resounding crack of its noise?

¹⁸Who is capable of such immense power and explosive show of lightning with its blinding flashes of illumination?

¹⁹Who is able to give directions to the waters as they flood the land—those torrents that gouge deep channels into the soil as it is swept out to sea?

²⁰Who is mightier than the universe that defies explanation and clarification—who can provide enlightenment concerning the solar system and its fabrication?

²¹When I reflect and ponder on these breathtaking phenomena, I find myself surrounded in awe and reverence for You, my God.

²²I see no other explanation aside from Your majesty and vastness—I stand in awe of You—Your capabilities are truly frightful and defy human comprehension.

²³The comfort I receive in knowing there is none greater than the One who created all these things is beyond my mortal grasp.

24 Only the Creator is greater than the created object or purpose!

25 I find contentment in knowing there is no other god who is greater than You—what an absolute relief to know that You are my God.

26 There is none like You and You have no equal—each display of your handiwork has pointed this out.

27 What a comfort Your Word has been to me—it has clearly shown that anytime I am afraid, I will be miles ahead by trusting explicitly in You.

28 Apart from Your Holy Spirit I am no different from a filament inside a glass bulb without electricity—You are my source of power and I honor You for that.

29 O praise and glory to the everlasting Lord and God—I will always put my trust in You.

Psalm 6

Your Salvation Overflows All Around Me

1 I am anxious to see how this day unfolds and what You have lined up for me—may I go forth in boldness and confidence.

2 Today I take pleasure in knowing that You are at my side—joy comes my way because every aspect of my day is at Your disposal.

3 You have encircled me with angels of mercy and they guard my life at all times—O praise Your name.

4 You are my God and on a daily basis I seek You—You are my overseer—I search for You like a private eye hunts for a criminal.

5 One thing I ask is strength for today because I realize there is no guarantee of tomorrow.

6 Let those who speak against me be bound up and put into Your prison until they see the error of their ways.

7 I will be blameless as long as You cover me with Your righteousness—unblemished and spotless in Your sight.

8 The assurance of Your Word is as comforting to me as a downy blanket is to a toddler—an oath of promise unto all who believe.

⁹Your blessings overflow in my life like a downpour overflows a rain barrel after a summer storm—Your favor supports me on every side.

¹⁰The flashlight of Your Word illuminates my way with truth and understanding—it provides interpretation as well as clarity of thought.

¹¹My heart is chomping at the bit like a thoroughbred at the Kentucky Downs—it awaits Your arrival on the eastern horizon.

¹²Let my eyes be watching—my ears be listening for Your soon return before I sleep in death.

¹³You bring joy to my heart each time I think of Your superiority—O how Your name rings of excellence—just like the caroling of the bells at Christmastime.

¹⁴You were pleased to believe in me when I didn't believe in myself—for that I will ever praise Your matchless name—that name of unrivaled worth.

¹⁵When I have searched for the time You have forsaken me—each and every occasion I come up empty-handed—for You have never abandoned me.

¹⁶In my diligence I can only recount the many ways You have been there to uphold me—You are my advocate and defender.

¹⁷The saints of the Most High have become intoxicated with joy because You are their mainstay—a support that drives all gloom far from them.

¹⁸To all the peoples of the earth God bestows His good pleasure in abundance.

¹⁹To those who have eyesight He blessed with the beauty of the flowers—He added the delicate scent so that those with no sight might also enjoy His creations.

²⁰He made the loveliness of the birds for those with sight—the sounds of the songbirds for those without.

²¹Come worship Him in His fullness—for by Him and through Him everything is made complete—He has already made the finishing touches, which are awaiting their proper times.

²²His salvation has covered the earth and is readily available to all who choose to accept it—let them call upon His name and appeal unto His mercies daily.

Psalm 7

You Cause Sweet Melodies To Flow From Me

[1] You are my conductor—the maestro of my concert—I need no other.

[2] It is You who brings me scores of music for my heart to play—you invite me to learn transcripts of the heavenly anthems.

[3] Hymns from a heavenly realm have delighted my soul—flooding it with a glorious sense of Your presence—it is always with me.

[4] Your melodies have spoken a new language into my soul—one for which no earthly interpretation is possible.

[5] I listen intently for Your leading—You set the tempo with precise rhythm.

[6] Even when I miss a beat, You are there to get me back on track—You gently correct my inconsistencies and regulate my pace.

[7] Your hand guides me—much like a conductor directing his musicians.

[8] You look at me and nod the go-ahead—I follow Your signal and at Your direction I lead out—I closely watch all of Your gestures, for they indicate Your desires.

[9] I play in tune—I strive to keep my heart in tune with Your ear—it is dead on as I adjust it to the proper pitch.

[10] Others around me listen as I closely follow Your guidance—we are in harmony as a unit and there is no dissonance among us.

[11] Your smile tells us we are in rhythm—we reach the cadence together—our pitch and timbre resonate with Yours.

[12] As we crescendo to the highlight, my heart swells with bliss—I shall never want any other conductor but You.

[13] You have transposed the joy of my heart into beautiful music as I play my instruments for my King.

[14] Music pours out of my piano; You, O God, touch my heartstrings and they ring with joyous reverberation.

[15] The contentment of the Lord erupts in triumph as I lift up my voice to You in praise.

[16] Even my voice, such as it is, belongs to You—let it be a sweet sound in Your ear, for You delight in the tone of my voice!

¹⁷Be pleased, O Lord, with my praise—with my tribute that ushers forth as a pure and holy sacrifice unto You—even as You were with Abel's.

¹⁸The organ plays with a splendid sound as You anoint my fingertips—its magnificence comes only as a result of Your anointing.

¹⁹You cause songs of delight to bubble into a symphony of praise for my King—You lavish on me melodies unbeknownst to man.

²⁰I am privileged to be the conveyor of Your songs—I have become a bearer of glad tidings.

²¹You allow my fingers to dance on the keys as I come into Your courts with thanksgiving.

²²You transpose my praise into different keys as I exalt You with excellence—keep me from becoming obsessed by technicalities so my worship may be pure.

²³You flood the depths of my soul with Your Majesty—Your voice is as a gentle rain that calls out melodies of praise to my Creator.

²⁴At Your command my heart is fed with the sounds of angelic choirs—whose singing is like none ever heard—O praise Your pure and matchless name.

²⁵At times my spirit becomes quiet before You—no music can ring out—I calm down and listen—in the silence I am hushed before Your presence.

²⁶O Jehovah Jireh, You are the provider of songs that play through my mind quietly in the night, but in the morning they are no more.

²⁷You rock the seas in their cradles—You sing them a lullaby with the breeze—You croon a nighttime song to my soul.

²⁸The oceans crescendo to a mighty roar—like a kettledrum of worship, their climax rises to You in a forceful culmination of praise.

²⁹I have heard the pines whispering their adoration to You—it ascends to Your throne on the winds at their bidding.

³⁰The birds of the earth warble and trill their thanks to You for all of Your provisions.

³¹The creatures of the forest scoot along and in their own way pay tribute to their Maker—only You are aware of their language and song.

³²All of us who have breath sing to You in fulfillment of our appreciation of Your might.

33 You established music from the beginning of creation as the planets and stars sang out to You in hymns of praise.

34 As a merry brook ripples along its course, so does a heart in tune with its Maker.

35 My heart dances before the Lord and whistles in delight—He has brought merriment to my soul and laughter to my spirit.

36 The strains of a heavenly anthem soothe my weary soul—giving me strength for the journey ahead—it is a sacred song known only to the godly.

37 Whenever my spirit touches Yours, a joyous cacophony explodes in heavenly music like fireworks that light up the firmament.

38 Your greatness peals loudly as the bells of heaven toll Your magnificence.

Psalm 8

The Bitter Cup

1 Blessed is he who is made to drink the cup of bitterness and does not revile in return—his failure to bring censure has met the approval of the Father.

2 Disappointment and distress come when the words of a best friend are harsh—they are like a dagger to the midsection.

3 In despair my spirit was crushed and trampled down — despondency besieged me and called for my surrender.

4 The choice of words used was heart-rending and agonizing without thought for my benefit—a painful line of reasoning was initiated.

5 Like drinking quinine or gall my spirit was poisoned with hopelessness—bleakness rushed in to attack.

6 The acidity came from being misunderstood and resentment became my partner—bitterness marched along beside me.

7 Sleep fled from my eyes and my mind would not be quieted—my thoughts were on a merry-go-round as at an amusement park.

Psalm 9 - You Saturate Me With Honor

⁸My stomach was in turmoil like a rider on a bull—strife and upheaval became my song.

⁹My spirit was full of trouble and my pride was wounded—the insult carried me away and soon became my problem.

¹⁰Offense was my nightmare and stalked me at every turn—resentment turned into indignation—discontentment turned out to be a slap in the face.

¹¹The enemy had shot me full of arrows and reveled at my fall—he took pleasure at my downfall and relished my defeat.

¹²My demise seemed certain had You not intervened on my behalf—woe no longer plagued me like a bad dream—You brought to an end the approaching disaster.

¹³The adversary is now on the run because You rescued me—because You set me free—Your defense has become my salvation.

¹⁴I will sing a new song of praise to You, my God, in return for Your deliverance—there is no one like You, Lord—no one in all the earth.

Psalm 9

You Saturate Me With Honor

¹I am drunk with the pleasure of Your presence—I reel in Your closeness—I am under the influence of Your authority.

²You have made me giddy with pure joy, yes I delight myself in You because I am made lightheaded with Your good pleasure.

³I am under Your control and yield myself to You—Your wish becomes my inclination because there is a fondness in my heart to please You in everything I do.

⁴Your deliciousness fills me and its taste is sweet on my lips—You have charmed my heart and senses with pure ecstasy—gloom has left me to vex another.

⁵Consume me as one does with a glass of wine, drained to the dregs—let me be consumed to the last drop.

⁶My mind is a gateway for Your Word—the entrance to my heart—fill it with wisdom and let perception be evident and unmistakable.

⁷I am at Your disposal 24/7 so that You may have free access anytime—Holy Spirit, open the door and enter at Your leisure.

⁸My talents and abilities I have chained to Your desires—expand my gifts and aptitudes beyond my capabilities.

⁹You fulfill my deepest yearning and need—it resides in Your mercies—I hunger and thirst for more of Your righteousness.

¹⁰I am wrapped in the fullness of Your joy—to be immersed in the rapture of Your love—let Your friendship be like a bathrobe after a relaxing shower.

¹¹Saturate me, O God, with honor and purity—may my reputation be impeccable—allow my life to be a tribute of my worship.

¹²O that the essence of Your presence would ooze from the very pores of my being—that it would radiate outwardly with glowing splendor.

¹³Percolate me by the power of Your holiness so that Your Spirit would permeate me with authority and dominate my life for Your primary calling.

¹⁴Your Word cultivates the garden of my heart—let it pulverize the clumps that remain—crush any persistent chunks of hard ground into fine earth.

¹⁵The blessings You send bring rain upon my garden and cause the plants to grow—they are well watered with blessing.

¹⁶The warmth of the sunshine of Your Word brings truth—and truth leads, in turn, to maturity and wisdom.

¹⁷Your laws add substance to the soil of my mind and promote growth for its garden.

¹⁸You rain righteousness upon me—You shower me with honor and respectability—a crop of purity springs up.

¹⁹You have raised a harvest of hope within my spirit—You cultivate me by the refining of Your Word—it enriches my inward man.

²⁰Knowledge from Your Spirit works through me to reach other lands and territories where I may not personally be able to go.

²¹I will exalt You in all I do—never missing an opportunity to lift Your name on high.

Psalm 10

You Order The Steps Of My Journey

¹When the depths of my soul are like turbulent waters, the tranquility of Your peace calms their churning and quiets them like gentle streams.

²My mind is clouded with confusion whenever it becomes sidetracked from thinking about Your ways—uncertainty dogs my path, leaving commotion in its wake.

³Your rules are a prescription for godly living—the man who lives by them will do well because Your laws have settled his mind.

⁴Knowing You are in charge of everything sets my mind at ease—You never fall asleep as You keep watch day and night—O how wonderful You are.

⁵The righteous cherish Your name—for it is above all others—they prize it more highly than earthly riches—more than untold possessions.

⁶The corrupt man gives no thought to Your honor—he is crooked above all measures—may numerous others insult him.

⁷As for me—I will give reverence and bow down before Your throne—I uphold the name of my God in worship and respect—blessed be the Lord God Jehovah.

⁸You alone know the number of my days—they are held in reserve for Your summons—I pledge each one of them unto You.

⁹You mapped out my journey before I began the first step—not a single effort that I have put forth has taken You unaware.

¹⁰My thoughts are on You as continually as each breath of air enters my lungs—I endeavor to think on Your goodness as persistently as my lungs demand that I breathe.

¹¹With each heartbeat I am closer to my final destination—to be in Your presence eternally.

¹²You have requisitioned my steps—You have decreed that they be set aside for Your purpose—their order is known only to You.

¹³I request Your help in arranging my itinerary—be my travel guide—most prominent King—for You are the capable and expert planner.

¹⁴Today is the day You have planned for me—with deliberate intent You have created it—I look on it with delight and a sense of wonder.

¹⁵I hesitate to walk alone—without Your hand I will certainly fall!

¹⁶From the earliest times Your promise to me has been—I will never leave You nor forsake You—it is on this promise that I stake my claim and that You pledge Your reputation.

¹⁷I am troubled whenever my thoughts become scattered and distant—help me gather them as a rancher corrals his cattle in a roundup.

¹⁸The enemy has tried to derail me as I come closer to my goal—keep me on the right track and guide me safely home.

¹⁹These fleshly eyes dart about in search of You—trying to behold Your countenance—but You have wisely withheld that glory for a future time.

²⁰I have tasted and seen that You are so good—my ears perk up listening for Your voice.

²¹My senses come alive in my quest to experience all I can of You—my heart is bowed before You and my spirit lies prostrate at Your feet.

Psalm 11

You Keep My Heart Clean

¹My Father, forgive me when I do not ask You to test me—when I say that I will do anything for You—for I may speak as a foolish man —uttering vows I cannot possibly keep.

²Let the measure of my words be meaningful and few—so that You would be honored in all of my utterances.

³You do not take pleasure in the volume of expressions that proceed from within a man, but You look for that sincere language of the heart.

⁴My heart is an open book before You —before it was ever written You knew the entire story—cleanse it from all sin.

⁵I must have every conviction and

Psalm 11 - You Keep My Heart Clean

belief I own uncontaminated before You—sterilize my heart as it might need to be in a hospital emergency ward—so that it is absolutely pure.

6 Wash me whiter than snow by the light of Your Word—make my heart as transparent as a glass house and may the motives of it be favorable to You.

7 When my heart betrays my faith, my prayer is that You will keep me true to You—O God—bring me back into alignment with Your will.

8 Should my feet seek another path and my ears fail to hear Your voice—if my eyes look anywhere other than to the light of Your Glory—shackle my rambunctious thoughts forever.

9 When those thoughts turn out to be like an undisciplined child—gently restore me in Your mercy—forgive my waywardness—then I will once again seek You with my whole heart.

10 I will be a testimony to those around me because of Your faithfulness—a confirmation of Your nearness.

11 You have given me a heart that is modeled after Yours, O God—You were pleased to have fashioned me in Your image and likeness—now I am created to praise Your deity.

12 You created me with Your hands—You are the potter—I'm just the clay—shape me into a useful vessel of honor and value to the Kingdom.

13 My heart will sing yet another new song of thanksgiving unto Your name—a prayer of gratitude and blessing.

14 I worship You, not because I have to—Lord, I worship You with all that I possess;

15 I worship You every chance I get to —Lord, I worship You because I love You.

16 Your Word makes me aware that all I have belongs to You—I know that You never promise the next breath—You give me free choice and for that I am sincerely grateful.

17 My soul magnifies and sings the praises of Your mighty power—it searches the universe for the proper words with which to exalt Your Majesty.

18 The elusiveness of words to a man's soul can cause it to become bruised—let the glory of the Lord bind him with liniment—and may Your Word be an ointment to soothe his aching.

¹⁹He will then announce Your goodwill to all who will listen—his heart will be encouraged with glad tidings—his speech will bear a good report.

²⁰Let all those who love You present unto You high praise—it will be transported upward with tongues of elation.

²¹I will worship You with earnestness—thanksgiving for Your glory shall forever be on my lips—I will praise You with all that is within me—You are never wearied by it.

²²My soul is stirred by the gentle breezes of Your Spirit and left in awe.

Psalm 12

You Are Rich Beyond Measure

¹Though I am poor and needy—You are rich beyond measure—the treasures of Your wealth are incalculable.

²Who are we that You are not only mindful of us but You share the riches contained in the earth with us—those tucked away in every nook and cranny?

³Every jewel, gem, natural resource, and mineral deposit belongs to You—You have allowed us to not only search and discover Your precious stones, but they are ours for the taking.

⁴By the generous and loving nature that is part of Your disposition we have become recipients of Your great abundance—O praise Your Majesty.

⁵The Lord Almighty deposits His benefits into my account daily—He keeps tally of them all and adds to them at His discretion.

⁶My ability to withdraw from my account is not dependent upon my deposits into the account—He has placed them there for my blessing.

⁷The storehouse of His heavens contains infinitely more riches than this earth—were we to know the amount of His resources, we would be uncomprehending.

⁸The interest of heaven is far more valuable than the dividends of this world—this is what I am counting on.

⁹No man is able to buy his way into heaven with silver or gold—nor

any precious metal or stone—because it all belongs to the Father anyway.

¹⁰Material possessions do not matter to Him—for they will burn up with fire—what He longs for is the yielded heart—how precious that is to Him.

¹¹His harvest will be one of surrendered hearts—those who have not relinquished theirs to an ungodly world, nor given up in defeat to the enemy of their souls.

Psalm 13

You Quiet My Yearning Soul

¹I will apply myself to seeking after You—to knowing Your ways—to pursuing You and leaving no stone unturned—yearning only for Your friendship.

²Then my mind said—"Where are You, my God—have You abandoned me—why have You deserted me like a man who leaves his wife and child for other interests?"

³It appears like You have gone into hiding—much like the sun when it slips behind the darkest clouds and can be seen no more.

⁴When I cry out to You and my ears hear no answer—then a veil of darkness obscures my understanding—ignorance becomes my blindfold.

⁵I say to myself—"Where has my God slipped away to—has He departed to other worlds and left me all alone?"

⁶Depression holds my thoughts fast—much like an anchor keeps a boat grounded—melancholy slips inside my tent.

⁷Your departure grips me like a steel trap holds its prey—then as a drowning man going down for the last time—my spirit cries out in utter desperation.

⁸Suddenly my mind is soothed and quieted—my thoughts are subdued—Your Spirit speaks peace to my intellect and it is instantly hushed.

⁹The light of Your Spirit shines brightly as the sun reappears from behind the dark clouds—

18

You sweep away the rain clouds with the winds of Your presence.

10 The stars that are seen are recognized by man—yet vast multitudes of the heavenly hosts are unseen—these are established and known only to God.

11 My soul and the heavenly beings magnify You, my God—I will yet praise You—I seek to know You in power—Your blessings must be secondary.

12 You have placed within me a heart to know You, yet I want to know You more—my mind has become like an undisturbed pool of water waiting in stillness for You to come and stir it.

13 My spirit will be content with Your goodness—Your blessings come at me from many directions—though I do not stop and count them—for they are numerous!

14 Praise the Lord—praise the Lord—all I am can't help but praise Him!

Psalm 14

The Lord Our Provider And Salvation

1 As the days, weeks, months, and years go by—so will my hope always remain unshakable in the Lord my God.

2 Your Word is a beacon of hope that shines as an eternal light upon my footpath—it has been an utterance of truth from out of the mouth of the Almighty.

3 His vantage point illuminates my way like light from the moon and the stars—it blazes brighter than burnished brass in intense light—there are no shadows of darkness in it.

4 Your Word gives sustenance for my soul—it provides refreshment for the weary and a respite for the exhausted.

5 When hunger pangs growl with the ferocity of a pack of wolves, You make them cease—they lie in wait for me to break down—but You become my strong arm.

6 I praise Your name because You supply my daily bread—my rations come from Your hand.

7 Your storehouse supplies all I have ever needed and is inexhaustible

—Your cupboard is always available and is infinitely supplied.

⁸Bread is for the body but Your Word provides rations for my spirit—it feeds my inner man and keeps me filled with good things.

⁹Your laws are good for me and because I keep them I am blessed—Your commands have never been unbearable—blessed are all who follow them closely.

¹⁰The statutes of the Lord are correct and complete—declaring man's need of a Savior—they only call for a repentant heart and a sorrowful spirit.

¹¹Man is in essence morally deficient and bankrupt—he is in a state of ruin and poverty.

¹²There is none righteous—not even one—all humanity is flawed and has been left wanting—imperfect and unfinished without His intervention.

¹³The Lamb of God came to rescue us from our broke and penniless circumstances—He paid it all—in full—for a debt He did not owe—how marvelous is that!

¹⁴My heart overflows with unceasing gratitude—the blood of the Lamb has cleansed me.

Psalm 15

Chosen, Favored, and Blessed

¹Beauty is revealed in all the works of His hands—God is good and His entire creation displays His excellence.

²Your color palette with which You paint the sky and landscape is far more complex than the most sophisticated high-definition television man has ever produced.

³When I looked out on my world this morning I saw the smile of my God—lighting up the horizon—it shone with the beauty of a million stars.

⁴I saw and felt its warmth radiating across the earth as it spoke out, "I love you."

⁵You have often written Your love for me across the sky as I have watched an eagle or a hawk soaring so majestically in Your heavens.

⁶My soul takes pleasure in Your won-

derful kindness and revelations.

⁷My basket overflows with Your benevolence as I have experienced Your love through the sweetness of the wife You have granted me —I am truly blessed and favored among men.

⁸She has become my treasure, companion, and best friend—You have caused her to become the object of my affection and You are the only one I love more.

⁹I hear the music of my God in everything I do—His songs overflow the deepest reaches of my bosom.

¹⁰The breath of God exhales and the wind causes the leaves of the trees to flutter— rhythmically they vibrate and rustle to form the percussive section of His symphony orchestra.

¹¹I have heard the staccato beating of the rain against the window pane as it telegraphed me of His amazing love.

¹²Hark!—are those angels I hear, singing sweetly and so clear— singing words no man has known, except for those around the throne?

¹³Angel, sing that song to me, sing it with sweet harmony—let me sing along with you, giving praise to whom it's due.

¹⁴Now I've been chosen by His grace, chosen by His grace—O praise the Lord for His marvelous grace:

¹⁵It's not by works that I have done, but it's through God's only son— yes I've been chosen by His amazing grace.

¹⁶I give glory to the Lamb of God who sits upon the throne—I will crown Him with praise—for His seat of power is above all others.

¹⁷As I endeavor to draw closer to You, my God—You are reaching for me at the same time—gently pulling me to Your side.

¹⁸You have wrapped Your loving arms around me so that I might feel the warmth of Your embrace —I relax while You hold me close —all is calm and I feel secure in Your arms.

¹⁹You are truly the lover of my soul— I am at peace—I rest safely and securely in those mighty arms—You have cared tenderly and compassionately for me.

²⁰Let the glory of the Lord fill this temple—I am Your temple, O God —overwhelm me with Your manifested presence.

²¹My body is a temple of the Most High—I desire for You to take Your rightful place within it— without You it is no more than a piece of clay devoid of godly form.

²²Inhabit my praises as I fill this temple with them—let them rise like incense in Your courtyard—may they be a fragrant aroma unto You.

²³You are here in this place—I'm surrounded by the presence of my Lord—what these earthly eyes can't see—in my heart I will believe—You are right here in this place.

²⁴Show us Your power, show us Your glory—fill us Holy Spirit, Lord we need You right now.

²⁵O how I praise You for Your marvelous grace—it has calmed my fears and dried my tears.

²⁶I cannot yet see the victories of the coming day—they are waiting for me to discover them—like a fortune in a treasure hunt—they may even be just beyond the sunset.

²⁷Children of God can proclaim trust in their God each time they enjoy His blessings—their childlike delight is a testimony to those around them and brings Him pleasure.

²⁸They are prepared to soak up pure delight in each single moment—for God loves to put a lifetime of pleasure in just a single heartbeat—His children relish these times, even though brief.

²⁹Praise the Lord, O my soul, praise the Lord!

Psalm 16

Cherish Your Time With Him

¹Time exists at Your command, O God, and You have created it just for man—You have no need for it because You occupy an entirely different dimension.

²Like a mighty army it keeps marching on without looking back or to the side—generations and lengthy life spans are but a moment within eternity.

³Jehovah Almighty holds all time and space in His hands—they are of no consequence to Him —He is the Beginning and the Ending—the Alpha and the Omega—the First and the Last.

⁴Since we are mere mortals, we do not have the ability to grasp this concept—nor have You granted us the faculty for unearthing the

Psalm 16 - Cherish Your Time With Him

mysteries of substance without beginning or end.

⁵O that I might have the wherewithal to treasure my time here on earth —that I would be able to see it and value it through the light of eternity.

⁶May Your hand rest upon and cause me to prize this precious commodity You have given me—it is like no other asset.

⁷My lifespan is but a gasp of breath to You—I can best summarize the brevity of my life as fleeting and temporal.

⁸Which man can honestly say he hasn't wasted any of this precious resource?—no one can!

⁹Forgive us, Lord, for squandering this costly possession that should be valued more than pure gold, diamonds, or even pearls.

¹⁰You recorded the minutes of my pilgrimage long before I ever came to be—You had written each one of them in Your ledger.

¹¹My life has always been in Your hands—from now on I entrust it completely to You—every waking moment and otherwise.

¹²That You, O God, would be glorified through my time on this earth and that I would remain faithful until I reach the other shore—this is my prayer to You.

¹³I have made my choice to serve You all of my days and have set it in stone—the enemy has tempted me to change my allegiance but to no avail—for who is like You?

¹⁴Extend the days You have marked out for me—not that I would use them for worldly pleasure or temporal gain—rather that I would be allowed to complete all You have in mind.

¹⁵And should You choose another to polish the jewels I have left behind when I return to You—what is that to me?—I will praise You even in my absence from this body.

¹⁶I really get pumped whenever Your joy becomes my strength—Your delight provides motivation beyond any other earthly pleasure.

¹⁷I am smitten by Your love—it has affected and influenced every area of my life.

¹⁸Mark me with the branding iron of Your affection—let Your love be the identifying mark that labels me as Your son.

¹⁹Power wash the cobwebs from my mind—let any failings present be washed away so that I may dance before You with boldness and singing.

Psalm 16 - Cherish Your Time With Him

[20] Purify me and remove my sin—burn it in the incinerator of Your forgiveness—place my iniquities in the crucible of Your furnace so they may be purged from my spirit.

[21] Any earthly passions and worldly desires rooted within my spirit—I bind as a farmer bales his hay and ask that You uproot them at once.

[22] Don't let Your hand strike me nor reproach come upon me any time I have not been properly thankful for Your gifts and kindnesses—or I will go the way of all flesh before my time is up.

[23] Turn aside my faults so my enemies will not hold them against me—as they love to do—my flaws are always before You—yet Your mercy has not condemned me like I deserve.

[24] Keep in mind that I am but dust and have no recourse when You come to oppose me—who would ever be able to outdo You in a contest of any sorts?

[25] Where has gratefulness gone—has it gone next door or around the corner—or maybe up the street to the marketplace?

[26] I will call out to it and summon it to return to me—to join me in celebrating the greatness of my God—we will sing, dance, and make music unto Him.

[27] My heart will rejoice greatly—with hilarity it will praise my God—yes how I will exult in the seasons He has brought into my life.

[28] Lulls and waiting periods are the change of scenery for my soul—a new and fresh perspective of my great God—they provide a pause for ripening.

[29] I will bring a sacrifice of praise and thanksgiving unceasingly, Lord—You are the central theme of my song—You provide the interlude between the movements of my anthem.

Psalm 17

He is Still God When the Brook Dries Up!

¹God is still God when the brook has dried up—when all around me the ground is parched and thirsty!

²When the stream refuses to flow and the ground is bone dry and scorched—when God has closed the valve and shut off His waterway—He still reigns supreme.

³His promises have never failed—as the Almighty He is our source for everything—what do we need that He cannot supply?

⁴All those who trust in Him have witnessed His hand of provision and praise His name—their reliance on Him has never been frustrated.

⁵His arm is not short and He does not limit Himself by our circumstances—His supplies are never depleted.

⁶His name is Jehovah Jireh—He is our provider—the all-sufficient one.

⁷He is pleased to work on our behalf in ways that often surprise us—He catches us at our point of desperation and takes over.

⁸His mercies are new every morning—yet this does not cancel the fact that our faith must be refreshed—as surely as the dawning of a new day.

⁹Does God lie—does His Word deliver empty promises—has He not spoken words of truth unto those who believe on Him?

¹⁰He speaks forth in boldness—His words are clear and lucid—His speech is not ambiguous—nor does He speak with vagueness.

¹¹Be still, listen to His heart, and hear what He has to say to yours.

¹²"I am concerned for your welfare—I saw your needs before even one of them came about—My warehouse has reserves you cannot fathom and I am able to supply your every need.

¹³Will you marvel at the ways I am able to bring an end to your needs?—I am able to cover your scarcity with My sufficiency if only you will lift your arms to Me.

¹⁴Have you not read that I am able to open the very windows of heaven and pour out blessings that you cannot contain?

¹⁵Do not look on Me as though I were a man like you, who could not take his next breath if I, the Almighty, didn't allow him to.

¹⁶Reinforce your supply of faith in Me so you can stand when there is no other way out—when only darkness of night lines your pathway.

¹⁷"My people, if you claim Me as your God then why do you deny My power—why do you push Me away as though you do not need Me?

¹⁸Why do you distrust My Word—have you seen anything too staggering for Me to accomplish—is there something you believe would be too difficult for Me?

¹⁹What it all boils down to when you consider these facts—I did create the universe—I am God and there is no other like Me!

²⁰I rest My case, need I say any more—the remainder is up to you—I am still God when the brook dries up!"

Psalm 18

O Great America – How You Have Fallen!

¹"O great land of the West—how I have blessed you—from your birth I have watched over you while keeping a close guard upon your ways.

²I have cradled you from infancy while teaching you My ways—I have shown you righteous paths to walk on.

³Your ways were established upon My principles—your founders were devoted to My Word—they did not fail to acknowledge Me.

⁴You were devoted to Me and proclaimed My name to many nations—you were a leader of righteousness—honor and respectability went before you.

⁵I was pleased to call you Mine because your fathers were instrumental in leading this nation as a free world.

⁶Now you have forsaken My ways and become a stubborn people—turning from My commands with a rebellious heart.

⁷You speak words—professing to be

Psalm 18 - O Great America – How You Have Fallen!

Christians—but in reality they are empty—the shallowness of your expressions is without substance.

8If only you would turn back to Me in earnestness—it would fill My heart with gladness once again.

9I have loved you with an everlasting love—that is why I have reached out to you through My prophets and holy men—still you turn a deaf ear.

10You have let the carnal pleasures of this life take the place of the life I desire to give you—you have turned the things I destined to be clean and wholesome into impure.

11I have given you My Word as a blueprint—a road map—a detailed outline—to show you how to live.

12You have seen numerous examples of other nations who have tried doing things on their own without me—but you have not learned from their lesson.

13You have not only turned a deaf ear to My prophets but a blind eye to My Word as well—how much wiser you would have been had you listened and experienced My knowledge.

14My Word clearly shows that My Spirit will not always strive with man.

15The door is quickly closing and I will come soon to snatch those who have taken note of My words and followed My teachings to be at home with Me forever.

16How much longer will your flag fly free over the lands I have given you—will you continue to provoke Me with your disobedience?

17Indeed I have numbered your days—and it's with a sad heart that I am turning my back on you—My heart has desired only the best for you but you have disregarded my ways.

18O America—so tall and proud—how you have fallen from the heights of My mountain!

19If you would only humble yourselves and forsake your evil ways—I would once again be your God—nurturing you like a favored son.

20I know your heart—how you have forsaken Me—you have abandoned My exhortations and brushed away My disciplines.

21Because of this you will be taken captive by a people—another nation—because you have failed to attend to My Word.

22One other thing I hold against you is the sin of turning against My chosen people—and for that you must be punished."

Psalm 19

You Purchased My Healing

¹My infirmity was a blessing in disguise even though You had hidden its purpose from my view—and had not made it known to me.

²If I had only seen Your hand in it from the onset—my mind would have been at ease and no complaint would have ventured forth from my lips.

³On those occasions when the temptation to pity myself was present—I solicited You for help—I sought Your wisdom in managing what I viewed as my misfortune.

⁴You have chained my misery in a dungeon and placed a sentence of life without parole on it—You sent my despondency to solitary confinement.

⁵You gave my faith a pardon and Your clemency soon set it free in worship—Your mercy gave it a new outlook.

⁶Wisdom became my nursemaid and bandaged my wounds—she applied salve and ointment to my suffering.

⁷I have seen the rain fall on the just and the unjust—the righteous and the unrighteous—thus showing forth Your leniency on those You would have compassion on.

⁸My eyes have been exposed to the misery of others—the width and scope of my vision has been enlarged with understanding.

⁹Wisdom has introduced empathy within my being for the problems of others—it has imparted to me a commiseration I would not have known otherwise.

¹⁰When I view the calamities of others in comparison to my own—mine have been like a sliver in the finger—nothing but an irritation for me to deal with.

¹¹Jehovah Rophe—I have heard Your voice and it has spoken clearly and with emphasis—highlighting my need for dependence upon You.

¹²You have purchased My healing and paid for it in full—its possession is left up to me to receive in faith.

¹³Lord, I believe; yes, I believe! I believe the Son of God has died for me—Lord, I believe, take my unbelief; by the power of faith I can now receive.

¹⁴Your assurance has been like an umbrella in a rainstorm—Your authoritativeness has been my awning against the burning rays of uncertainty.

¹⁵When You put things together in Your time—they will shine like well-polished silver—gleam like a burnished doorknocker.

¹⁶At that perfect moment when time aligns with Your will—You will reveal my healing in power—making manifest Your might and authority over all disease.

¹⁷You will receive glory through it—Jehovah Rophe shall be declared the conqueror once again—because His foes have been vanquished.

¹⁸Time is a cruel drill sergeant and all humankind has been its slave—we have been made to grovel at its beck and call.

¹⁹Wisdom has shown me that time is no stranger to You—it is Your servant—it has travailed in servitude to You and You alone.

²⁰My spiritual eyes have peered through Your eyes and seen my healing—Glory to the Lamb—who by the stripes He received—has suffered and taken my sin upon Him.

²¹I wait patiently before the Lord for His glory to be revealed in and through me—Praise the Lord, O my soul—praise Him, O my soul!

Psalm 20

Listen Earnestly for His Voice

¹Lord, my heart is hungry for You—Your Spirit fills me yet I long for more—I am ravenous, like a bear after a long winter's hibernation.

²Listen for the Lord—listen earnestly for His voice—He will speak to those who pay attention in sincerity.

³Shut out all the noise around you and concentrate on Him—use earplugs if you need to—fasten your mind upon Him and Him alone.

⁴Be all ears when He speaks and hang onto every word He makes known—do not become distracted from all He tells you.

⁵Call to Him with persistence and He

29

Psalm 20 - Listen Earnestly for His Voice

will not fail to answer—His ear is attuned to your call.

⁶Though it may seem delayed—it will be there at your time of need—He does not answer according to man's timetable—but He renders a reply in His time.

⁷His heart is moved by your appeal—it will arouse His compassion and He will come quickly to your relief.

⁸Whenever I need encouragement I put on praise as my overcoat—then the Holy Spirit fills me with peace and power—whooh—Hallelujah!

⁹Distractions come and go but I am listening attentively for Your voice—for the sound of Your footsteps.

¹⁰Focus your eyes upon the Lord like a hound on a rabbit—let your spirit be directed to His Word so you can receive guidance.

¹¹Like the new fallen snow—His Word is fresh and clean each time I read it—it is from the days of old—yet it retains an innovativeness that only His Spirit can add to it.

¹²Even as a baker rises in the wee hours of the morning to bake his bread—so is the freshness of Your Word, O Lord.

¹³I feast on it daily—it is strength and nourishment to my inner man—nutrition for my bones—food for my thoughts—sustenance in life.

¹⁴The revelations of the Spirit are vitamins for the soul—they are healthy and wholesome.

¹⁵Like a freshwater spring coming out of the mountainside—so is the thirst-quenching refreshment that gushes from Your Word.

¹⁶The Word of God goes before us in strength and power—with the force of a mighty army marching into battle—it sweeps away the powers of darkness and lights our way.

¹⁷Our great Savior and King has marched victorious into battle and has borne the brunt of it for us—now we may follow Him in mighty triumph.

¹⁸He guides me even when there is no light because I trust in Him.

¹⁹I have kept Your Word close to my heart so that I will never look aside—to the right or the left—but only straight into Your marvelous face.

²⁰It was His privilege to become our Redeemer—so how can we do less than to follow Him all the days of our life with gladness?

Psalm 21

Your Amazing Strength Covers My Weaknesses

¹I am weak but You are so strong—mighty in strength and power—who can stand against You?

²When I put my strengths and weaknesses on a scale—the weaknesses cause the strengths to slide off the other side with alarming speed.

³If I were to put my strengths on a scale next to Yours, O Lord, it would be like having the Rock of Gibraltar on Your side and a grain of sand on mine.

⁴I have taken inventory of my strengths and I find that apart from You, I have none—any that I lack, You more than make up for.

⁵My weaknesses stack against me—all my imperfections overshadow me like Mt. Everest—my faults are many—like those that lie beneath the crust of the earth.

⁶You have covered them with the cloud of Your glory so that they cannot be seen—You have been my guardian.

⁷Praise be unto God who has seen my humiliation and covered it as the oceans cover their beds—Your kindness has not allowed You to exploit my embarrassment.

⁸Your Word has revealed that You use those things that are weak to shame the strong and the foolish things to disgrace the wise.

⁹Because of this I feel confident that I can be useful—my security is dependent upon Your faithfulness—and You never disappoint.

Psalm 22

You Breathe In Me Wisdom And Power

¹Your Word is my seatbelt of protection—it keeps me safe and secure—but only as long as I use it properly.

²The Word of the Almighty gives me power so I can speak truth—anoint me, Holy Spirit, and I will proclaim Your majesty.

³I have been dealt a handful of thoughts—God's wisdom allows me to discard those of little or no value while I retain those of high value.

⁴The Holy Spirit has become my trump card with which I can render useless any card the opponent throws my way.

⁵All my thoughts I hand over to Your Lordship so I can be pleasing in all I say and do.

⁶Let the purity that flows from Your throne sterilize and decontaminate my thinking.

⁷Censor every particle of my thoughts and viewpoints—permit my intellect to join hands with Your wisdom.

⁸At times the tedium of each day grabs me and threatens to pull me under like quicksand.

⁹Often the vibrant watercolors of life have faded to a black-and-white drabness and monotony has set in like a dull toothache.

¹⁰Doubt and disillusionment rake me over the coals—they badger me with needless uncertainty causing me to question my self-worth.

¹¹The Spirit of God enlightens me while improving my maturity—the reassurance of His voice keeps my feet steady and on level ground.

¹²As I regain my equilibrium I find praise even during the normalcy of everyday living.

¹³I will let my praise intensify and swell like the crashing of the waves in the ocean—like the crescendo of the kettle drums at the end of a clamorous symphony.

¹⁴With sincerity let us rejoice—let the praise of His people grow with intensity and power.

¹⁵Let it rise like the smoke from an evening campfire—praise the Lord, O my soul—praise Him with pure delight.

Psalm 23

You Set Me Free When I Abandon All

¹Holy Spirit—You are the helium in my balloon—the source of my strength and power—the basis and purpose for my existence.

²While the skins of many balloons are varied and colorful—You have made mine plain and nondescript—Your wisdom has afforded me great contentment with that.

³You are developing within me a desire to rise to heights unknown—a yearning for ways unfamiliar to me—for a heavenly home that is home to my spirit.

⁴Even while my flesh binds me to this earth with tethers, I still feel Your tugging within me to go up—the heavenlies are pulling against this earthly encapsulation.

⁵I must release my will in complete submission to You, O God—only then will You cut free the ties that bind me and those ropes that are holding me back.

⁶In my vision—You have shown me that total abandonment is the cost—a rejection of all earthly sentiments must come first.

⁷Each day I must strive to set that last mooring loose so that You may release all restraints—then I will have no fetters binding my soul to this earth.

⁸I lay aside my hopes and dreams in surrender to Yours—my preference must be to Your everlasting Kingdom, O God, not my will but Yours be done.

⁹Then I will be free at last to be in Your presence forever—Hallelujah!

Psalm 24

The Joy Of Knowing You Brings Peace and Quiet Assurance

¹Why am I ecstatic that my heart no longer condemns me?—Because the blood of the Lamb has washed it spotless and that puts me on cloud nine.

²The enemy can no longer bring reproach and censure against a child of God who has given his heart to Him.

³Blessed is the one who pursues You with excited and passionate devotion—for that is one thing You desire above all.

⁴When I searched I found great treasure—greater than that of an untapped diamond mine—now I have chosen to be a devotee of You and to make Your principles my daily life's focus.

⁵My heart is tender before You, O God, as a young plant breaking forth through the earth—although my heart is delicate and easily crushed—I place it under Your protection.

⁶Give Your servant an impressionable heart so it may be easily influenced by Your Word—pliable within Your hands.

⁷Shield my heart from those who want to destroy me and then revel in my downfall—all those who would party in the wake of my demise.

⁸When I rise in the morning I feel as if I am looking into a thick fog before I put on my glasses—but when I read Your Word—then I find clarity for my whole day.

⁹Your Word, O Lord, is a light switch for my soul—it lights up the darkened room so I will not stumble and fall.

¹⁰It is a lantern to expose any ruts that cross my pathway so I will not be tripped up—it is more valuable than a kerosene lamp in a storm.

¹¹Teach me, O God, to walk along fresh trails of exploration—for in so doing I will avoid the deep potholed paths of routine and monotony.

¹²Your Word is like a flare that a traveler sets on the roadside to warn of impending danger.

¹³It has been my radar to keep me on track and heading in the right direction—it has become my course of action at all times.

Psalm 24 - The Joy Of Knowing You Brings Peace and Quiet Assurance

14 The joy of the Lord brings peace and a quiet assurance that You, O God, are in control—I find You working behind the scenes even before the curtains open—that is true joy.

15 The godly will hang onto Him as a picture hangs onto a hook—their will has been securely fastened to His so that they will not fall.

16 The warmth of Your embrace, O God, is more intimate than that of a lover—I have cherished those private times in Your presence.

17 Having close fellowship with You is warm and personal—it is far better than snuggling up with an inviting blanket.

18 Can I count the sands of the sea—is it possible for me to number their grains?—Neither can I count the thoughts of the Almighty—they are limitless and immeasurable.

19 The futility of such an undertaking would frustrate even the wisest man on earth—his mind would be stymied by any effort to measure Your vastness.

20 Eternities on end will never reveal even a small fraction of Your inexhaustible storehouse of thoughts—Your wisdom is unparalleled and beyond compare.

21 Each newborn baby imparts a creative and fresh thought of God—a new point of view and revelation from Him to us.

22 I have noted Your commands and Your words—I have written them on my tablet—they serve as reminders of Your dealings with me.

23 My heart is a notebook containing Your teachings—I keep them close and become wise by them—You impart truth and wisdom to those who seek for it.

24 Renew my life, Holy Spirit in the same way a retread adds new life to a worn tire—so that I may continue and finish the works You planned for me.

25 Only You, my God, know the end from the beginning—my humble prayer is that You bless the latter portion of my life in a much greater proportion than the former.

26 Apply Your truths to my mind as a fresh coat of paint to an old weather-beaten barn.

Psalm 25

Worship In The House Of The Lord

¹Welcome to the house of the Lord—welcome to the house of the Lord Almighty—we have gathered here to lift Him up—welcome to the house of the Lord.

²Does He dwell in a house of wood or stone—is the Lord of the universe—the One who created all things—willing to be confined?

³His presence does not need a container in which to live—the very heavens and the universe He created cannot hold Him.

⁴He is held captive any place where praise and adoration for Him emanates forth—anytime our praise radiates—we have His attention.

⁵Come reverently into His house—give Him the honor due His name—pay tribute to His majesty with singing—let your praises be lifted unto His throne.

⁶Prepare your heart to receive His Word with anticipation—He will fill it with good things—He will organize your thoughts and set them in order.

⁷Those who are His children gladly come into the hallowed place of God—they have found pleasure and joy within His dwelling.

⁸They have learned His law of praise and blessing and look to Him for anointing—they have made their worship holy unto Him.

⁹The truth of Your decrees, O God, has proven itself over and over—when our praises go up, Your blessings come down.

¹⁰Since You no longer require a blood sacrifice—we bring You a sacrifice of praise in its place—we have renounced our worldly ways and relinquish our gifts unto You.

¹¹I have witnessed sinners who enter Your house in search of something—but they do not know what they are looking for.

¹²Your saints have been blessed with ministering spirits and lift their voices with songs of worship in adoration to You, O God.

¹³Music is the vehicle that carries our praise to the very throne of the Most High—the instruments are merely conduits for our worship that is transmitted heavenward.

¹⁴As praise is raised to You, the outsider is touched by the presence of the Holy Spirit and moved to respond.

¹⁵The Spirit of Truth continues to draw the unsaved through the preaching of God's Holy Word—those who are lost are stirred by what they have heard.

¹⁶We have heard the bells of heaven toll out God's promise that He is with us—they toll perpetually—few have heard their summons—they have shut their minds to heavenly things.

¹⁷The godly have learned to hear the peal of those bells through the din of daily chores—in the midst of the cacophony of worldly living the minds of God's children are tuned heavenward.

¹⁸You are glorified each time we come into Your house and seek Your face—we will esteem and build up Your greatness as we despise our inadequacies.

¹⁹Let us gather to lift Him up and exalt His righteousness—we will assemble to add strength to the lifting of our hearts.

²⁰Welcome to the house of the Lord—where His glory fills the temple as He is lifted up—it fills the hearts of those who enter in.

²¹Come and be blessed in His sanctuary—the shelter of the Lord Almighty.

²²O praise the Lord, all who have breath—praise Him with honor and affection by showing respect for His nobility with upraised hands and grateful hearts.

Psalm 26

Praise For Your Unfailing Love

¹How I praise You for Your mercy and grace—they have kept me from crossing that line of no return—watching me closely in spite of my blunders.

²Is there a man who has lived without having even a single regret—and who has not lamented the error of his judgment?

³I lay all my pangs of conscience before You and sacrifice it on the altar—remorse will not pester

Psalm 26 - Praise For Your Unfailing Love

me forever—for You have taken it away—contrition will be my strong supporter.

4 The single biggest ache of my heart is that I did not follow Your ways devotedly and bring more pleasure to You as my gift from my youth.

5 Wisdom has been my ally and taught me that I cannot change the past—I freely and gladly accept Your generous offer of forgiveness.

6 It takes a steady hand to guide the needle as it mends the cloth—You guide my heart—Holy Spirit—as I am made new by the Word.

7 I must make this a daily choice in my pursuit for more of You—I will concern myself only with Your business.

8 The saint shall live the ordinary life while wrapped in a sheath of godliness—he will shed the mundane like a duck dispersing water off its back.

9 How can a man please You—do You find delight in his carnal ways—does not the mindless ways of a man annoy Your Holiness?

10 If a man was able to control his tongue perfectly and speak only cheerful and kind words—perhaps then You might find a measure of gladness in a man.

11 My tongue is a sentinel who guards the gateway of my heart—I will instruct my mouth and my lips to tell of Your greatness.

12 It is certainly no secret to speak publicly the depths of my love for You—I will openly proclaim on earth what is noised abroad in the heavens.

13 Your fame and glory have been dispersed abroad—each of Your stars has broadcast it to the nations while beaming the light of truth—it will pierce and penetrate to the uttermost distance.

14 The planets of the Almighty will showcase His excellence—they will feature the works of His hands—they will unmask truth in broad daylight and display it to all.

15 Who is able to hide truth from the Almighty—has anyone never spoken a falsehood or fabricated a deceit of some sort?

16 No one can maintain this claim and retain integrity—the honesty of the heart must not be tarnished by a corrupt mouth and a deceitful tongue.

17 You have absolved and washed clean the guilt of my lying lips—Your only censure was to go and sin no more.

¹⁸Put Your seal on my lips, O Lord, so that my tongue may speak only truth—yes You delight in truth.

¹⁹May I never cease to praise You for Your unfailing love—let truth forever be the refrain to my verse and the coda to my song.

Psalm 27

I Sing Your Praises For Another Day

¹Help me cherish each day as a present from Your hands—it is an endowment to attach importance to—a grant of superb value.

²The best part of waking up is anticipating what You have in store for me that day—besides the pleasure of another day to praise You, my Lord.

³Thinking upon its freshness with absolute marvel—delighting in its uniqueness—these are the proper things to do.

⁴I intend to look upon this day as a gift from You and to delight in it as one might savor a fine dessert or choice cut of meat.

⁵Show me how to treasure each day along with their God ordained moments.

⁶I live knowing You have prearranged for me a precise number of days—hours—minutes—and even breaths—that I may experience while here on this earth.

⁷Our lives are the sum of the number of breaths You have allotted us—and no one can add to that number—it is not up to us—nor is it our right—to take away from that number.

⁸I do not know which breath will be my last—yet I am confident in Your ability to complete the work You have begun in me in the amount of time You have set aside for me.

⁹Shall I look for tomorrow in expectancy—or to those things yet to come?—I think it would not be judicious seeing Your Word cautions against it.

¹⁰Instead I will rejoice—yes, I will glory in today—for You have shown me the glorious path—and only You know what is ahead—just around the bend.

¹¹You never promised the road would be trouble-free—You only promised You would never leave me nor forsake me.

¹²Today I will eat with gladness and joy—the bread You have set before me—yes, You know what I need and You are willing and able to provide such things.

¹³The hungry heart has sat in the classroom of quietness and learned to hear the voice of the Master—He has taught it to carry His stillness and revel in His peace.

¹⁴This is the day that the Lord has made—I will rejoice and be glad in it—I will sing for joy at another chance to worship His majesty—this is the day that the Lord has made for me.

Psalm 28

You Are A Safe Haven For My Thoughts

¹I find satisfaction and contentment when my way of thinking is riveted on You—when I am preoccupied with Your ways I will not drift off course.

²You have planted thoughts of peace and righteousness and caused them to grow as a hedge around my mind.

³Take my thoughts captive as an indentured servant—I surrender them to Your care.

⁴When I contemplate You and Your grandeur, Your vastness crowds out unruly thoughts and gives them the boot.

⁵All unfocused thoughts will render a man ineffective in battle—distraction and daydreaming has meant the loss of many crusades.

⁶Sometimes my meditations are as stammering lips before You—once they quiet down and hold their peace—Your tranquility becomes my chamber.

⁷I strive to make my deliberations as obedient as a slave to his master—I will reflect on Your greatness and not disregard Your truths.

⁸Your plans erase all of my vague notions and fill them with design and purpose—forgive me of my absentmindedness.

⁹I have put my thoughts through a rigid training process as one might do with a new puppy—for its owner must keep it on a leash for tight control.

¹⁰Quite often my ideas disrupt my focus on You—like a classroom full of children—at times they are unruly and entice me to go down the wrong paths.

¹¹My thinking delights to be held captive by You—let it be confined by Your authority—it is proud to salute Your majesty.

¹²I have sought to find a communication with You that is beyond mere words—let the expressions of my spirit be pure before You—my God.

¹³My thoughts and musings have found such a niche and often take me to that hiding place—my spirit has often taken them by the hand and led them there.

¹⁴This retreat is a cleft in the rock—a place where no one abides but You and me—it is there in sweet quietude that You bring our spirits together.

¹⁵O what solace I find there—a refuge and protection—You are my fortress forever!

¹⁶Whenever I am afraid, my thoughts make a beeline for Your presence—where they find shelter from the attack.

¹⁷My thoughts have found a safe haven in the protection of Your sanctuary—a place of retreat and solace.

¹⁸I will praise You with my intellect and understanding—but my faith finds deeper levels still—places where Your wisdom sidesteps my rationale and reasoning.

¹⁹You have helped me find that secret place—a place of security and refuge—a haven of rest for all who go there.

²⁰O what joy to meet You in secret—just the two of us—it is a place of no disruptions where trespassing is not allowed.

²¹My inhibitions head out the door—along with my uneasiness and anxious perceptions—my apprehensions disappear like frost melting off a window.

²²Your countenance assures me that this is where I have always hungered to be—You make my yearnings complete in Your presence.

²³I bask in Your embrace—peace flows over me like anointing oil streams down Aaron's beard.

24All my thoughts have taken off and deserted me—I feel no alarm because I am lost in Your presence.

25I will not postpone the giving of all glory and majesty for my God to future days—let me magnify Him in this present moment—even now!

26When this instant has passed—then I shall continue to exalt Him for all eternity—my soul shall praise Him forevermore!

Psalm 29

You Are The Commander In Chief

1My God—You are our Commander in Chief—underneath Your supreme authority You govern and direct us.

2The Private answers to You as well as the General—all are under Your rule because You preside over all.

3All the leaders under You seek Your guidance—esteem and high regard belong to those who respect Your leadership.

4You are supreme and direct with a mighty hand—Your authority is undeniable—You rule with dominion—lead on, great Jehovah!

5There is no other as knowledgeable as You—as mighty in power—as thorough in command—Your expertise is more apparent than a highly decorated General.

6You have enlisted me as a soldier in Your army—I am pleased to be Your recruit, O Lord, and my every effort will go into making You proud.

7Although I am just a novice I will go forth bravely—confident in my God—because of Him I am able to slay the powers of darkness.

8You grant me protection from those who try to harm me—You have put a safeguard all around me and are my shield of safety.

9You have declared victory at the onset of the battle and I will trust in You, my God—You have outlined the reckoning of conquest and it is firmly in Your grasp.

10You have armed me for battle with the proper weapons—I go forth in Your strength and will not be defeated.

¹¹You have drawn the battle lines—all soldiers have taken their formation—their weapons are ready for service.

¹²You lead with an upraised hand and victory goes before You—Your name is known abroad and goes in advance of Your company.

¹³At the clear sound of Your trumpet the battle cry is raised—the ground trembles and quakes in awe when Your voice is lifted high.

¹⁴The enemy flees in every direction as Your troops go forward—the adversary is routed in terror and has taken flight in a panic with no regard for his own safety.

¹⁵Which sovereign nation or foe is able to stand against the forces of my God—whose leaders are capable of defending against His authority?

¹⁶When the battle is over and all combat has ceased—You will give me the flag of peace and a banner of reconciliation.

¹⁷I will wear a victor's crown and revel in Your greatness—a garland of righteousness will be my reward.

¹⁸Because of Your honor You have caused even my enemies to be at peace with me—O praise Your Worthiness.

¹⁹Who is so strong as to stand against the Lord—to scorn His Might—to despise His Majesty—to disrespect His truth?

²⁰At the final chapter all shall bow before You, my God, in reverence—proclaiming Your Lordship—acknowledging Your eminence.

Psalm 30

A Plea For This Land I Love

¹I am surrounded by You, my God—You are my refuge and the One I love—I have made You my sanctuary.

²Your presence is like a veil of light that boxes me in daily—it overshadows my way—I sense You have been there all along even though I may not have known it was You.

³That You would bid me come into Your presence is more than I could ask or think.

Psalm 30 - A Plea For This Land I Love

⁴O Lord, give me a careful and reverent spirit so that flippancy will not come near me—let all my days be filled with admiration and awe for Your Holiness.

⁵Your Spirit, O God—has instilled words for my soul when I have learned to be still and listen—You are made glad with a wise heart.

⁶Now is the time to get down to business—for the work of the Kingdom is at hand—we need to be busier than a bat at a mosquito convention.

⁷I spend my energies like a kid in a candy store in order to receive Your delicacies—Your sweetness is like a treat of luxury to my soul.

⁸Recollections of my past serve to remind me of the error of my ways—like a sheriff with a court order—I am then encouraged to follow Your course more closely.

⁹Thoughts and imaginations abound in generous supply—sometimes they escape me like a horse out of an open barn door.

¹⁰Generally they are like a flock of sheep attentive to the voice of the shepherd—they usually mull around without regard for any dangers lurking about.

¹¹It is when my requests to You are dried up like a drought in a parched barren land that I call to You for advice.

¹²Daily I face my own frailties—then I look to You and face Your strengths and I see hope—the power of Your Word builds me up—in it I find fortification for my spirit.

¹³I ask that You will sit on the throne of my affections and rule my heart—do a mighty work through me so that I will rise up to be a man of God.

¹⁴Humbling myself I realize that I am entirely at Your mercy and dependent on You as my reservoir—the mainspring of my fountain.

¹⁵I deny myself food for the body so that I may reach out and grab hold of Your graciousness and experience Your mercies once again.

¹⁶My stomach rumbles like an approaching thunderstorm or a freight train rumbling down the tracks at full speed.

¹⁷The adversary tries to distract me with wild illusions of hunger—he is a master at trickery and deception.

¹⁸Voices inside my head have a footrace in an attempt to sidetrack me from my purpose—they try to tear me away from my objective.

¹⁹My cry to You is for this land I love—the home of my dwelling—this nation of my ancestors—we are in dire need of You.

²⁰I pelt the throne of heaven with my petitions for Your mercy—like a hailstorm on a tin roof they assail the very portals of the heavens.

²¹Your kindness has surpassed what we deserve—Your mercies have exceeded our quota—You have doled out our rations with liberality.

²²One thing I know—of this I am certain—our power and strength come only from You.

²³Is there a single click of the clock that we do not need You—a chiming of any hour when we are not dependent on Your care and favor?

²⁴Which nation can exist beyond its allotted time—do not all nations rise and fall at Your Word?

²⁵Open the eyes of America before they are closed in the face of death—let us see You as our Redeemer and look to You for a revival of unprecedented proportions.

²⁶The unceasing flow of evil has eroded a land where truth and liberty once reigned free and proud.

²⁷Are You ready to give up on us, O God, to cast us upon the heap of discarded rubbish—are we able with truthfulness to blame You for a shortage of patience and long-suffering?

²⁸Your faithful ones look to You in hope—let the breath of Your Holy Spirit fan the glowing embers of those You have called—so that they might burst into fires of revival.

²⁹From Your outstretched arm comes all might and power—from You comes deliverance.

³⁰Transfer to me the ability to grab hold of Your hand and be an extension of that authority and I will continually praise and exalt Your name forever.

Psalm 31

You Are Always Listening For My Call

¹I never get a busy signal when I call on You—my plea always rings straight through—You never put me on hold.

²A cell phone or a satellite does not have the crystal-clear reception of Your signal.

³No wonder I call on the name of the Lord—there is never an answering machine or voice-mail to deal with—the reassurance of the sound of Your voice brings me comfort.

⁴I have abounding joy each time I speak directly with Your Majesty—my call is never handled by operators standing by.

⁵The joy of the Lord invigorates like a cold shower—sometimes it makes me gasp for breath.

⁶Each morning I can rise and bless Your name, O God—strike me with a godly jealousy so that thoughts of You would be the first to cross my mind.

⁷I will come into Your presence to magnify, to exalt, to praise and lift You up—I will raise my hands in total surrender of my will—casting aside all worldly thoughts.

⁸You, O Lord, have allowed the righteous works of the godly to precede them into glory—they have gone ahead of them to the other side wherein they are causes for great rejoicing.

⁹They will arise as a fiery burnt offering—and the host of heaven will be set loose in joyous celebration—in this way the godly honor the Lord of Glory and are made perfect.

¹⁰Lightheartedness overwhelms me as I am overcome in the presence of Almighty Jehovah—Your saints join with me to give glory to You, my God.

¹¹In the briefness of a moment—joyousness is overcome by peace.

¹²In the quietness of this hour, You direct my thoughts upward—they desire only to extol Your faithfulness.

¹³Are You more pleased with calmness than with joyful exuberance—does not Your Word show that each one has its place in our worship?

¹⁴Holy Spirit—let the sweetness of the Savior illuminate and brighten the atmosphere all around me in tribute to my God.

¹⁵The righteous will let their lamps glow with intensity—thus bringing glory to God.

Psalm 32

My Heart Beats Strong For You

¹My heart beats strong for You, my God—it is not wavering in its desire—there is a passionate and deep-seated force that keeps it beating fiercely.

²Though storms of life may send doubts my way—my heart marches resolutely on.

³Fear does its best to overwhelm me at my weakest point—I beat it back with a good tongue-lashing and call quickly on Your name.

⁴A good dose of the Holy Spirit makes fear hit the road in a quick retreat—it is gone for a while—but if I let my guard down it soon comes slinking back.

⁵Your Word is the entrance to my mind, O Lord—put Your flaming cherubim, yes even a host of Your mighty angels there to defend it.

⁶Your Spirit sends me words I do not know or understand—they shield my life and keep me protected.

⁷An unknown tongue takes control of my speech—I speak forth praises in a heavenly language—words too wonderful for comprehension.

⁸Satan has no answer—no interpretation comes his way—he is stymied for a clarification.

⁹O Lord, how great You are—that You would speak a word to me—You have not denied me truth—it has even risen from dust and ashes and erected a tower for all to witness.

¹⁰My soul will bless Your name and I will sing for joy because I am the work of Your hands—created in the image of the Most Holy One.

¹¹I will bless Your name—yes I will—in submission I bow before Your Majesty.

¹²You have blessed me with and deposited Your loving kindness into my account—not because I

deserve it—but because of Your great love.

¹³You have pinpointed my strength, O God, it is You, it is You—and it is not found in my good virtues or anything belonging to me, it is only found in trust and quietness.

¹⁴I am refreshed and lifted up—my soul rejoices with singing—my lips soon follow suit.

¹⁵Hallelujah—Hallelujah—Hallelujah to the Lamb—I will praise You—King of Glory—for You are the Great I Am.

Psalm 33

Laid Bare, I Will Praise You

¹The neediness of my heart has been exposed before You—it is a gaping hole that only You can fill—but it is certainly no hardship for You.

²The heart of the devout is passed on as a legacy to ensuing generations because they chose to follow Your commands without reservation.

³O Lord, they have forsaken all things to follow You, and Your reward will rise to greet them on that great morning that awaits them.

⁴Who do I have but You my Lord, and is there another so faithful who would have stayed by my side as You have?

⁵You so carefully hold me up and strengthen me with power hidden to this mortal—You are mightier than a Delta Force elite tactical combat detachment.

⁶Where can I go when my knees are weak and my body trembles?—I shiver at random and my eyes are unable to see directly in front of me.

⁷Nausea covers me with a bedspread without finding warmth—infirmity grips my bowels—yet even then You are with me—as a faithful nurse with her patient.

⁸I have been traveling through a passageway of darkness—optimism has all but dwindled—light begins slowly to appear toward the end of the tunnel—it is the light of Your glory.

⁹Through all of this I hear Your call—Your voice sounds like a golden harp at a wedding—You sweep

me upward and set my feet on a higher elevation—my strength is renewed.

¹⁰Once again victory has tapped me on the shoulder—I turn and embrace it with a warm hug—to You belongs victory and You have blessed me with my portion.

¹¹Darkness has left me for another day—the energy of Your Almighty power has given me new life—I am overjoyed and give glory to God in the highest.

¹²You are my Redeemer kinsman, and have paid the full price to rescue me—I am capable of trusting You more completely because of my victory—praise Jehovah.

¹³The shaft I was confined to—along with all of its darkness—taught me many things about Your law—but in the end I can only praise You, my God, for the light that came my way.

¹⁴Your Word is my light—more to be desired than wealth and possessions—in it I observe truthful precepts upon which I base my certainty.

¹⁵I will praise You, O God, upon my bed of ease—I will praise You upon my bed of pain and discomfort—I will praise You upon my bed of roses and yes—even upon my deathbed.

¹⁶The evidence that Your angels of mercy have walked before me—and beside me—yes, even behind me—You have made clear within my soul.

¹⁷In my love for You, my God—works have forsaken me—they have left me unattended—I am left holding the bag.

¹⁸You have shown me paths of righteousness, O God, and I have walked upon them with You—they are carpeted with the moss of truth and lead straight into Your glorious Kingdom.

¹⁹When Your children pass through times of weariness—You supply them with needed rest—their thirst You satisfy with fresh rains.

²⁰Where are You in their time of great need?—You, O Lord, are never far away.

²¹Indeed I will let my soul speak forth —for all my desires are spread out before You—I will praise You for Your love—Your great mercy has followed me all the days of my life.

²²I rest my heart securely upon Your Word—knowing that none of Your promises will come up empty—no—not a single one will be left unfulfilled.

23Exalt the Lord today with Hallelujahs and Hosannas—let your heart be lifted with glad tidings for the Savior.

24He will be exalted with praise—so it might as well come from you—humble your heart before Him and lift high your joyful praise.

25The glory of the Lord is great—for He heard the cry of my soul and added strength to it—now I am able to sing praises unto Him.

26I rejoice—I sing—I shout aloud—for You have done great things—not because of who I am but because of whose I am—and because of who You are.

Psalm 34

Rising In Humility, I Run To You

1My soul was bowed before Your presence, O Lord, not in despair but in humbleness of spirit—never in arrogance for that would not be pleasing to You.

2Now it rises in humility and blesses Your name—unto You it sings—my soul magnifies You—my Savior and my God.

3In the stillness of the night I sense Your presence—in the blackness of the dawn I find You waiting—You are never far from me when You fill my being with Your presence.

4My first conscious thoughts are of You—I am quick to fill them with You—I only have to whisper Your name and You are on my lips.

5I am desperate for You like a sheriff who is hot on the trail of an outlaw—I will hunt for You with a sense of urgency and abandon.

6Obsession over You is my passion, fill my longing, O God—my fervor drives me past my human limits.

7I am thankful that You haven't punished me for the foolishness of my youth—it is evident that Your grace is beyond measure and reaches past my recklessness and folly.

8You have dismissed my yesterdays and filled me with eager joy—Your mercy has not charged me on account of them.

9Walking in new light and gladness I am doused in unused mercies—

hot off the press—daily He gives me a clean slate with which to begin.

¹⁰I have praises to spare for my King—it's with honor and joy that I bring—sacrifices of praise for the rest of my days—with my voice and my heart I will sing.

¹¹How much distance is there between my Lord and me?—There is none because He fills me with His Spirit—He is the hand and I am the glove.

¹²Confirm Yourself in and through my life O God, that I may have the courage to trust You for greater things.

¹³My heart and flesh call out to the Living God who rules and reigns over all—His reign is without end—He is the Immortal One—Ruler of eternity.

¹⁴I exalt and lift You up, my God, as You are enthroned upon the praises of my heart—You are the mighty God and everlasting Father who rides on the wings of my praise.

¹⁵My heart accepts Your longsuffering with tender thanks—You do not treat me as I deserve.

¹⁶Sever those heartstrings—which may still be fastened to this world—so that I will aim my pledge of allegiance upward.

¹⁷The insecure heart He will strengthen—if He is allowed access then He can shore up those weakened timbers that have started to sag over time.

¹⁸A brother with hatred in his heart has no regard for Your compassions—he is to be pitied for his malice and spite—Your gentleness can cause him to discard the callousness of his heart.

¹⁹Expand my devotion, O God, as when air is added to a flat tire—so that it will increase and become more like Your never-ending love.

²⁰Just like the air inside a tire touches all parts of it—so let my love be far reaching—let it touch not only those around me but those out of my range.

²¹Blessed are they who run to the place where God is working in the moment—He has met with me in my place of need—His words have become my strength.

²²Your enduring tenderness has guided me up the path to heaven—day by day You teach me Your ways—Your instructions are the illustrations to my story.

²³The godly have refused to be bullied by the shortcomings and frailties of their flesh.

²⁴Without Your Word, the godly are like a man who cannot take two steps without His cane—it is the crutch they depend upon.

²⁵He has given the discouraged and downhearted the opportunity to release their burdens and heartaches to Him—their sorrows are no more than a dropping of pebbles into the ocean to Him.

²⁶If you let your spirit rise from the valley floor—and let it carry you to the mountain top—then He will show you marvelous things.

²⁷All those who belong to Him are His children—He has made them heirs of His Kingdom.

²⁸Those that live unto Him will walk the perilous path without fear—they will not shudder at any crossroad they come to—the season of His Kingdom will live in their heart year round.

²⁹I have made up my mind—and no matter what comes my way—I have made up my mind, O Lord—I am going to serve You today.

Psalm 35

Saints Of All The Ages Will Praise You

¹Does the Lord want only the early years of a man's life—is it only the formative part that matters to Him?

²No!—emphatically no!—He is seeking the man who will dedicate all of his years—the latter years are equally as important to Him.

³I have seen wicked men waste their youth on madness and reckless living—but the Lord replaces their old ways with righteous living in their later years.

⁴Yet at the same time righteous men have surrendered their youthful years only to lose out in their prime of life—how grievous is that?

⁵Our days on earth are much more than an athletic event or a sporting rivalry—yes we fight to run a spiritual race.

⁶Does the race become less exhausting the longer we run it?—No, it actually becomes more grueling and requires renewed effort and determination to finish.

⁷Fatigue sets in like a twenty-six-mile

Psalm 35 - Saints Of All The Ages Will Praise You

marathon to a first-time runner—it is then I must place my weariness upon the Lord so I will not succumb to burnout.

⁸His Spirit propels me onward with a new burst of resilience—He kicks my stamina into overdrive and fills me with rejuvenating zeal.

⁹Interference is before me everywhere—disruptions clamor for my attention and often turn into a hindrance or delay.

¹⁰I must not avert my eyes from the finish line—my resolve must not veer to the right or the left—but must remain fixed steadfastly on the prize.

¹¹I have decided not to dilly-dally or waste time—for that could be my undoing and cause me to lose the race.

¹²Anyone can start the race strong—but the finish belongs only to those who are fully committed to the Lord.

¹³My heart will be unswerving in my commitment to You all the days of my life—let it be staunch and unshaken before You, O God.

¹⁴There is a victor's crown set aside for the faithful and persevering—I intend to cast it down at Your feet, my Lord.

¹⁵I will dance before You if I am able to stand—otherwise I will just lay prostrate in Your presence.

¹⁶Singing—such as has never been heard on earth—will emanate from the children of God in a glorious harmony.

¹⁷Angels will long to worship You as we can—but they will not be able to sing the songs of Zion—the songs of the redeemed.

¹⁸As I lead the heavenly choir in a stirring chorus—all of heaven will be compelled to pronounce holy Your Majesty—in a melody that will honor Our God—El Shaddai.

¹⁹The throne is surrounded by the saints of all the ages—singing and praising The Lamb who sits upon the throne.

²⁰I will praise You with my whole heart—with each breath I give You praise—I will lift my heart in worship—and I'll serve You all my days.

Psalm 36

Your Word Is The Lifeblood Of My Spirit

¹Holy Spirit—You are my tutor—You guide me so I will not be as naïve as a schoolboy—You instruct and train me in pure living.

²Tears cloud and dim these earthly eyes whenever I direct my thoughts upon You.

³You have cleansed the eyes of my spirit through those same tears—much the same way a person uses eye drops.

⁴Let the eyes of my heart have 20-20 vision—Your Word gives them youthful eyesight and an understanding beyond their years.

⁵The more a worker practices a profession the more he acquires a skill—it is the Lord who gives him competence in all he does.

⁶We must seek to be accomplished in attitude as well as aptitude—neither should eclipse the other—let your mindset be a godly one and you will do well.

⁷You, O Lord, only desire that we give You our very best in all we do—by doing so we will bring glory to the Father.

⁸A man's heart is set on the things he desires—Your Word, O God, has the upper hand in all my longings.

⁹He places fresh thoughts into the minds of those who seek steadily after Him—to those whose minds are captivated by His Spirit will He grant success.

¹⁰To them He will spread His love upon their hearts like jelly upon a peanut butter and jelly sandwich.

¹¹Sometimes I have to stop and pinch myself to realize that Your love for me is real.

¹²My heart is set on pleasing the Lord so that I might avoid displaying offenses against Him.

¹³I put Your Word into practice daily—then I will become skillful and handle it maturely.

¹⁴Your Word is a prerequisite to the start of each day—it is imperative that it begin the launch of my upcoming hours.

¹⁵The Word of the Lord is more powerful than a Howitzer artillery gun—faster than an F-15 Eagle fighter plane

Psalm 36 - Your Word Is The Lifeblood Of My Spirit

¹⁶As soothing as a cough syrup to a sore throat—refreshing as ice water on a one hundred-degree day.

¹⁷More skilled than a tenth-degree black belt martial artist—wiser than "Jaguar"—the world's most powerful super-computer—far more fearsome than the most potent nuclear bomb.

¹⁸Your Word provides the traction I need to bring my thoughts under control when they occasionally go sliding and spinning away like a car on a patch of ice.

¹⁹I find life for my spirit bound up in Your Word—it becomes like a transfusion to an ailing person—it is the lifeblood of the spirit.

²⁰Your Word protects my life like a wall around a castle—it serves as a pharmacy stocked with antidotes against the cares and burdens of life—sustenance comes from it.

²¹Plant Your Word in the garden of my heart in order that it might be like an invasive bamboo plant that takes control—let it be more nourishing than a well-supplied food buffet.

²²I write Your Word on the stationery of my heart so that I will be pleasing to You—I will not fail to jot down Your truths upon its notepad.

²³The marvel of Your Word comes to light every time I see the works of Your creation—I am left in awe and astonishment.

²⁴Wisdom demands that a man refrain from speaking all the things he is thinking.

²⁵It is the godly who have set aside the reasoning with their wits and are content to know that He is God—by this they have driven a stake through the heart of fear.

²⁶Let me direct my life so that it becomes a living message to all I come in contact with—proclaiming the truths of Your Word as on a billboard.

²⁷My purpose in life is to be a banner of light and a promotion of Your Gospel, my Lord.

²⁸In Your kindness You never fail to provide for my protection—a cadre or more of angels is dispatched if necessary—O praise Your glorious name.

²⁹Because I trust in Him—He will bring me safely through all of my days.

³⁰The promises of our God are powerful—it is on them that we have anchored our faith.

Psalm 37

Your Spirit And Mine Unite

¹When I reach the state of exhaustion and I have depleted my storehouse of energy—my eyes look to the heavens because that is where I find my help.

²Acquaintances are a dime a dozen but a true friend is like a crown jewel—of high value and to be closely guarded.

³Now and again You allow us to struggle and learn things on our own—You are never far away—like a teacher waiting for her pupil to ask for help.

⁴Your Word, O Lord, awakens a hungering in my spirit with godly notions and fills it with good things.

⁵I thirst to drink from the fountain of Your righteousness—fill my vessel to overflowing so I can be a wellspring of truth and life to others.

⁶The finger of God has signed His name across the entrance to my heart showing I belong to Him.

⁷You dazzle me with Your creation—I only have to look at the heavens to be moved with admiration by the work of Your hands.

⁸I am blessed in private ways whenever I am hushed before Your presence—it is then I hear Your voice and release my stress to You—it melts away like chocolate in the hand.

⁹As a resourceful woman knits yarn to produce a beautiful sweater—You also knit the fabric of my individuality with Your Holy Spirit to produce a worthy garment.

¹⁰I come before You as a man of prayer—let Your heart be glad anytime I offer praise and worship to You.

¹¹Sometimes the wages of sin wriggle their greedy fingers of enticement in front of me—but I have designated that all my inclinations be directed unto Your ways.

¹²I leave no stone unturned in my search to get nearer to the heart of my God—I seek to probe the depths of His Wisdom for truth.

¹³Your ultimate design mapped out my life long before I was born—but it is still up to me to make wise use of the free will You have given me.

Psalm 37 - Your Spirit And Mine Unite

14The opportunity to praise and worship You, O God, presents itself with every breath I take—and I seize each chance with eagerness.

15There are no words that adequately exalt Your Majesty—which language can reveal the greatness of my God?

16In a declaration of Your holiness any utterance of many words is gibberish—no one but the Holy Spirit is able to convey my heartfelt homage to my God and King.

17I am delighted for each new day He gives me—looking forward to meeting with Him is captivating.

18It is a chance to discover what He has in store for the day ahead—stir in me an eagerness to link up with You, my God.

19Just to think that I can meet with Him—the Master of the universe—talk about incredible—it doesn't get any better than that!

20How simply thrilling it is to linger with my Creator—the Lover of my soul.

21And even more astounding than all of this (as if this were not enough)—He looks forward to our encounter even more than I do—how utterly mind-boggling is that?

22O how marvelous—how divine—when our spirits unite—His heart and mine.

23Lost in the moment—caressed by His love—peace has descended—down from above.

24The wisdom of Your Word has shown me that I never need to come into Your presence as long as I abide in it daily.

25My ears are guided by the voice of the Holy Spirit—they are in tune with His mission.

26Within Your Word, O Lord, are answers to each of life's problems.

27I search it intently so that all of the questions that plague me will be fully revealed—on occasion I find answers to questions I never had.

28Let all of my deeds be clean before You—not out of vain righteousness but from a humble holiness.

29You send the rain in order to purify and refresh the air we breathe—so the Holy Spirit cleanses and purges our impure spirits and worldly contaminations.

30I take note of the judgments in Your Word and apply them to my heart—I will use them so that my steps will remain upon Your path.

Psalm 37 - Your Spirit And Mine Unite

³¹Earnestly I seek Your face today so that I might know the full assurance of Your love—Your Word is the oath that I trust in.

³²What do You ask of Your children—the nation that is called by Your name—is it consecration that you solicit?

³³Surely it is not sacrifices of meat you desire—for You have provided the Lamb—the Son of God.

³⁴It is with humility and clean hands that You are pleased—not a false righteousness or holy piety.

³⁵A rejection of sin and shameful ways—a reverent acknowledgement of You is all You expect.

³⁶A return of wholehearted devotion to Your ways must be made in order to receive Your blessings.

³⁷As long as You are leading and guiding my footsteps I will never fear or dread where it is I am going.

³⁸Lead on, Yahweh, for You know the direction I should take—why wouldn't I rely on You for counsel and wisdom?

³⁹The wise have learned not to live beyond their next breath—they are not ignorant of the fact that life can disappear instantly—then where are their health and riches?

⁴⁰The Lord bestows some serious blessings upon the lives of those who fear Him because they allow Him to be their guiding hope all the days of their lives.

⁴¹How blessed are those who have cast off their ways of independence and rest securely upon His Word in complete dependence.

⁴²Are the godly not doubly blessed when those steps lead them into the presence of their God?

Psalm 38

Open The Eyes Of America

¹O God, when You speak—is there a single word that does not come to pass?

²You love us enough to warn us through Your Word and Your prophets.

³Open the eyes of America and remove the scales that cover them—we have plugged our ears—my cry is that You would open not only our ears but our understanding also.

⁴Things of this world have dulled and blunted our minds—renew and restore them through Your Holy Spirit—so that we may give heed to Your warnings.

⁵Your grace and mercy demand repentance—they are not to be trampled on or to be taken lightly.

⁶Our ways have led us down other paths—those not chosen by You—our way has been foolhardy and uncontrolled in Your eyes.

⁷It is not Your desire to destroy us or You would have already—but Your justice requires that we return to You with our whole hearts.

⁸Our worship needs to be pure before You and not tainted by worldly stench.

⁹We say, "How have we forsaken God—where are our idols?"

¹⁰They are many if we will but open our eyes to the things that take our focus off Him.

¹¹We say we have no Asherah poles—no gods to Baal—no high places—yet our land and our hearts are polluted with other gods.

¹²Are we truly God's people?—if so then we will follow Him with all our heart, mind, soul, and strength.

¹³We have grieved Him by not electing godly men and women but instead choosing the popular route—this has been the root cause of many of our problems today.

¹⁴He longs to bless us if we would turn our hearts back to Him—but the choice must be ours—He will not make it for us.

¹⁵He has loved us with an everlasting love but His love can be turned into judgment—take heed for He is coming soon and His Word will not fail.

Psalm 39

In The Presence Of The King

¹I come into that secret place of the Lord Most High and shut myself in—it is a private place of meeting between us.

²All my preconceived inklings of worship I toss on the burn pile—my stubborn heart I turn over to You, my Lord.

³You place new paths before me when I seek Your wisdom—when I try to find what my worship should truly be.

⁴Your Holy Spirit takes over and moves me into new dimensions—You show me aspects of Your glory I have never seen.

⁵Soon worship pours from my vessel exalting Your name—Your majesty—Your dominion—like emptying a container of liquid.

⁶Then I find myself sitting quietly before You as I wait with longing—my heart wells up in gratefulness and my eyes fill with tears.

⁷Grant me the ability that my thoughts and deeds would be godly so my worship might be pure before You.

⁸As I sit in solitude my thoughts are fixed on You—they are waiting for You to take them captive—mesmerized by Your royalty.

⁹My one aim is to praise You, my God—not only in this life but for all eternity.

¹⁰In the stillness of this hour my soul waits patiently for You—it will not grow weary seeking after You.

¹¹Indescribable beauty flashes before me as peace floods my soul like a waterfall coming out of the side of a mountain.

¹²I hear all of heaven's angelic beings singing the persistent chorus, "Be still and know that I am God."

¹³Its melodic line is joined by the instruments of praise so that all of heaven is lifting up and exalting my God.

¹⁴Suddenly I burst forth singing with the heavenly voices in an energetic chorus of "Be exalted, O God, above the heavens and let Your glory be over all the earth."

¹⁵I grow quiet as my worship subsides for the time being—I delight in Your presence and glory as it moves about the room.

¹⁶Bowing my knees before You I seek to honor You—Your face is all I want to see.

¹⁷Your ear is quick to take note of the prayer of the saint—so with my voice I call out to You.

¹⁸In my spirit I bow low before You—I prostrate myself before Your throne—I am broken before Your Majesty.

¹⁹I am sobered by the fact that I am in the presence of the King of Kings—Jehovah—my Heavenly Father.

²⁰You utter words unknown to man but my spirit obeys unaware—I rise to my feet in awe.

²¹I am standing before You—stripped bare—my modesty shrieks in horror unable to grasp my shame.

²²With embarrassment I catch a glimpse of myself but to my sheer bewilderment I see that I am clothed—covered in a robe of righteousness that my Lord has put on me.

²³I stand amazed in the pure light of Your glory—bathed in the radiance of Your splendor.

Psalm 40

You Give Joy To My Daily Life

¹If I were to tally up the dollar amounts of every blessing You provide—I would discover I am a wealthy man.

²The riches of heaven have become the Dow Jones of my portfolio—its stock market has never had a loss on record.

³Examine my heart, O Lord—scrutinize it thoroughly—give it a good tune-up so it will continue to run well.

⁴The prayer and focus of my heart is to walk unwaveringly before my God—the man who does this will please Him and be blessed.

⁵I have considered my life and it is evident that I am just a mortal man with flesh and blood and spirit.

⁶I am a man into whom You have planted a seed of faith and I eagerly watch to see how You will use it.

⁷I am sure, no, let me be more spe-

cific—I am unhesitatingly certain that I will serve You all of my days—however few or many they may be.

⁸As a child of the King I need the boundaries You set for me—they keep me on the straight and narrow.

⁹I pledge my life to Your care as a man does to his bride—forever and always—would it please You if I were to swear an oath vouching for my word of honor?

¹⁰Your hand of conviction bears down on me at times but it only serves to draw me closer to Your side, dear Lord—usually it brings sorrow and regret, which leads to repentance.

¹¹To live a life on the mountaintop is for the extraordinary moments—I dedicate myself to living and making the most of my run-of-the-mill days.

¹²The view from the top is spectacular—but where the line is drawn in the sand is when my daily life—which is hid with Christ—is exposed to others for the glory of God.

¹³You dwell inside my vessel, O God, when will You overflow and spill over the outside like the morning mist?

¹⁴Would You make my goblet transparent so that You shine out and others will see the light of Your glory coming from within?

¹⁵I will probe to know You more deeply until I am captivated by Your presence—I keep my eyes open for Your return each day, my Lord.

¹⁶You have marked my soul for resurrection and I will sing for joy of my Redeemer.

¹⁷My praises ring as a tolling bell to You and as a scourge to satan and his cronies—they are a nuisance unto his efforts to harass me.

¹⁸All of my days are blessed because of Your mercies—they are never repeated—but I find every one of them to be unique and original.

¹⁹All my thoughts are well known before You, O Lord, each one is disclosed in the light of Your omniscience—but death has swallowed up many secrets.

²⁰My loneliness slips away as I rise in the early dawn because You are there to greet me.

²¹When you sit at His feet nothing else will satisfy—sitting in His presence causes you to hunger and thirst after righteousness.

22 Let His thoughts be opened unto your spirit—then your eyes will not be closed unto heaven's truth and you will be established in greater faith.

23 The troubles of this life are many—You bid me to thrust them on You, for You are strong.

24 A thankful heart and grateful lips will always draw me closer to the Master—it will not fail to open the door into His presence—let it flow freely and not hesitatingly.

25 The Lord is my caregiver—who else do I need?—whenever I require help I just ask—He is the keeper of my soul at all times.

26 He has played a new song unto my soul—the notes have rung out with different tones because He writes them with excellence.

27 His love has called forth the music of my soul and we have made sweet harmony together—now my soul rejoices each time I hear His voice.

28 O how my heart loves to praise Him—to sing songs of thankfulness to Him with joy.

29 Godly praise strikes a chord in His heart and leads to His favor—He is blessed and, in turn, passes that right back to us.

30 The praise of man is not necessary to validate His character—His attributes stand on their own and do not need our affirmation.

31 Our praise draws us unto Him like the needle of a compass cannot resist pointing north.

32 I have learned to trust You, O Lord, because You have my best interests at heart—my welfare is of the utmost importance to You.

33 My soul delights in the increase from Your hand—I am filled to the brim.

34 You send me trials and testing—essential for my spiritual growth—to receive the most favorable results I must allow myself to be steered by the Holy Spirit.

35 No one knows the heart of a man like God—is there anything hidden from His awareness?

36 In my search for the signpost that will draw me closer to the Father—wisdom has shown me humility as the marker.

37 My God—You are the essence of humility and are jubilant when You find a humble man.

38 Your scrutiny disrobes all my pretenses like a paint stripper on an old coat of paint.

[39]The Holiness of God Almighty is not something to be calculated like a math formula.

[40]Integrity leads to virtue—virtue leads to honor—honor leads to respect—respect leads to morality—and morality leads to holiness.

[41]Holiness is not the things we do as much as it is the attitude we do them with.

[42]How can I, a man of unclean lips, be holy?—Unless my heart is renovated by the transformation and washing of the Holy Spirit—I cannot!

[43]You set my feet a dancin'—my heart overflows—I've got the joy of the Lord inside—from my head down to my toes.

[44]Search me, O God, and You will see that the dedication and craving of my moral fiber is to lay at Your feet a humble heart.

Psalm 41

Shaped Into His Image

[1]Which flask is able to contain His power—is any canteen capable of storing His glory?—there is none—for His glory is like an all-consuming fire.

[2]At various times my zeal has clashed with His wisdom—I have spoken without knowledge and understanding and my ignorance has brayed in triumph.

[3]At times, my soul has clamored for Your power to fill me—yet it could easily consume me if You filled this tent in which I reside.

[4]I would be incinerated as a fire cremates a corpse—reduced to nothing but ashes as a nuclear holocaust does to its victims.

[5]Holy Spirit, be my regulator valve—govern and pour the proper amount of the Lord's power into me.

[6]Make me as a piece of earthenware that's been fired in the kiln to give strength to the clay.

[7]Glaze me, O God, with Your Holy Spirit that I may be fused with You—that my pottery may be more useful.

[8]Does the vessel dictate to the potter how to make it?—Of course not!

Psalm 41 - Shaped Into His Image

—Imagine how ludicrous and absurd that would be.

9 I am delighted that You are shaping me into the image and likeness of Your son—what more could I ask?

10 Contentment will reside within me as a pitcher with a useful purpose rather than as an exhibit at a museum.

11 Time and eternity are on Your side. —Though they are enemies of mortal man, make me one with You so that I may also be on Your side.

12 The endlessness of eternity is all You have ever known—it belonged to You before You created time—it stretched beyond its beginning and ending.

13 Is the creator less than the created —or the one who forms things with His hands less significant than what He formed?

14 I just look at the works of Your hands and see how monumental they are—You create everything with excellence.

15 The vastness of the heavens testify to Your overwhelming size— when I take this into account my mind fails me—why such a great God would even consider such a pauper as I.

16 Yet in spite of my misgivings You show in Your Word that I was on Your mind before You fashioned the world—how incredulous is that?

17 Let all praise go to the Rock of my Salvation—the eternal God of all the ages—the Infinite One who is ageless and everlasting.

18 Whenever I run to the Rock of Ages He shields me from temptations as well as the storms of life that come against me.

19 Thus if I fail to enter that place of safety I become a target for the enemy—my well-being is in grave danger.

20 Whenever satan throws a roadblock in my path I just praise my Lord all the more—I will rejoice with hilarity and exaltation.

21 It is up to me to take responsibility for all You have entrusted to my care—You have called all of Your saints unto steadfastness and devotion.

22 You prompt me through Your Word—it is the burr under my saddle to seek Your ways—it reveals wisdom to my soul.

23 The citation from Your Word summons me to praise Your authority with all that is within me—there is none like You, O Lord.

24It is not up to me to question Your leadership because You are truly sovereign—You reign with power and might and depend upon no one else.

25Your nature is flawless—You are not prone to shifting frames of mind like mortal man—You are steady, stable, and ageless—praise be to Your Magnificence.

Psalm 42

I Need To Know You Intimately

1I dare not lose my single-mindedness in the quest to know You, my God—if I do, my mind will be dissected and my tenacity will come to naught.

2Reward me with persistence so the motives of my heart will come to fruition—let my aim be to diligently seek godly purposes for my life.

3It is the baptism of the Holy Spirit that saturates me and produces an urgency to see my Savior—sometimes I can barely contain myself.

4Who can see into the depths of the soul besides our Maker—to know the thoughts that abide there—the schemes that lie hidden in the recesses—all the dreams lying in wait?

5Seers and diviners cannot—mind readers and fortune tellers cannot—sorcerers and witch doctors cannot—neither can clairvoyants or mystics.

6Only the Lord God Almighty is able to peer into the remoteness of our souls and perceive our aspirations—Your presence in my life at all times is the thing I covet the most.

7Moments I wish I could have hidden from Your examination have come and gone—those less-than-proud moments—even bursts of fleshly desires.

8I can hide nothing from You—my strongest desires cannot conceal my intentions from You.

9The crater in which my deepest longings and desires exist—You have seen by Your great insight—Your wisdom has penetrated into the abyss of my soul.

10Bring to remembrance those periods of devotion where You united our spirits.

¹¹Lord, recall to my mind again how I must walk by faith and not by sight—nor by feelings—I need Your daily prompting.

¹²To please You is a moment-by-moment undertaking—walking by faith is mandatory.

¹³When I lay down the mantle of this life and draw my last breath, You will lift me to glory—Beyond this veil of tears, past the heartaches of this life—forever in Your presence.

¹⁴To be at home with my Lord is better than ten thousand earthly lifetimes.

¹⁵At the proper time all creatures of our God and King will give Him a standing ovation in honor of His majesty and triumph, O my soul, praise the Lord.

Psalm 43

You Fill Me Up

¹O Lord, my God—I am steadfast in my desire to stand up and protect Your honor—to wave the banner of Your dignity unto all nations.

²I want to stand on the top of Mount Everest and call down curses on all of Your adversaries—to heap troubles upon their heads.

³Now isn't that comical!—it's not like a God of Your power and might would need someone to defend Him—especially someone as weak and defenseless as I.

⁴That would be comparable to a gnat standing up to fight for a dinosaur—how preposterous would that be?

⁵It will be my privilege to respect You and esteem You above all other gods—out of reverence and admiration.

⁶Let me not be ashamed to stand up courageously—to witness and confirm Your glory by the demonstration of my walk.

⁷Your Word testifies of Your Majesty—how You have so aptly defended Yourself.

⁸It speaks also of gods of wood, stone, and precious metals which have no life—idols of no intrinsic value.

⁹In the short span of my lifetime, I have witnessed the lifelessness of those gods but I have also

had the privilege of a true encounter with the Living God—Jehovah Almighty.

[10] What a pleasure it is serving You—the one and only God of life, love, and mercy—I will praise You with all my soul for You make sense of my life.

[11] You have chosen me—not because You needed a servant (although I would gladly be one)—but You have adopted me as Your son—glory to Your name.

[12] As I yield myself to You I am filled with Your righteousness—and my will becomes relinquished unto Yours.

[13] I have never gone away empty handed after seeking Your will—You fill me up.

[14] Delight floods my soul each time I enter Your courts with songs of praise—I will let my heart perspire with love for You, my God.

[15] Prayer and offerings of gladness escort me into Your presence.

[16] When I dwell on Your Word, it satisfies me—like tasty morsels of meat at mealtime.

[17] In my pursuit to know You better I have been diving into Your Word as a swimmer dives into an Olympic-size pool.

[18] Wisdom teaches me that as a swimmer must surface to receive air, I must also have periods of renewal if I am to continue searching You out.

[19] My way is smooth and my path is on level footing because I trust in You—You have leveled its ridges and hills.

[20] I have found the highway that leads to heaven—it is a highway of holiness, which has bypassed the turnpike of pleasure.

[21] Fall in behind, seeing that it is a narrow road—our Lord leads the way and only the pure in heart can travel on it.

[22] Those redeemed by the blood of the Lamb will walk it in confidence—for the Lord is their guide.

[23] Impale me by the Word of truth and run me through with righteousness—then my walk will be blameless and pure before You.

[24] The longer I live the deeper my love for You grows—As my life on earth winds down my excitement is spurred on thinking of how I will soon be home with You.

[25] My list of "to-dos" gets longer the closer I get to the end but You, my Lord, are at the top of my list.

²⁶For I know if I sleep in the dust of the earth I will rise in power at the sound of Your mighty trumpet blast.

²⁷I will awaken clothed in everlasting life—dressed in robes of righteousness—presented to my King spotless, before His throne.

²⁸And if You come back before I taste the sting of death—I shall be raptured to be with You in the twinkling of an eye.

²⁹While on this earth I have lived under the judgment of other men—as You have permitted—but ultimately Your judgment rules over all.

³⁰You alone are the Lord Most High and my praise will ever follow You —with an aching in my heart and a yearning in the depths of my soul will I seek You all my days.

Psalm 44

You Fill Me With Pleasures Unending

¹I reach out and grab in order that I might catch hold of Your Spirit —You are reaching for me at the same time.

²Draw my heart close to Yours, O God, so I can glimpse Your vision through my eyes.

³Pulverize any pride that may be hiding within me—whether it would be real or false—grind it into ashes of humility.

⁴The law of the Lord is like an umbrella and covers all who live—it is righteousness and a precious gift tied with a bow.

⁵His laws are unalterable and cannot be maneuvered—they are more certain than the law of gravity—which belonged to God long before Isaac Newton discovered it was there.

⁶God's laws in the spirit are as surefire as those in the natural—His promises are more certain than the most iron-clad guarantee you will find on earth.

⁷I woke up singing—joy bells were ringing—looking for my home on high—His hand will feed me—His light will lead me—straight to that home on high.

69

Psalm 44 - You Fill Me With Pleasures Unending

⁸There's a heavenly dwelling—He has made for all, all who worship Him—there's a heavenly dwelling—waiting in that home on high.

⁹The quickest cure for my sadness is to run into the arms of my Father and get a hug.

¹⁰When I am running short on strength, I ask God for a transfusion of His strength.

¹¹The breeze of Your Spirit plays a cheerful melody on the chimes of my heart and fills it with delight.

¹²Blessed be the Lord—You fill me with wonder—pleasures unending—Your Spirit guides me—I hear Your voice saying, "This is the way—walk in it and be righteous."

¹³Then I will lift up holy hands and a clean heart to You for You have made me glad.

¹⁴The most amazing thing I've found is Your grace in my hour of need—it is great enough to cover every one of my sins.

¹⁵As simply as the warmth of the sun ripens the grapes on the vine, I look to the Son of God to produce the maturity I need.

¹⁶He is the vine—I'm just a branch growing out from Him.

¹⁷As the Master Gardener, He knows precisely how to prune and cut back the dead growth—to thin out and shape the remaining blossoms in order to produce healthy fruit.

¹⁸Holy Spirit—let Your sweetness come forth as the fruits of my spirit are pressed in the winepress of God's vineyard.

¹⁹Why has it taken me so long to learn to trust You in all of my ways—the only conclusion is that I am just a slow learner.

²⁰When I obey Your Word—and set aside following my own sense—I grow more comfortable trusting You.

²¹You place trials across my path to test my trust in You—I am becoming more accustomed to being on familiar terms with Your ways each time I allow You to be my guide.

²²I find delight in talking to You in the same way I do with my brother Milton, but You alone are the desire of my heart.

²³I wait upon You as a baby bird waits for the next meal from its parent—I am fed by Your Word, through which I receive my daily nutriments.

²⁴The joy of the Lord is the fireworks of my soul—I discover new levels of passion as I wait with excitement for His soon coming.

²⁵When sickness has sapped my body—and the strength to pray has left through the back door—my only hope is in You, Holy Spirit.

²⁶Translate the prayers of my mind and take them to the Father that He might have pity on my feeble body—then He will pass His healing onto me so I might praise Him for one more day.

²⁷Glory unto Jehovah Rophe—my healer—my God.

Psalm 45

Your Presence Is My Home

¹You have selected me to wander in search of my homeland—by faith—like Abraham when You called him—help me find contentment and peace of mind knowing I am in Your will.

²Guide my steps, O Lord, so I may find the place You have determined—You have a preferred location for each of Your children—a selected spot of Your choosing.

³You have placed me on this earth as a pilgrim in search of a better residence—this earth is not my permanent home—just the boulevard that takes me to my heavenly abode.

⁴My soul longs to be with You, my God, forever—in Your presence—that is where I have always wanted to be.

⁵While on my travels here below—I find only temporary gratification—a dulling of the senses—a fleeting fulfillment of pleasure.

⁶You have given me spiritual eyes and a willing heart that constantly search for You.

⁷How I long to be at home in Your dwelling place—that eternal spot You have prepared for me—a home of unending worship and endless praise to Your majesty.

⁸You created this world in beauty—but what a mess and shambles man has made of it.

⁹Forgive us of our destructive ways, O God—they have been detrimental to the beautiful atmosphere You gave us in the beginning.

¹⁰We have failed to follow Your laws and have not made Your precepts our practice—we have made our ways higher than Your ways.

¹¹Where have we missed the mark and strayed so far from the path You have laid out for us?

¹²By following other gods and going our own pigheaded way—look where it has landed us.

¹³Those who prefer to follow darkness and decline to follow the light will be left in the lurch—like a spinning top that is almost finished with its spin cycle.

¹⁴As darkness settles across the earth—so it is with an evil man—he is wrapped in a cloak of darkness—he is not anxious to see the light for it will surely expose his deeds.

¹⁵Search my heart with the penetration of the light of Your Word—and I shall be clean and free from the guilt and condemnation that would infect me.

Psalm 46

You Created Everything From Nothing

¹I weary myself, O God, to obtain my portion of You—like a mountain climber struggling to reach the peak.

²Be pleased with the fragrance of my offerings of praise that I seek to honor You with.

³I wait submissively for You—enable me to remain immersed in Your glory.

⁴It is not my desire just to be sprinkled by You, Holy Spirit, but to be totally drenched with the essence of my God.

⁵The godly honor You without taking any forethought—they bless Your name with their deeds—their words are gracious and accompanied by righteous actions.

⁶They seek no reward but are content to be used by You and in Your service—Your joy is their payment—their gift is in seeing You meet the needs of others.

⁷Smiles that light up their faces belong to those who trust in my God—these are countenances that beam with the glory of His authority.

Psalm 46 - You Created Everything From Nothing

⁸Their faces are the evidence of Your sunshine coming through the clouds.

⁹Anytime smiles turn into laughter it becomes music—like a melody straight from the soul.

¹⁰Long before You created time, You, the Master Architect of the universe drew the plans for my life in full color and in vivid detail.

¹¹As a designer there was none Your equal—the inventor of all that is, that was, or ever will be—a Master Builder who is capable of creating substance from nothing.

¹²Your blueprint, O God, was without flaw and with great purpose—You knew the end from the beginning.

¹³You sketched and traced my frame in preparation for the object of Your affection.

¹⁴With painstaking precision You modeled my life before it ever came into existence.

¹⁵When it came down to the nuts and bolts and the nitty-gritty of Your plan—You did not miss a beat—You laid out every element in Your drawing.

¹⁶Knowing what it would take to bring my flesh into alignment with Your will—You instilled within me a set of yearnings and desires so my heart would follow after You.

¹⁷You fashioned my temperament and my disposition according to Your diagram—You knew my nature and character full well.

¹⁸You formed me with a unique personality—a distinctive trait that You specially endowed for me.

¹⁹Your hand shaped my physique—both inwardly and outwardly—it was with great care and purpose that my being came to light on Your drawing board.

²⁰You produced me with the skill of a specialist—an artisan—a true craftsman—You worked out every part in minute detail.

²¹Then You assembled the parts together—machined to the exact tolerances according to Your draft.

²²You engineered me with strictness—With purpose and deliberate intention You fabricated me as an original.

²³With exactness and precision You stitched my parts together as a tailor would produce a garment with care and meticulousness.

²⁴At times I look and see what Your hands have made—and I am truly in awe with wonder.

25It is with dismay that I ponder and see where I have focused on outward nobility instead of viewing other qualities of merit—such as inner growth and beauty.

26Mortification and shame reprimand me—I confess my murmurings and offenses against the marvelous work of Your creation—I have talked foolishly with little regard for Your handiwork.

27You have made me with much refinement—I have no right to protest to You—my Maker—concerning my makeup—take away my sin and reproach—my Redeemer.

28You hold me accountable—now direct me to be the man You established—a man after Your own heart.

29I bow my heart before You in reverence—I ask for Your supervision and oversight in all my ways—the moorings of my soul hold fast because they are firmly attached to the Rock.

30Steer me in Your path—keep my life in check with Your Holy Spirit.

Psalm 47

You Establish Your House Upon The Prayers Of The Saints

1The halls of my God are lined with the praises of His saints—like a room's walls are covered in wallpaper.

2He delights in carpeting His courts with their praises—His inner rooms with their shouts of joy.

3You have established Your house upon their petitions—You have fortified it with the cries of passionate saints.

4I—the Lord your God—present Myself among them at the sounds of their weeping—their cries are like magnets to My heart—I am stirred by their tears.

5Their songs of worship make Me smile—I am cheered at the very sounds of adoration—they are sent from their hearts to My throne.

6It is not just with loud sounds and much clapping that I am honored but with the gentle and sweet song of the heart that rises to hail Me in highest esteem—in that I take pleasure.

Psalm 47 - You Establish Your House Upon The Prayers Of The Saints

⁷Even in the silence of the saints I am exalted—in the quietness of the moment I will pour forth My Words—may you learn to apply them to your hearts.

⁸I bestow blessing and honor upon the godly—those who do not fail to seek Me at all times.

⁹I have chosen My servant to anoint you with blessing because he has listened to My words.

¹⁰The prayers of My people are like salve to a wound—they benefit much before Me.

¹¹The aroma of your worship fills My nostrils—the sacrifice of your praise permeates the heavens—I have opened the windows of heaven to let it drift upward and in.

¹²Destiny has been changed through the prayers of a single widow—how much more will it be changed when you seek Me in chorus?

¹³Do not think your prayers are pointless or redundant—for I cherish each one of them—I am saving them for a special day.

¹⁴You are invited to bring Me each petition—all are significant—they melt My heart as a candle melts under the flame.

¹⁵If you really believed in Me as your heart says it does—what would you not ask of Me?

¹⁶Am I too small for anything you might conceive—or is there anything you could possibly imagine that would be too great for Me?

¹⁷I cannot lie—but aside from that I can do anything else.

¹⁸I have thrown down the gauntlet in My Word by bidding you to test Me—to try Me—to ask for anything in My name—and see if I will not stand by My Word.

¹⁹My Holy Spirit rests in your midst—I fill your vessels daily—I am overjoyed to give you life that you might praise Me.

²⁰I have been blessed by your dedication of prayer—now reach out and take hold of all that I offer.

²¹My heart longs to fulfill each of your godly desires—worship Me in Holiness—for I am Holy and there is none like Me.

²²I—Myself—will go before you and My Glory will be your rearguard—I have declared it!

Psalm 48

He Chooses My Path And I Follow

¹Remove the cataracts from my eyes so I can see You clearly—otherwise I can only see You through cloudiness and haze.

²Am I any more than a clay pot to which You have loaned Your Holy Spirit—an earthen vessel into which you have breathed the breath of life?

³I have pledged my whole life to You—not just those spare moments I can grab now and then—I want to spend all my time on You with no change coming back.

⁴Sharpen my mind, O Lord, as one sharpens the lead of a pencil that has become dull—then I will be more useful and productive.

⁵You have chosen the path I take—let me walk it with dignity and acceptance so that I might be neither proud nor ungrateful.

⁶Whenever my walk becomes difficult I choose Your Word to be my crutch—the support upon which I can lean.

⁷I have discovered that when things don't go my way—I just shrug them upon You.

⁸I strain to draw closer to You—like a long string of railroad cars laboring to hold on to the locomotive.

⁹How can I help but find pleasure in Your Word, O Lord; I practice it daily so that I will follow all of its requirements, so that I may hear and heed its warnings.

¹⁰If I reject Your Word, that is proof I have no wisdom within me.

¹¹My soul magnifies You, Lord, and my spirit maintains an atmosphere of worship continually.

¹²What can I do for You today that will bring a smile to Your face—something that might make Your heart glad?

¹³As I point my full attention upon You, my God—allow my worship to be undisturbed and full strength.

¹⁴Clarify the Word—Holy Spirit—that I might hear what You are saying—empower me to put Your truths into practice.

¹⁵I will enter the gateway of heaven and abide daily in Your presence—while I agree that every breath of my life longs to be spent in Your glory.

¹⁶The express purpose of my heart is to be faithful to You all the days of my life—I will set up a guard against the seed of unfaithfulness so it will not be allowed to take root.

¹⁷Opportunities come and go to worship Your Majesty—but none are more prevalent than this present moment—I inhale Your grace and exhale Your mercies.

¹⁸The powers of darkness are a mighty force—but none so powerful as my God who created them—for He is mightier than the greatest enemy.

¹⁹He created everything that exists—there is none like Him and no one is His equal.

²⁰When I think of You—the Almighty God who could demand strict obedience of us—I marvel that You in Your superior might—have left us the choice of being obedient to You.

²¹Gratitude and praise piggyback with a sense of indebtedness as I proclaim Your Glory.

Psalm 49

He Speaks Peace To My Turbulence

¹I love growing old with You, my Lord—every day grows sweeter than the day before.

²Without glasses these eyes would be of little value—so it is for my spirit without Your Holy Spirit.

³Each day You replenish my resources with fresh and new ones—You stock up my pantry so that I will not be in need.

⁴Daily I will seek You in order that You will be foremost in my thoughts and actions—then Your Spirit will point the way for each decision I make.

⁵This daily walk is furnished with its share of rough times—I have experienced both mountaintops and valleys.

⁶Oftentimes my strength has failed—sometimes I have stumbled and You have helped me get back up.

⁷Now and then I have lost my way but Your hand prevailed and got me back on track.

[8]There were times I desperately needed Your Word of encouragement just to keep going—You were my solace in the raging storm.

[9]In the face of all of this I am determined—it is my emphatic and unhesitating goal to cross the finish line with my torch still burning brightly.

[10]Holy Spirit—be the DNA of my bloodline—the origin of my lineage—the filament of thread that holds my humanity together—the kernel and center of my being.

[11]You quiet the turbulence in the deepest parts of my soul by speaking peace to it.

[12]Whenever the evil one dangles his objects of temptation in front of me, I call upon the Spirit of my God to sweep them away.

[13]Eliminate the fleshly desires from my heart, O God, as an exterminator would eradicate those pests that attack earthly homes.

[14]Your Word, O God, is truth—it has been uttered and will not be taken back—nor will it be changed.

[15]Time brings all things to pass—You will not leave so much as a single letter of Your law unfulfilled—for as You have spoken it, O Lord, it will be done.

[16]Your Word is that pillar of truth unto my life—and it speaks reassurance to my heart.

[17]Each time I wake up I find You have given me added and beautiful opportunities to praise You—how can I help but be joyful?

[18]Your joy makes my life burst into song—Your affection for me makes up its sweet notes.

[19]You have applied a badge of courage to my garment so that I might go forth boldly—giving high praise unto Your name.

[20]When I sit and ponder life's mysteries—that gives me a headache—every time I ponder Your greatness I am at a loss for words and find great peace.

[21]The glories of the Lord are reserved for the righteous—for those who seek His face daily.

[22]He delights in storing up His treasures for the pleasure of His saints—because they are pleasing to Him.

[23]It was good for me to take notice of the reason for my sickness—it taught me a deeper trust in You, my Maker.

[24]Your hand of affliction upon me was meant to draw me closer to Your side.

25Though the storms of sickly health pounded my body—my spirit was on solid footing—anchored firmly upon the Rock of my Redeemer.

26While the winds and rain eroded some of my joy—I will sing to You a new song—one of hope and recovery.

27Restore to me the joy of my reward so that my heart can rise again in worship—my soul magnifies Your greatness, O God.

28I will be as the wise man—for I am building my house upon the solid Rock—upon Jesus the Master Builder—who cannot be shaken or moved.

29Let the tempest blast its fury and blow violently upon my homestead—for I am hunkered down safe in the Rock of Ages—for He is my surety and protector.

Psalm 50

Your Sleep Rejuvenates Me

1See how often this fleshly body grows exhausted and drained—it is constantly in need of daily recharging of strength.

2By the work of Your hands, O God, You created and designed sleep to restore our energy levels.

3Just as the Sabbath provides a break for our week—so does sleep for our daily labors.

4Each time I lie down to sleep and close my eyes I prepare my heart before You, my God.

5Often I acknowledge my frailties—sometimes realizing I am only a heartbeat away from awakening in Your presence.

6Sleep comes to me with the reassurance that this may be my last conscious waking moment on earth.

7I have no fear or alarm—sleep comes as a sweet peace—I drop off into a sound slumber.

8Should You choose for my term to expire—my labors to cease—my good work to have been completed—the last chapter to have been written;

9I can smile knowing that in a twinkling I will be rejoicing in Your presence—dancing evermore—

singing Your praises with choirs of angels—living forever with You.

¹⁰And if, perhaps, I have another mile to go—or just a few more steps in my journey here on earth—I arise rested and refreshed—pleased that You see fit to use me in Your Kingdom.

¹¹As the body requires rest—so my spirit must also find a lull in order to rejuvenate.

¹²You—Holy Spirit—breathe new life into my spirit and cause it to become reenergized.

¹³My soul finds rest in You, my God, for I can find strength in no other place.

Psalm 51

Your Word Intervenes In My Heart

¹Whenever I sense danger nearby I make a beeline for Your Word.

²Your Word, O Lord, becomes a safety net beneath me when I am on the tightrope of life—it provides protection and security in case I fall.

³With audacity I declare that You are my God—in full assurance I speak forth Your praises.

⁴The words of Your truth are propelled through these lips of clay—declaring Your worth and supremacy.

⁵I have resolved that neither the world nor its powers will intimidate me—for You are the Ruler of my heart and life.

⁶You have entered my change of address and I am looking forward to the day I move into Your house—You have prepared a special room for me.

⁷You inspect my thoughts and motives and are faithful to show me my faults.

⁸The rebuke that comes from Your mouth is gentle and full of mercy—it speaks to my heart with tenderness.

⁹Nowhere are Your mercies more evident than when You daily send angels to escort me wherever I go—they are ever present—surrounding and hemming me in.

¹⁰Godly men have heard Your call and are quick to comply—they act

Psalm 51 - Your Word Intervenes In My Heart

in accordance with what they have understood.

[11] They are quick to sound a word of admonition in exactly the same manner a smoke detector blasts its horn to warn of an impending fire.

[12] The righteous give no thought to what others may say but are quick to get down to business—the fool says, "I will wait for a more convenient time" and thereby perishes.

[13] You break the yoke and bondages are smashed into fine powder at the cry of Your servant.

[14] You release oppression and I gain freedom when I call upon Your name.

[15] Is there a specific thought—one solitary action—even one isolated breath—where I don't need You?

[16] No—I need You for all of these and so much more—You fulfill the very purpose of my being—You are my sole desire.

[17] The mind of the Lord searches out and discerns a man's heart long before even one act of his behavior causes him to trip up and divulge his true nature.

[18] Let all I do and say be pleasing in Your sight, O Lord; let it be God-honoring in every respect—point my steps in the best direction and keep them on the desirable track.

[19] Right choices come as a result of a heart in tune with the Master—for He keeps the heart strings tuned up.

[20] It is my Father's objective that I inherit His spiritual tendencies—I make it my goal to absorb His characteristics into my persona.

[21] I am hemmed in by an abundance of joy every time I come into Your presence—it safeguards my life from the bitter moments that come my way.

[22] Sin and the cares of this world have caused me to do an about face—now I look toward Your commands to bail me out.

[23] I am listening intently for the sound of Gabriel's horn—to usher the return of my Messiah—it could be any minute now.

[24] My gratefulness knows no bounds, Lord—I appreciate You because every time I have taken my concerns to You—You have never given me the run around.

[25] One of the best things I have learned is to base my life on the "good Lord willing" factor—because if He is not, then I don't even want to go there.

[26] A smile lights up my face like an eastern sunrise whenever I think of Your goodness and mercy; You grant unceasing mercy, O Lord, without a down payment of any kind.

Psalm 52

I Have Eagerly Answered Your Call

¹The Spirit of God is searching the earth for a man who is anxious to be wholly sold out to Him—without reservation of any kind.

²My hands shoot up into the air like a student eager to answer a question—as I volunteer to be that man of purpose You are looking for, my God.

³Place within me a receptive heart so I can latch on to Your mind, O God.

⁴My heart has dared for a moment to surrender—shake it to its very foundation so that I will totally give it to You.

⁵Lord—I am a desperate man—I am in dire need of You.

⁶You heard my cry of desperation—the cry of my heart—You came to meet with me—to draw my heart next to Yours.

⁷Outline the course of my day, Holy Spirit—so that I may walk in the ways of my God.

⁸I present my alms to God as a token of my love and adoration for Him.

⁹Take my gifts, Great Jehovah, and use them in Your Kingdom—no matter how small and unimportant they seem—I must remember that little is much when it is in Your hands.

¹⁰The widow's mite was a powerful token—a gesture proving the capacity of the heart was mightier than the coin.

¹¹I take no pride, therefore—indeed I have no pleasure in what I have to offer You, my Lord—my abilities are of no use in and of themselves.

¹²When I come to the end of my self-sufficiency—only then can You begin Your work of grace.

¹³Your grace has chosen my soul and You move me about at Your good pleasure—as a knight on a chessboard—Your full armor upon me—as the King, You lead me into battle.

¹⁴Any works that I do, or have done for that matter, are for the express purpose of glorifying Your name—praise the Lord, O my soul.

¹⁵The Word of the Lord cuts to the core of all my weaknesses—exposing my defects.

¹⁶It cuts to the heart of the matter—digging to the root cause of my sin—repairing and correcting my mistakes.

¹⁷Each day I awake—I arise to go forth as a living testament of God's grace and mercy.

¹⁸You clothe me in humility, yet also in power—in order that You may show through me the glory of my God in splendor.

¹⁹There is great pleasure in obedience to Your Spirit, O God—it requires sacrifice but not knowledge.

²⁰There is much to be gained from it—it provides ointment and great peace for the conscience.

²¹You answer the prayer of the righteous each and every time—perhaps not always to their satisfaction and understanding.

²²The faith of a godly man causes him to stand firm in the darkness—when answers elude his grasp he will remain confident in his God.

²³You fill a man's life with a series of God moments—it is up to him to capture those by recognizing and acting upon them.

²⁴Pilot me by the assortment of God moments You send my way.

²⁵I seek You, O Lord, and one thing I ask; never withdraw Your favor from my life or Your anointing from my resolve.

²⁶Never remove Your presence from my days or I will be like those who go to the grave full of misery and anguish.

²⁷Forgiveness has cleansed me—but still I find a loathing in my heart against my past.

²⁸Cleanse me and I will be clean—wash me and I will be whiter than snow—crucify those memories of my past and I will be free from condemnation.

²⁹I get excited like a little kid at a birthday party—when I think about all You've done for me.

³⁰The signs of the times are more evident than a man's reflection in a mirror inside a brightly lit room.

³¹They beckon to us loudly—calling forth with great persistence—insisting that we take immediate action.

³²With my back to the wall—You called my name and chose me to be on Your team.

³³I have left the worldly side and crossed over to God's side—His record is unbeaten.

Psalm 53

You Breathe New Life Into Me

¹Give me a well-ordered heart so I can praise You in sincerity.

²Anytime my thoughts go awry—I lasso them and replace them with selections from Your Word—it keeps my mind focused on You.

³Your Word is a microscope under which I view my life—it magnifies and shows me my shortcomings.

⁴The storehouse of the Lord is open to all who believe—come into the treasury of the Most High freely and receive His blessings.

⁵Boldly I hand over to You the key to my heart—asking that You will come in, take possession, and make it Yours.

⁶If good intentions were diamonds—sinners and saints alike would be wealthy.

⁷I will glorify my God wherever He places me—whether near or far—the choice to praise Him is mine.

⁸In the past I have despaired when asking—"Why does it take so long to grow up but such a short time to grow old?"

⁹Now I console myself with growing old because it draws me much closer to You, my God.

¹⁰Live life as if you will spend your next breath in the courts of heaven—then you will have nothing to trouble you.

¹¹Lord—keep my spirit sweet like honey from the rock—do not allow it to become cantankerous and resentful.

¹²The joy of the Lord gushes up in my soul like an underground geyser.

¹³The wisdom of the aged saint is a gift from God and is to be highly treasured.

¹⁴If perchance I have grieved my Lord—I quickly go to Him with a penitent heart and He is swift to forgive me.

¹⁵You have made this day so that I can rejoice in Your strength, Your power, and Your holiness.

¹⁶I will exhaust and use every praise that resides within me—then You will fill me with more—for You alone are worthy, my God, of all praise.

17The Word of God opens my eyes to my sin so that I might not be oblivious to it.

18Last night I was an eyewitness of Your handiworks as You displayed them in the heavens—they far surpassed any light show man could produce.

19You lifted up and encouraged my spirit as I viewed the magnificence of You, my God—praise the Lord, O my soul, praise Him forever.

20The Holy Spirit is my teleprompter—He gives me the words to speak when this natural mind comes up short.

21Your Word not only cleanses me from the stain of sin but also from the dust of the road I travel on.

22Brighten the corners of my room—shine Your light on my pathway—illuminate the course of my intellect so I can increase my knowledge of You.

23I will not ask for or receive any special merits or commendations for each occasion I think of You, Lord—but I do derive sweet communion with You in the process.

24Every child of the King is a recipient of untold joy and everlasting blessings.

25Holy Spirit, these two things I ask—be the guardian and protector of my soul and the overseer of my cause.

26O Father, forgive us our sins and draw us back to You; unless You forgive us and change our hearts we will perish and Your judgment will swallow us up.

27Your Word has spoken forth our sentence and shown clearly our guilt—we must forsake our idols and return to You—our hearts must be set on seeking You wholeheartedly.

28My heart is heavy with grief for my people—forgive us our sins against You—revive us and draw us back to You.

29Revitalize us from our lethargy—stimulate and arouse us so that we might come to our senses—bring to our minds the ways we have forsaken You that we might be ashamed.

30Breathe new life into us, Holy Spirit, so we might be refreshed—awaken us with a sense of urgency—so You might renew us once again.

Psalm 54

Your Creation Is Immense

¹You sweep my soul clean through the purity of worship with You, my God and my Creator.

²When I dust away all the distractions that surround me—when I focus my concentration on You—even the stillness of the night often bids me to come into communion with You.

³The night belongs to You—the stars twinkle in their eagerness to speak forth Your majesty—they shoot across the skies as they praise Your name.

⁴The stars and planets testify to Your character—they are steadfast and reliable—their course is unchanging—because You have placed them in the skies and govern their destinies.

⁵They impart a testimony of Your faithfulness that is as true and certain as Your Word.

⁶Your Word, O God, has used many different sources yet none contradict the other—each points the way to You.

⁷Creation itself is evidence of Your existence so that man is without excuse in his search to find You.

⁸I delight to know You daily—I seek You and You are always there; as sure as the sun, moon, and the heavenly bodies You have appointed to run their courses.

⁹Your Word—on which I stand firm and base my case upon—reinforces the certainty of this.

¹⁰I am constrained in the grips of trepidation and amazement—when I consider the immenseness of Your works I am blown away.

¹¹My bird's-eye view cannot take it all in—it simply cannot do justice to the awesomeness of Your creation.

¹²It is good for me to meditate on the works of Your hands—the marvel of Your majesty—the enormity of Your creation.

¹³My thoughts are swallowed up—unable to process what my eyes are seeing.

¹⁴Feeling as a deaf mute—unable to express the way of thinking that lies hidden inside—I am inadequate to respond to Your loftiness—wisdom—and understanding;

¹⁵I wonder exactly who I am that You, O Great Jehovah, would take notice of one as miniscule and trivial as I.

¹⁶Although Your Majesty outranks everything without exception—You never purposefully make me feel meager or worthless.

¹⁷Who is capable or wise enough to build an argument against You, O God, to put Your omniscience on trial; to put it to the test by assembling infallible proofs against it?

¹⁸No mortal man can even begin to make heads or tails of Your brilliance.

Psalm 55

Your Seal Of Approval Is On My Heart

¹Has my soul consciously sought self-righteousness?—If so then I seek Your forgiveness.

²I must search after You and You alone; to desire You more than anything, to live a life pleasing to You; then holiness will overshadow me seeping in unaware.

³You are a holy God—Holiness is Your name!

⁴In quietness I lift up my soul to You, my God, so that You might replenish it with wisdom and strength.

⁵Add to it sublime peace—which cannot be found in the natural life—but is an abundant gift You supply to Your children who ask for it.

⁶Holy Spirit, won't You usher my spirit into the throne room—right up to the throne of the Lamb of God?

⁷What a relief it is to know that anytime I need You—there You are—as close as the mouthful of air that I breathe—the words that I speak—or the thought that crosses my mind.

⁸May the songs I submit to You be more than just noise—the music that flows from my innermost being never ceases to soar in praise.

⁹Be pleased with the worship of my heart—let it be pure and undefiled before Your throne.

¹⁰The praise on my lips follows the song in my heart—and before I

Psalm 55 - Your Seal Of Approval Is On My Heart

know it—it ascends to the heavens—touching all it encounters as it heads up to the throne room of my God.

[11]That it would move Your heart with gladness is my deepest desire—fill my longing with Your glory.

[12]The Word of God serves to challenge me—to dare me to trust it implicitly—as a young child does when he jumps into his daddy's arms.

[13]For improved and carefree living—try following the Lord's plan—let it guide you down the path you are traveling on.

[14]Never miss the chance to share the gospel with those you come in contact with—let God's purity and righteousness shine through you like the sun shining through a stained glass window.

[15]Use words as a reinforcement and support of your life's message.

I Heard The Angels Bidding Me (a poem)

I heard the angels bidding me to come on home,
to join them in praising the Lamb upon the throne;

I know my spirit's willing and my soul says yes
but I haven't finished working here on earth I guess.

I'm anxiously waiting just to hear that trumpet sound,
this body will be changed as I'm heavenward bound;

And when He speaks the word just be sure of one thing,
I'll be over there in glory praising Christ our King.

[16]The light of the heavenlies shines into my soul—like the sun passing through a prism, it fills the surrounding space with color and beauty.

[17]Let every detail of my life be stamped with the approval of Your Presence, O God, like the President does when he signs a bill into law; his signature is his stamp and seal.

[18]I store Your Word in my heart so it will be available at the first sign of trouble—it will be readily on hand for sharing with those in need.

[19]Sometime while soldiers keep the night watch I remember You—even during my daily activities I will strive to be thoughtful of You, my Lord.

[20]Your Word is to be cherished more than a letter from an intimate

lover—how it brightens the eyes and brings happiness to the heart.

21The philosophy I have found to assist me in getting through any trial is to first measure my problem and then measure my God.

22I looked into the heavens and saw the beauty of the moon and its fullness—It saddened me to think of how mankind has chosen to worship the created instead of the Creator.

23As the moon is merely a body that is a reflection of the sun—so let me be a shining reflection of Your Son, O God, that I may provide light to those in darkness.

24Although the moon is not the source of light—it still receives glory and honor along with the sun.

25Let me direct any praise that comes my way back to the Father of Lights to whom all praise belongs; I will praise the Lord, O my soul!

Psalm 56

Your New Life Is Contagious Joy

1I am contagious with pure joy—it consumes me like a plague in an epidemic—let it spread among everyone I meet.

2Lord—give me an excited and single-minded heart to follow determinedly after You—voluntarily—with my eyes wide open and without any reservations.

3I have shed the old life like a snake sheds an old skin—in its place a brand new one has become my dwelling place.

4This new life finds its delight and fervor wrapped up in devotion to my Savior and Lord.

5I have yielded it to Him in its entirety—my soul says "take it now—take it all—take what You desire."

6The gentleness of the Lord refreshes my spirit and fills me to overflowing with His mercies—His kindness restores my soul for future days.

7His grace exceeds my wildest expectations and causes me to sing with delight—Who has not experienced His matchless grace?

Psalm 56 - Your New Life Is Contagious Joy

⁸The good deeds of a righteous man are stored up for him in heaven—like money deposited into a savings account.

⁹It will sustain him on rainy days as he withdraws it with interest—it is like nourishment after a long hike.

¹⁰Satan, take notice!—I have posted a No Trespassing sign over the door to my heart and my home, and the blood of Jesus is there to enforce it.

¹¹Jesus will cast out every unclean thought and impure intent that shows up before either can gain a foothold.

¹²You, O Lord, have rewarded me with Your presence each time I direct my thoughts toward You—Your presence has become the desire of my heart and has replaced all earthly things.

¹³Your faithfulness heaps good things upon me—You have drawn Yourself near to me.

¹⁴Holy Spirit—You have become sweetness and joy to my spirit—filling me with inexpressible longings.

¹⁵Your presence, O Lord, has become my daily sustenance and has become more valued than life itself.

¹⁶I run to You when circumstances are perplexing and do not make sense;—without wasting a single minute You are quick to clear things up.

¹⁷Book me with a life sentence of service to You, my Lord, and I will spend the rest of my days devoted to You.

¹⁸Even the righteous bump up against the snare of usefulness—Your desire is to teach them to ignore these signs and to keep the eyes of their faith set solely on You.

¹⁹I search Your Word unceasingly in an effort to learn more of You and Your ways.

²⁰Submerse me, Holy Spirit, in the Word of God so You can wash me clean—scrub spotless those parts soiled by unrighteousness.

²¹Smite the pride of my heart with a death blow—so I can stand clean before You.

²²I covet Your blessings so that I may in turn bless others freely—now let the yearning of my heart be pleasing unto You.

²³The angels of the Lord surround me better than a huddle surrounds a quarterback.

24 I make it my goal to serve You, my God, with no ulterior motives of any kind—to know and love You—and You alone.

25 The follower of God is complete and satisfied in Him—even in the absence of blessings You have made him whole and content.

26 You fill this shell of mortality with life—like when a balloon is filled with helium.

27 As I breathe in, it is Your air into my very being that animates me and fills me with life—I am quickened by the very breath of my God.

Psalm 57

My Sacrifice of Love To You

1 Have I ever given extravagantly to You, my Lord—in a totally unselfish manner?

2 My love for You is urging that I make such a sacrifice to You—one I give from the depths of my heart with no regard for cost.

3 Like the woman who poured the alabaster box of expensive perfume on the head of her Lord just for the love of Him.

4 King David pouring out the water that three of his best fighting men risked their lives to obtain tells of a love beyond words.

5 I have inquired and even pleaded—that You reveal the sacrifice I might make to show this sort of love—now I submit the last twenty-five verses of this psalm to You as my gift.

6 They were already written—some of the finest writing I had put together—when I felt moved upon to sacrifice them to You, my Lord—deleted and gone never to be retrieved.

Psalm 58

Your Word Purifies The Heart

¹A God-fearing man is guided by tribulations and adversities—they are tools to shape him into an instrument for Your glory.

²The Word of God acts as a filter—to strain out and extract all the impurities that invade the life of the godly.

³The Lord loves the pure in heart—for they bring radiance into everyday situations.

⁴Blessed is the devout man—he walks uprightly no matter who is watching because he fears the Lord—he knows His eye is upon him at all times.

⁵A sinful man loves to profane the name of our God—he wears crude and coarse talk as his raincoat when the sun is shining.

⁶In matters of the heart a saint will not be neglectful—he is always mindful to have an encouraging word and a cheerful countenance for those in need.

⁷Opportunities abound to become more Christ like—they show up daily as a multitude of irritations we must face.

⁸I have tasted the absence of Your presence and it is acidic—like the taste of a green melon rind or bitter herbs.

⁹Without Your presence life is meaningless—I find it futile and empty—so much that there is no joy in living without You, my God.

¹⁰You will have pity on the man who is quick to acknowledge his need of You, and fill him to overflowing with Your Holy Spirit.

¹¹Let Your Spirit fall—let it fall on me—let Your Holy Spirit fall like rain on me.

¹²Blessed is the man who is anchored in Your Word—it shall become a lifeline that will prevent him from drifting away.

¹³The motivated man leads a peaceable life and has established guidelines to rule his existence according to Your bidding.

¹⁴You perpetually pour your blessings upon the grateful—because they will not take a single one of them for granted.

Psalm 58 - Your Word Purifies The Heart

[15] Enlarge my capacity to love You, my God—build within me a large reservoir where I can store up a supply for the season of drought—enable me to love You even more than I already do.

[16] Your Spirit has spawned within me a fierce desire to please You—it has stirred up longings not reserved for mortal man.

[17] I was blind until the power of the Word applied ointment to my eyes—it opened my eyes to Your truth—the truth of Your Word—it made my eyes see when I first believed.

[18] If we are not revealed to be fit in the small things—how can we ever hope to rise to the occasion when the big crisis comes along?

[19] The strain of the storm reveals the preparation of a man's heart.

[20] Can a man show his God in public if he does not know his God in private?—I think not!

[21] These eyes look to You—to Your hand of provision—for my daily bread.

[22] Each and every moment of this life provides me with an occasion to admit my need of You.

[23] My spirit must often view You, my God, shrouded by the shadow of darkness before You will be revealed in the light of day.

[24] I wait in quiet confidence for Your clear revelation—knowing full well that You will be justified at that hour.

[25] Your servant searches diligently to find the place where Your presence abides.

[26] When he finds it—he hides it away in his heart—in that secret spot reserved only for Your Spirit.

[27] Who can make paths straight—the mountains tower majestically—the valleys lush and green—the storms that fiercely pound the land;

[28] The sereneness of the island beauty—the calmness of a peaceful stream—the vastness of heavens unending—the darkness that becomes light?

[29] It is only Your great power that does all these things—You exhibit Your greatness so that we might see and believe—Lord I believe!

[30] Your Word also tells us of Your mighty power—I have witnessed it with my own eyes and thereby stand in awe of You.

Psalm 59

You Replace Sin With Celebration

¹The light of Your Word brings illumination to my soul and brightens my understanding—it chases away the darkness.

²The location to the secret of happiness can be found when you fasten your thoughts upon our God and linger in His presence.

³As I sit among my elders I am blessed—by the wisdom and knowledge they impart to me.

⁴Eradicate any vacuum—any empty space prevalent in my life—fill it with Your wishes.

⁵The righteous overflow with graciousness—like a river overflows its banks during the monsoons.

⁶A godly wife is a blessing from the Lord, like a pacemaker to a man with a failing heart.

⁷She is like honey to bread—like sugar to tea—like a sword in the hands of a valiant warrior—like a scalpel to a competent surgeon.

⁸Her smile brings beauty—her words bring encouragement and comfort—cheering the soul.

⁹My life has truly been enhanced by the helpmate You have placed by my side—she has enriched it in a multitude of ways.

¹⁰The sadness and disappointment of a man's heart quickly leads to a soured stomach unless he allows himself to be filled with the sweetness of the Holy Spirit.

¹¹A smile to the hopeless is like a candle in the dark—bringing cheer to the weary.

¹²You have established limits of time on mortal man—I will honor You as a wise steward in this area so I may accomplish each purpose You have planned for me during my allotted days.

¹³You are my strength, O God—You are my hiding place—the Rock that covers me.

¹⁴When the storms of life prevail—Your love will never fail—and in Your Spirit I reside.

¹⁵I am pleased to be identified with You, my Lord—wearing Your mark emblazoned across my life as a public emblem is a joy to me.

Psalm 59 - You Replace Sin With Celebration

[16] As the rolling thunder announces the coming storm, so Your Word broadcasts the soon return of our Lord and Savior Jesus Christ.

[17] A display of godliness will exude as divine transformation alters the servant of God.

[18] Not only will inner beauty radiate—but wisdom will come to focus in the forefront.

[19] I cannot resist Your invitation to come into Your presence daily—with certainty I trust Your every decision.

[20] Sin bumps into righteousness and is put into a headlock—it is rendered incapacitated by the power of the Holy Spirit.

[21] Righteousness guards the path to the house of the godly man—the angels of the Lord watch over his affairs.

[22] It is my persuasion that I am drawing nearer to the heart of my God and that is precisely the direction I am aiming for.

[23] Each time the enemy hounds me with temptations I race in the opposite direction with breakneck speed—straight into the arms of my waiting Savior.

[24] Let my understanding be split wide open—like a ripe melon—and filled with Your wonders.

[25] I will ostracize all evil and unkind thoughts that creep into my way of thinking—banishing them with great disdain.

[26] All heaven rejoices with a grand cosmic celebration when the powers of darkness are defeated—when a sinner sees the light.

[27] The voice of God speaks and darkness flees—life springs forth in obedience to His commands—galaxies move to do His bidding—my heart bows in response to His whisper.

[28] In spite of Your unchanging nature—I have never found You to be dull or boring.

[29] You are faithful to bring about a change of pace whenever life starts to become humdrum.

[30] The curve balls of life are often baffling—but in their midst, You are my one constant.

[31] The core of my foundation trembles with awe and excitement when I realize You created me for Your good pleasure and held nothing back.

[32] I am beside myself to think the very God of the universe would know my name—or that He even knows where I reside.

³³I live to sing Your praises, O God, to express the pure joy of my soul, to release adoration as I magnify the King of Kings and the Lord of Lords; praise the Lord, O my soul, praise Him.

Psalm 60

Your Spirit Is As Fresh As The Early Morning Sunrise

¹The anxieties of life cause a buildup of barnacles on the soul—they need the Holy Spirit to remove them.

²As drops from the morning dew refresh the grass—squeeze out a freshness of Your Spirit upon my spirit, O God.

³The unpleasant people we face are the speed bumps on the roads of life.

⁴Brush my soul with the scent of heaven so its fragrance will be given to others.

⁵The redeemed of the Lord are His—they have become a pledge and a token unto Him.

⁶My primary goal is to capture the essence of Your glory within my mortal body.

⁷The wilderness holds no terror by night or by day as long as I am following my Lord.

⁸Your Spirit of power, O God, enables the godly to do all the things they are not capable of doing on their own—yet You never force submission.

⁹Love and a righteous man join hands and walk together—they are companions of the Most High God.

¹⁰The chosen of the Lord are confident of His calling and wear His banner proudly.

¹¹Whenever I am enticed to think the ungodly are getting off scot-free—You remind me that nothing escapes Your attention—and I am comforted.

¹²Preparation is the key ingredient to a consecrated life—one that has discarded every remnant of offensiveness.

¹³The man after God's heart has been instructed in His Word—like a grounding rod buried deep in the soil.

Psalm 60 - Your Spirit Is As Fresh As The Early Morning Sunrise

14Whenever my mind clouds up like the haziness of a steamy window—I seek clarity through communion with You, my God.

15I wash my hands from the contamination of sin each time I immerse myself in Your Word.

16The fool has no regard for God's Word but is totally reliant upon feelings—and is justified by them in his own mind.

17The true believer will not rely on feelings unless they line up directly with the Word of God.

18The wise man is quick to learn from other people's mistakes and refuses to repeat his own.

19The righteous decide that integrity is the foundation of their principles—truthfulness establishes a strong cornerstone to build upon.

20Little sins have a way of growing into big ones—unless we are quick to nip them in the bud.

21My heart swells with praise for You and it bursts forth with songs from my lips—I cannot restrain it—nor would I ever want to.

22These vocal chords serve as an instrument of praise—to speak forth Your majesty—to sing of Your faithfulness.

23I am drunk with enjoyment at the prospect of being a friend of the King—the Almighty One.

24My thoughts are quickly sobered when I think of who I am and what He has done for me—O how can I cease to praise His Holiness.

25There is no pining away in this soul of mine—for You have made me glad—thankful for each unmerited favor sent my way.

26With the dawning of each new day—the appearance of another sunrise—You encourage me to step out in a brand new walk of faith.

27Each successive generation inherits Your faithfulness afresh—as a witness to Your Majesty and Glory in new and unique ways.

28You are more than my portion—You have become my all in all—my source.

29O Great God of Israel—the Almighty Jehovah—You are my fortress—the Rock of my safety—the wall of fire that surrounds me.

30You are my castle, the castle of my heart—into which I can run for security.

31Armies and foes of all kinds have come against You and You have remained impenetrable—for You are truly the Rock that cannot be moved.

Psalm 61

The Mantle Of Your Voice Gives Me Guidance

¹You have laid Your mantle upon my life—it gives me guidance—it is the touch of Your Spirit that covers me.

²Open the eyes of my spirit and prepare me to do the works of Your hands.

³Your anointing bursts over me like water explodes over the top of a waterfall.

⁴The godly man will shun every self-righteous thought and bury it in the graveyard—his prayer is for purity of heart and a wholeness of soul.

⁵A wise soul will leave a heritage by doing noteworthy accomplishments—not by seeking an everlasting name.

⁶Since I have tasted the good things of heaven this world is not the least bit appetizing to me.

⁷The children of the Lord can feast from his banquet table whenever they desire.

⁸Blessed is the man who walks close to the cross of his Lord so he does not traverse the line of temptation.

⁹I keep my heart tender before You, my God—like a piece of young veal—desiring to be sensitive to Your passions.

¹⁰You have ordained praise from each of your creations—none is exempt—even the inanimate objects of Your creation praise You for Your wonder.

¹¹The Lord has taken my flaws and made them into something distinct and special—exchanging my weakness for strength—my inabilities for sufficiency.

¹²There is nothing commonplace about our God—He doesn't mind using the uncommon and eccentric commodities of life to portray His lessons.

¹³The aches and pains of this mortal body only serve to point us to a better life awaiting us in Your presence, O God.

¹⁴If You were to grant us that proverbial "bed of ease"—"pie in the sky"—or "rose garden" status perpetually—what incentive would we have to look for something better?

Psalm 61 - The Mantle Of Your Voice Gives Me Guidance

¹⁵If the sun always shines—how are we supposed to learn to appreciate the rain clouds?

¹⁶Without the rays of Your mighty sun life would cease to exist; everything, including man, depends upon You and Your very creation for survival.

¹⁷The unbalanced man ceases to be well-rounded and becomes lop-sided in all of his ways.

¹⁸The godly seek to please You by demonstrating a well-balanced life in all areas.

¹⁹I grab hold of and hang desperately onto the faith that I possess—because darkness has swallowed me—and my assurance is all I have.

²⁰This valley is dark and there is no light that I can see—but You are there with me—to comfort me with Your presence.

²¹Your voice reassures me—Your touch guides me—I cannot see my way—yet You are there.

²²Even the darkness would terrorize me were it not for Your presence.

²³I have desired a closer walk with You, my Lord—You have darkened my way so I cannot see—You have hidden my path in order that I must only follow Your voice.

²⁴The enemy would try to distract me with other voices but I know Your voice—I strain intently so that I can heed it.

²⁵Although I am unable to see Your face, Your words lead me—they guide me as a service dog guides a blind man.

²⁶You allow me to come close and lean upon You for strength and rest.

²⁷I am seized with anticipation at the marvels and wonders my mind is not capable of conceiving in its present state.

²⁸There are untold volumes left only to our mind's eye—and at that—the best we are capable of is a feeble attempt at a sketchy and incomplete description.

²⁹You are not lured into allowing my cravings to be given a sneak peek at the world to come—knowing a glimpse would never be satisfactory.

³⁰On the contrary—You bolster my life of faith by not going along with my wishes—knowing that in the end I will be richly rewarded.

³¹Bring into living color the wildest dream I could ever envision and don't deny me the chance to be grateful for that.

³²Your secrets are locked up and held in storage—out of reach to our carnal minds—but You will reveal every one of them in the eternities to come.

Psalm 62

You Give Me Strength And Success

¹We are the people of Your creation—the work of Your hands—You premeditated us with purpose.

²You wanted our peculiarities to somehow be threads—woven into a gorgeous tapestry to show off Your glory.

³You have made my thread multicolored—how I love to worship You with all of my colors.

⁴The wise man does not hesitate to do the Father's bidding—he lays aside his work to listen at the slightest urging.

⁵Wisdom flows as he joins forces with Your Spirit—uniting in prayer against the forces of the evil one.

⁶Grant me abilities beyond my capability—strength for the day—success in the struggle—victory in the battle.

⁷I walk the path You have laid before me—not with fear and uneasiness—but with delight and boldness.

⁸I give You praise in exchange for the breath of life—praise the Lord—O my soul!

⁹The upright let their light shine as easily as they breathe—the Lord blesses them abundantly.

¹⁰Sin has nipped at my heels since childhood—but praise the Lord—for You have delivered me.

¹¹You have been my strength and shield so I would not be devoured by it.

¹²You have filled me with the light of Your Word so I would not have to walk in darkness—where shadows obscure my vision.

¹³I have devoted my life to You—even when I have strayed from Your path.

¹⁴Your good promises have been my protector and put me back on the right track—the path of righteousness.

¹⁵Temptation has surrounded me and come upon me at times, like flies at a picnic table—but Your grace has bailed me out—O praise Your holy name.

¹⁶Now I look to You for my salvation—You are there every time I call upon You.

Psalm 63 - Will His Mission Be Yours?

¹⁷I am consumed by Your mercies—Your grace covers me like a tidal wave.

¹⁸You sweep over the righteous like the mighty Mississippi does to anything that gets in its way—Your compassions encompass the saints forever.

¹⁹You alone, O Lord, have put into my heart a desire and a passion to serve You the remainder of my days.

²⁰I make it my top priority to be filled daily with Your Spirit—until I have been completely formed into the likeness of Your Son;

²¹To be soaked by Your Word and to absorb it into my spirit, as a rag soaks up a spill.

²²I whistle a joyful tune—I know He is coming soon—it may be today—please don't delay—whether morning, night, or at noon.

²³Prayer and the Word of God are surefire antidotes for the ravages of sin—they provide me the only sanity I possess.

²⁴Your mouth, O God, will instruct the wise and they will become wiser still.

²⁵Those who choose to follow You find pleasure everlasting—You put their hearts at ease—and their spirits find comfort.

²⁶The Word of God has become my stoplight and blocks my progress before I transgress against Him.

²⁷I proceed with caution only after the Holy Spirit has prompted me to move on.

Psalm 63

Will His Mission Be Yours?

¹The proud heart has been calloused by the deceitfulness of sin and pays no attention to righteousness.

²My heart is fenced in by Your love, O God; I am secure and never need to leave Your presence.

³The blessings of the Lord shower on all those who call on Him—He swiftly takes care of those who wait expectantly for His benefits.

⁴Walking the streets of that sweet bye

Psalm 63 - Will His Mission Be Yours?

and bye is held in reserve for those who are ready for His return.

5 Blessed is the man who keeps an eye out for his Lord's appearance—he is careful to be on guard at any moment.

6 You have opened me like a pastry before baking and packed me with choice fillings—now I am complete with the sweet things of my God.

7 Happiness always comes from deep within—experiencing it is never dependent upon material things.

8 My obedience to Your instructions has unearthed treasures of rejoicing and revealed future blessings to come.

9 Those who are truly wise do not seek to become wiser still—they allow their conformity to His laws to push them closer to the Father.

10 Each name in a genealogy listing is precious to the Lord—He treasures them all for they are His creation—He has fashioned us in His likeness and made us for praise.

11 I have located the source of Your unending love and it has now become the wellspring of my heart.

12 If you were to put good under the cover of darkness, it would look identical to evil—it takes the light of the Holy Spirit shining upon each to expose it for what it truly is.

13 The child of God hears His voice in every situation—he is quick to put it into action.

14 Never forget to thank the Lord for each blessing you can call to mind—in fact stop right now and give Him thanks.

15 Those who disregard God's Word fail to receive even a fraction of the blessing He has intended for them.

16 I will let every breath You have issued to me—as incessant as the ticking of a grandfather clock—be destined for the praise and glory of my God.

17 All wisdom belongs to God but He so benevolently shares it with those who seek Him for it.

18 Wisdom without direction is like a race car without a steering wheel.

19 The Word of God is not only written on scrolls, tablets, chronicles, and ledgers—He has inscribed it on the heart of man in order that he would not forget His regulations.

20 All those who are prudent have His precepts etched upon their hearts like a sailor has a tattoo engraved upon his skin.

²¹Victory could never be sweeter than when it is shared with my Creator.

²²Christ came on a mission—which He fulfilled—He left a mission for you to fulfill—will you?

²³I cannot see the other side—the river is just too deep and wide—nor can I see around the bend—only the beginning and not the end:

²⁴There's coming soon a day when He—will open these eyes and let me see—the secrets darkness holds mystery—making known all throughout eternity.

Psalm 64

I Am Life and Everlasting Glory

¹The upright wear integrity as an undergarment with ethics as their outer clothing.

²They keep integrity close to their hearts—it is a protective armor against the sin that would try to penetrate their souls.

³Adhering to the principles of truthfulness, they model uprightness to their children.

⁴A life of accountability is a call of duty to those devoted to honor and true-heartedness.

⁵The gatekeeper to the house of the righteous has been committed to moral principles and is not swayed by a bribe of any sort.

⁶Your behavior will always reflect your beliefs when supervised by candor.

⁷The plans of a wise man are brought to fruition by the labors of a working man.

⁸The Master uses the prayers of the saints to accomplish His plans because of their steadfastness.

⁹You have spoken, O Lord, and I have listened—You give me songs in the night and words of comfort and hope.

¹⁰I have taken to heart the following words You have uttered to my heart—Your disclosures have stirred the depths of my soul.

¹¹"My son—you have expressed to Me your desire—to reach out and touch Me.

¹²I will grant your request—reach forth your hand and gently breathe upon it—now you have felt My very presence.

¹³Do you not know that I—the Glory that filled Solomon's temple—am the breath of life that resides within your own temple?

¹⁴So be comforted in this and know that I—the ever-present and everlasting Spirit of the Living God—am always with you—I will never leave you alone.

¹⁵I have placed more than the breath of life within you—My eternal promises are the life of your soul—Have My everlasting pledges penetrated your human conception?

¹⁶On that day when I withdraw My breath of life from your temple—your soul will live with Me forever and find joy in My unending presence.

¹⁷I have promised it and I am faithful; not just now, but forever and beyond all time.

¹⁸My Word is truth and I have spoken—trust only in Me—you will never be disappointed.

¹⁹When those times come upon you—when My presence seems to have vanished—always remember the great sun I have placed in your heavens.

²⁰Observe and learn a lesson from it!—The curtain of darkness comes between it and your eyes—but does it ever leave its appointed place?

²¹How about when the ferocious storms beset the earth on which you reside—does the mighty sun flee and hide in terror?

²²No—it stands steadfastly as a testament to My faithfulness.

²³Learn from this case in point—I am there all the time, even when you cannot locate Me:—My eye is still upon you, be at peace."

Psalm 65

The Love Of God – How Incredible

¹As when a piece of wood is soaked and steamed with water before it is bent—so our spirits must be through the words of God.

²Without this process the fibers of the wood will only break instead of bending into a graceful arch—our spirits are quite the same.

³I rise with a renewed hope and faith—trembling with an excitement that points me to His soon return.

⁴Will you call me foolish for realizing that today just might be the day that even eternity has been looking forward to with great anticipation?

⁵Eternity has been preparing for the greatest commencement since history began.

⁶Where is the expectation in living without hope for the future—which was sealed by the certainty of the cross and the resurrection of our Lord and Savior Jesus Christ?

⁷My soul longs to be trapped by His love—like a fly upon a spider web.

⁸Whenever I realize it is all about Him and not at all about me—I break through the realms of glory and into His heavenly presence.

⁹Grant me power and strength in the innermost regions of my heart and mind—then You can bring about Your will through my life.

¹⁰I will not allow the tests of life to pilfer my songs of joy—no matter what!

¹¹A wise man is able to keep his feisty tongue in check before he ends up eating his own words—they are more bitter than tonic water.

¹²How embarrassing it is to think that while I cared not a single speck for You—even then You loved me.

¹³In fact—You loved me long before I even knew of You—such love is more than this mortal mind can grasp.

¹⁴What value does a single grain of sand have—and who in their right mind would trade the riches of heaven for it?

¹⁵That is what comes to mind when I contemplate how You sent Your only Son to die for me—how can I abstain from praising You?

¹⁶When the enemy tries to get a rise out of me and urges me to curse my Creator—the only rise I allow him is a rise of praise.

¹⁷The Lord smiles on those who call upon His name—He delights in their praises.

¹⁸The peace of God eases the cares of a troubled heart—bringing quietness in a moment.

¹⁹With God, peace is not necessarily the lack of controversy—however, it is the presence of His abiding love in the midst of turmoil.

²⁰Although the righteous suffer many aches and pains in this life—they pale in comparison to the suffering of the Lamb of God.

²¹He has taken their agony and grief upon Himself—in response they will lift up their spirits in praise to honor Him for all He has done.

²²It is impossible to stifle my praises—my heart gives vent to adoration of my King—praise the Lord—O my soul—and praise Him again and again.

Psalm 66

I Trust You No Matter What

¹Truth restrains itself from showing up when pride is present because it is suffocated and snuffed out—it will not go where arrogance is found.

²The spiritual standing of the life of a saint is tested by their answers to the following questions:

³Would I continue to trust God if He were to cut off all of His blessings completely?

⁴Am I able to exhibit complete childlike trust—not caring for even a moment what happens all around me?

⁵Do I want my Father and not just the blessings He brings my way—would I thrive contentedly or merely exist?

⁶Will my soul hunger after You, my God, and not after power, wealth, or fame—can I be satisfied with You only?

⁷Now that is what the life totally hid in Christ and transformed into a new creation should look like.

⁸The godly are content to be placed in any circumstance He puts them in—resting confident in His provisions.

⁹I am searching for a life that is pregnant with meaning—where I number each day given me and pack it to the max.

¹⁰The joy of the Lord courses through my veins—it is the lifeblood of my existence—it has become rapturous to my soul.

¹¹Look to the creativity of the Master and not the student—for He has much to teach.

¹²It is easier to find an excuse not to do something than to find a way to do it—let love lead the way.

¹³The Holy Spirit bids the listening one to draw near to the Father—to come close and hear His heart—to sit contentedly at His feet.

¹⁴When the Lord found me I was a renegade and rebelled against His law—His love captured my heart and now I am His bondservant.

¹⁵Never start your day without first consulting the Word of God—that would be like starting a road trip without looking at a map.

¹⁶The tears of God are directed downward into life-giving rain—they shower our land and give it life.

¹⁷Whenever our compassion fails to take action we widely miss the mark—never fall short of allowing your humanity to touch another life.

¹⁸God loves to cheer us up by sending friends who come alongside and look after us—often they become partners for life.

¹⁹He gives power to the weak so they will not shrink back from His appointed tasks—they will go forth in boldness.

²⁰The unrighteous look on the frivolity of sin and smirk with a haughty look.

²¹The righteous refuse to even hazard a guess at the plans and purposes of the Lord—they just smile knowing He has them all in control.

²²He meets the godly at their greatest point of need because He knows their trust is fully in Him.

²³The bowels of this earth hold the mortal remains of the righteous as well as the unrighteous on deposit—they are held in reserve for judgment day.

²⁴Although the light of the godly man's candle may have dimmed with age, his light will continue to shine through the multitude of other candles he has lit.

Psalm 67

Your Light Shines Brightly Through Me

¹Those who fail to place the burdens they carry upon the Almighty are destined to cart them around needlessly under their own stamina.

²Nothing I possess—nothing I cling to—except Jesus, my Redeemer.

³All I have is borrowed—it all belongs to Him—as I myself do.

⁴Take your flowery words and save them for another—His sweet words are all I care to hear—"Well done, my son"—nothing else matters.

⁵No one has loved me like my Jesus—He did not stop short at words—His actions told the story.

⁶Holy Spirit—my oft forgotten friend—how I appreciate Your guidance.

⁷You lead through marsh and swamp—through rivers deep—we have even marched to the very mountain top together.

⁸My point is, You have always been there with me—as my Lord said You would be.

⁹My heart bows before You in repentance—because of my negligence to Your commands—and I ask that You apply pardon and mercy on my behalf.

¹⁰You have even led me to the throne of our God, carrying my griefs and passions there personally.

¹¹Through thick and thin—You have stuck with me when others have bailed on me.

¹²I revel in the attention that you afford to me as a child of the Most High God.

¹³You are the light of God that shines through this old clay pot—the light that brightens the way of all those who walk in His path.

¹⁴God's glory shines forth continually—sometimes it can by likened to the sun—it may not always be seen or experienced.

¹⁵Its brightness may be hidden by clouds of darkness or storms of fury—nevertheless it shines brightly on.

¹⁶Holy Spirit—all I have is Yours—to be used as You see fit and at Your discretion.

Psalm 68

You Join Us All Together

¹My soul harkens to the heavenly strains of that angelic choir and dreams of the day I will join them.

²I have opted to take the narrow road—the one less traveled—in order to reach my heavenly home.

³It is not only less crowded—but I will be personally escorted by the King of Kings.

⁴He who has been shown great riches will long for them with all his heart—his aim will be set on attaining them.

⁵When a wise man comes across an unfamiliar word or passage of writing—he will seek to know its meaning—and he will be wiser still.

⁶You have spoken things to my heart that You have hidden from ages past—and I have treasured them as nuggets of gold.

⁷The man whose heart is right displays Your truth daily—not to convince the skeptical nor to shame the wise—but to bring glory to his Father in heaven.

⁸If I were to count all of Your blessings it would take days on end—without repeating a single one.

⁹The glory of God can be seen through death and disease as well as through the life of a righteous man.

¹⁰God's power is something that must be reverenced—it is not a thing to be taken lightly or without awe.

¹¹Every time I view the beauty and majesty of Your creation—I am able to catch a small glimpse of You—O God.

¹²The seasons shimmer with change as they come and go—but my God never changes—He is stable and steady—as sure as time itself.

¹³It is this same God whose splendor is contained within the world surrounding us—it is He, who not only lives in us—but also calls us by name to serve Him.

¹⁴Let your mind continually mull over the goodness of your God—let it contemplate His mercies and then you cannot refrain from being thankful.

Psalm 68 - You Join Us All Together

Each Breath In The Life Of A Man [a poem]

Each breath is unhurried as it goes on its way,
determined to praise Him yet willing to pray;

Created with purpose designed for a cause,
whether singing God's praises or reciting His laws:

It spans but a moment and then it is gone,
sometimes faster than lightning sometimes brief as a yawn;

They are all joined together like links of a chain,
they can praise Him in sorrow they can praise Him in pain;

When they form one grand purpose in the life of a man,
they will point to God's greatness every chance that they can.

15 You, O God, welcome praise from a willing heart—and the one who is joyful in spirit will not be turned away.

16 The Lord will grant those who seek Him unreservedly, true knowledge and a heart of wisdom;—the common man He will not rebuff.

17 My soul has witnessed Your greatness and Your power countless times—still I stand overwhelmed in Your presence.

18 You feed me from Your banquet table—the rich delicacies provide fatness for my bones and Your bounty nourishes my soul.

19 My heart is made to honor You—how can it help but burst forth in songs of praise?

20 A prideful man is arrogant in his foolishness and fails to come to terms with it.

21 I especially like my odds whenever I bank on the Lord and put my faith and trust in Him—that is as sure a bet as I will find anywhere.

22 He speaks to me and each time I respond, His words continue to go forth unto new and unreached generations; O magnify His faithfulness.

23 His Word travels ahead of me—lighting my way—even before I reach my destination.

24 If you want direct access to God's resources and wisdom—try prayer—it is like a line of credit at a bank with no set limit.

25 Lord, when I am tempted to carry the pain of my past into the present—help me run it into the wall of Your forgiveness.

26You direct my gaze upon things I would have never noticed—at times You even need to gently turn my face so I can look into Your eyes.

27The intervention of God for mankind came through the cross of Calvary—and the sacrifice of His only Son—Jesus.

28Although God's provisions may not come early, they are never late—He always meets the need of the moment right on time.

29Your presence fills the sanctuary—but it also fills the temple of my heart—so I can carry it with me wherever I go.

30While the world is busy seeking pleasure, God is at work—searching for a yielded heart that is earnest for Him above all things.

31I have pledged my heart to Him as a token of my love and sincerity—He wears it as a ring on His finger.

32As workers of His vineyard—we are not asked to produce the harvest—merely to plant the seed and water it—He does not make us responsible for more than that.

33A picture does not need a frame to be admired with respect—at times the frame can detract and cause a person to miss the picture and the blessing.

34Is any man a solitary life unto himself—without any outside source of contribution—which man can truly say he was not influenced by others—that he is a self-made man?

35No one can make this boast—this claim does not belong to anyone.

36Truth has revealed that even the most learned men among us have been touched by others' lives—who can say they have not gained knowledge from other people?

37We are a composite of varied sources of teaching—this has enriched our lives with color and purpose.

38Those who allow themselves to be touched by the lives of others will be the more colorful mosaic for it.

39They will have added texture and beauty to the personalities they have brushed against with their own impact and effect.

40How marvelous that the Lord has made us recipients of the splendor of one another—and allowed us to be brightly colored hues in each other's lives.

Psalm 69

You Have Given Me Your Gifts

¹Blessed is the man who is capable in numerous areas—his anointing shall be shared with a lot of people—his cup shall overflow unto many.

²I—the Lord—am pleased with anyone who is willing to scatter his gifts among all who are around him—ministering to everyday folk as well as to nobility.

³The wise have figured out that life is a process of refinements—learning right choices and practicing them—discovering wrong choices and discarding them.

⁴God's gifts are granted to every believer even though they may not recognize a single one of them.

⁵Take time to search for them—they may be simple—they may be complex—they will likely be found amongst the things you enjoy doing the most.

⁶Use them every day to enrich the lives of others—for if you neglect using them, your own life will be left unfulfilled and wanting—maybe even empty.

⁷The sinner is drawn to the wisdom of the godly—it shines like a light in the window.

⁸He who lives in the past and only thinks of yesterday is shortsighted—he has no goals and ceases to be vigilant and wise in his ventures.

⁹Which seed—when held in your hand—will experience any working of power—a bursting forth of any kind?

¹⁰Only if it is planted—buried in the soil—is it empowered to spring up.

¹¹Your Spirit, O God, has given power to this mortal body; to bloom, and at just the right time display Your glory, if but for a season.

¹²A yielding of self-will must first break through the shell of humanity—to the power that lies dormant within.

¹³Then fleeting as it may be—His glory can burst forth in splendor and radiance—His purpose conceived in grandeur.

Psalm 69 - You Have Given Me Your Gifts

[14] The light of God dispels all darkness and chases away the shadows so that I might walk in confidence and assurance.

[15] You have made me rich through the prayers of the saints—their requests have made it possible for You to heap Your blessings upon me.

[16] Their intercessions on my behalf have benefited me greatly and have often come to my rescue.

[17] Whenever I come to a fork in the road—Your Spirit is there to guide me—that is, if I'm not too proud to listen to His directions.

[18] Your Word comes at me from many vantage points—but at times I am too dense to catch on to what You are saying to me.

[19] Perhaps the message does not come in the form I think it will so I miss it altogether: Holy Spirit, enable me to tune my spirit to the frequency of God, the Almighty One.

[20] At times we may become perturbed at how quickly time flies—how it marches on with a steady beat —irritated by the chiming of the clock.

[21] Lord—teach us to treasure our moments—value each instant—cherish the interruptions—marvel at Your workings—profit from every pause.

[22] You have given me a beacon of hope that lies in the gift of music—it allows me to become immersed in another world and transport others there.

[23] How humbled I am at each day that You allow me to take part in—it is planned to perfection as long as I don't throw a monkey wrench in it.

[24] Your love is undeniable—You constantly make me aware of it each time Your grace and mercies wash over me.

[25] You have purchased my ticket through the blood of Your Son— and I have packed my bags—I'm anxiously awaiting that heavenly homecoming welcome.

[26] How close can I get to You, my God —as close as skin is to flesh—as close as blood is to the veins— as close as air is to the lungs—as close as ligament is to bone—as close as tissue is to flesh—do I desire all these more than life itself?

[27] Since my vessel is full of Your Spirit, You have assured me that as a mortal man I cannot get any closer than this; O my soul, I will praise the Lord.

Psalm 70

His Love Revealed

¹The oceans are vast and teeming with life—all that is within them is the work of Your hands.

²I've witnessed the light of Your love as it glistened off the mounting waves—they rose up to the heights of mountains in the distance.

³The seas are rocking and rolling to the beat of the heavenly band—as they praise the Lord, their waves crash like resounding cymbals—exalting the Most High God.

⁴I have traveled to distant islands of the earth and His presence abides in every one of them—His glory covers all.

⁵Let my heart dance before You, my Lord—let the sincerity of it coax You to join the dance with me—until we show the story of Your love to the world.

⁶Quiet the pounding of my heart, O Lord, the wild beatings of my restless spirit; so I can be still and hear You speak in the quietness.

⁷I hear Your voice in a multitude of others—because I am listening.

⁸Your Word is a surety—to be counted on more than any of man's oaths or promises.

⁹The fulfillment of Your promises is not to be deemed a rarity—but a guarantee to all generations.

¹⁰My heart is anxious with longing to see my Redeemer—the One who paid it all and went the distance for me.

¹¹The soul that has been untethered has the buoyancy of the Holy Spirit to rise in exaltation before the Almighty One.

¹²It is then able to experience the freedom from burdens and cares—which tend to become an anchor—or a noose around the neck.

¹³The prayers of the godly are unlimited—presented to You without borders or boundaries—like a corral without a fence.

¹⁴Music is God's way of speaking to the heart of man—of dusting the cobwebs from his soul—of inexpressible utterances without the need for words.

¹⁵The wise man is willing to pour his soul into others—so they might share the joys he has experienced.

Psalm 70 - His Love Revealed

¹⁶As daylight ushers in the early morning dawn—I wait for the Word of God to usher wisdom into my soul.

¹⁷The truth of Your Word is the sunrise in my morning—it brightens the entire day.

¹⁸Sin has various sides to it—often people get caught up in trying to find a good side—you can look for an eternity and never find it even though you may believe you have.

¹⁹Unless the Holy Spirit reveals truth to a man—the Word of God remains as only ink on paper—nothing more than a good book to read.

²⁰I have watched a man whose walk had retarded slightly as he neared the end of his spiritual journey—yet his determination was unflagging—it never wavered for a moment.

²¹Transfer the precepts of Your Word to the tablet of my heart—just like carbon paper to paper when it is written upon.

²²How quickly the day has passed—I have enjoyed spending it in Your presence, O Lord—You have surrounded me like a cloud covering the sunlight.

²³As day fades away and I look into the night—there across the great expanse of the heavens I see the signature of my God—written in lights.

²⁴It is undeniably His handwriting—for it is clearly inscribed—I AM Jehovah—O how I praise Your greatness.

²⁵For the man who determines to walk daily with his God—there will be no mistaking the road he is traveling and where it leads.

²⁶Those who dare to draw near to God are satisfied as His presence draws them near.

²⁷The Lord supplies the necessities of the righteous before they call upon Him—He anticipates their needs ahead of time and is quick to provide.

²⁸Lord, let me find the ability to distance myself from the desires of this present world and to latch onto the riches that You have available for me.

²⁹My soul has commenced a lifetime journey with You, my God; beginning with a longing to find You—steps to follow You—and a desire to know Your fullness.

³⁰You have blessed the paths you have led me down with exceedingly picturesque landscapes of sereneness and tranquility—bringing beauty and light to my journey.

Psalm 70 - His Love Revealed

A Thanksgiving prayer [2014]

For the gift of life and of Your Son
For all we have and all You've done
We sit with thanks and gratefulness
For food and friends and happiness
Now to Your hand we look for peace
And thank You for this bounteous feast

Amen

31 I would rather have five loaves and two fish that are blessed by the Lord than warehouses full of food without His blessing.

32 My thoughts have strayed like errant passes from a quarterback—intercept them, O Lord, so that they might be useful to You.

33 My heart aches with sorrow over those lost chances to glorify my Lord—it weeps tears longing for another opportunity—a fresh start.

34 God leaves us memories as reminders—not of condemnation—but of redemption and a promise of hope for tomorrow.

35 Repentance bombards my soul like a cloudburst from a thunderstorm.

36 I am humbled before the Almighty when I am faced with the stark realization that apart from His mercy and grace—I am no better than the most vile and wretched sinner.

37 The past serves as a reminder of how far God has brought me and a revelation of the depths of His love.

38 This flesh that covers my bones lives and breathes in hope—all because of He who lives inside me.

39 All praise and glory goes to Yahweh—the great Jehovah.

Psalm 71

For Mom & Dad

¹My soul has searched in the recesses of the night for You—and found You waiting.

²I am a servant of the Most High God and You have chosen to speak Your words of comfort and peace through me.

³In fear and trembling I come in obedience to You—I come in honor not only to You and Your commandments—but also to those You would have me speak to.

⁴Your words have been quickened to my spirit—I am but clay in Your hands—without Your Spirit I am but dust—You are the very language that I speak.

⁵I rise up in honor to those who have raised me in the fear of the Lord—who have trained and nurtured me—as well as the other children born unto them.

⁶In respect I honor the godly parents who have taught me to walk in the fear of the Lord: You, O Lord, have made known that You send comfort and peace upon them.

⁷I know it is not within man's power to impart wisdom regarding the wonders of God.

⁸Often it can come through a vision—a dream—a song in the night—a prophetic word—or sometimes just a rock-solid assurance of the heart.

⁹Only You—Great Jehovah—provide a season for answers to the prayers of the saints.

¹⁰You alone are able to show forth assurances that their prayers have availed much—that the cries for the souls of their children have not gone unheard or unanswered.

¹¹Your Word clearly shows that matters of the heart are known only to You—we must never judge by outward appearances and through the eyes of man—as even Samuel, the great prophet of God was guilty of.

¹²In Your diligence—You have heard the plea of the godly—You are ever true to Your Word and answer each individual prayer in Your time—and according to Your plans.

¹³Holy Spirit—You have spoken—and I can add no more to Your words—let Your peace rest upon the righteous as they continue to

serve and honor You the rest of their days.

¹⁴Allow their lives to continue to be godly influences at all times—and may Your richest blessings saturate them with goodness and mercy.

Psalm 72

His Mercies Refresh The Weary

¹You have clearly revealed the plans of the enemy—You manifest them in visions to those who trust in the Lord.

²You have fashioned each life with a preordained number of seemingly haphazard events—but you have appointed every one of them.

³You bring these incidents about in order to give our faith opportunity to rise to the occasion—to show that You are interested in the mundane things of our lives.

⁴The difficulty lies not in the viewing of miraculous and exceptional feats—but in the faith required for the dull and boring things.

⁵God gives those who search for Him a full heart—one that overflows and spills out.

⁶Trusting in the flesh is the dagger that pierces the soul—directing our attention away from God.

⁷To be truly humble—a man must unload his insufficiency from his back and place it squarely on the shoulders of the Savior.

⁸I will learn Your language—Holy Spirit—though it costs me everything.

⁹I can find a sanctuary of prayer wherever my mind is focused upon You and Your greatness—when my heart is lifted upward in praise.

¹⁰Radiating the joy of the Lord is relatively easy as long as we do not resist it.

¹¹The weary find times of refreshment in His presence—their souls are revitalized and renewed with added strength.

¹²In times of desperation—the currents of God's mercy will carry the weak to safety.

¹³When one's heart is right—great peace abounds.

14The shadow of God's blessing is a covering for the righteous—to those who are willing to call upon Him.

15What causes the dark clouds of uncertainty to pass over—the storm to linger no more?—the prayer of the faithful will certainly bring about a reprieve.

16A fool clings to the past—the wise have learned to let it go—in order that they might embrace the future.

17Lord—You have made me a man of purpose who has applied himself to intentionally drawing closer to his God—O how I praise Your name.

18How certain am I of Your mercies, O God?—they are as dependable as fall turning into winter—winter into spring—spring into summer—and summer back into fall.

19All those who are godly strive to keep their vessels in top-notch shape and are prepared to take steps when it becomes in disrepair.

20They have applied the anointing oil and the bonding agent of the Holy Spirit to any leaks or cracks that may appear over time.

The Cross [a poem]

It matters not what others say – I'll let the cross light up my way;
The Son of God gives it the light – to shine into the darkest night.
Its light shines out for all to see – the Lamb of God at Calvary;
He died for sinners to atone – the cross became a stepping stone.
It led the way unto the tomb – the earth became the Savior's womb;
It could not hold Him there for long – His victory was heaven's song.
Although the cross was only wood – its destiny the greater good;
It held the final sacrifice – that for all sinners paid the price.

Psalm 73

I Am That Drifter....

¹The glory of the Lord never ceases to infuse those whose lives are dedicated to His purpose—those who are not ashamed to call Him Lord.

²The Rose of Sharon grows in my garden and delights my senses with fragrance and beauty—its aroma invades every corner.

³My garden paths are lined with the Lily of the Valley—they are shaded by the True Vine—it receives glorious light from the Bright and Morning Star.

⁴You have allowed a faithful man to peer into Your heart—to receive a glance—in return, You reward his pursuits with a breathtaking experience.

⁵With a cold and bitter heart comes only trouble and grief—a soft and pliable heart is pleasing and useful to the Father.

⁶You fill up my day perfectly as long as You consume it—without You I am incomplete.

⁷Without Him—I am like a lock without a key—He is more than adequate for every need that comes my way.

⁸He has never failed to make good on a single promise He has made—and I have no reason to suspect that He will fall short now.

⁹The roots of a well-established oak go down deep—anchoring it against the storms of life—my soul has been firmly affixed to the Rock of Ages—which is immovable.

¹⁰The lawbreaker has swept his sins under a carpet of indifference—he has a tendency to think that God does not see them.

¹¹Those who delight in wickedness will perish in their evil thoughts and desires—the enemy has taken control of them.

¹²The godly will walk in the Spirit—forsaking their sins—while calling on the Lord.

¹³A redeemed man confesses his sins to God and He tosses them into the sea of His forgetfulness—never to be remembered.

¹⁴Goosebumps have footraces over my entire body when I dwell on Your awesomeness and majesty—they stir me to the depths of my soul with wonder.

Psalm 73 - I Am That Drifter....

¹⁵Holy Spirit—overshadow me—show me the way that leads to everlasting life so I may dwell forever with my God.

¹⁶My heart has made a pact with You, my God—that I will follow You all the days of my life—that I might abide in Your presence evermore.

¹⁷Your presence graces my home daily—Your angels abide there to obey Your bidding—O how blessed I am.

¹⁸A brother's smile is more favorable than a jacket on a cold day—his kind words and generous actions bring warmth to the spirit—the affection of his hug is beyond words.

¹⁹The crack of the whip serves to remind those who are slaves to the world of their destiny—the master they serve is fear.

²⁰True servants of the Most High God serve Him in love and sincerity—with an upright and cheerful heart.

²¹Some have wandered the wastelands of life—haunted by the smoking guns of their past—with their vision dimmed they are in search of a brighter future.

²²Then the brilliance of Your glory shined across their paths so brightly they were blinded by Your light.

²³They heard only Your voice speaking—but in ignorance—chose not to heed it.

²⁴Your Spirit pressed on in tender persuasion to the precious few who acknowledged Your voice—You were pleased to offer them unprecedented levels of Your grace.

²⁵I am that drifter who was thrilled by Your outpouring of grace and a new way of life—praise the Lord —O my soul—and yes I will praise Him again and again.

Psalm 74

Your Greatness Overwhelms Me

¹When I make up my mind to ponder Your greatness I am drawn to view each and every perfect day You have created.

²What is the record of Your number of days—and who is able to match it?

³There is none among gods or man able to measure up to You—You have no equal.

⁴Although Your days are without number no one has been able to outdo You on a single one.

⁵O my God—there is truly none like You—in heaven or on earth—in worlds unknown or in the ages of eternity.

⁶Reasonable evidence lays convincing groundwork to establish proof of Your greatness—following a pattern of rationality.

⁷The proof is in the pudding—in the works of Your hands—if anyone needs to reckon the matter.

⁸You have settled Your identity throughout infinity—can anyone refute the data?

⁹There are facts You have kept hidden through the ages—things unmanageable by these earthly minds—they are stored up for future revelation.

¹⁰Your majesty extends to times before the world began—which man have You made privy to that marvel—the beginning started with You—that's why You are the Alpha.

¹¹When I even attempt to grasp a minute portion of Your magnitude, I am left unfulfilled—longing to take hold of more.

¹²I smile inwardly and my spirit leaps with joy—knowing that You will soon remove this veil that blankets my eyes.

¹³Who can devise a perfect plan like You, my God?—You are perfect in all You do.

¹⁴From my point of view—I am staggered at Your ability to make something out of nothing—each day is a brand new creation.

¹⁵All praise be unto You for Your excellence—unto You for Your omniscience and power—Your might is not limited—daily You set new boundaries.

Psalm 75

Swallowed By His Purpose

¹Each day is like a single step in a journey—hopefully it brings us closer to our desired destination.

²The man whose steps are not planned by the Lord becomes disoriented and loses his way—he becomes easily sidetracked and his confusion takes him elsewhere.

³He who is guided by his conscience will surely stumble—but the man who is led by the Spirit will not falter.

⁴When you see someone without a smile—share and give them one of yours—that is the way to spread the joy of the Lord around.

⁵The Lord blesses those who are willing to share with others what they have received—whether small or great.

⁶The sacrifices of the godly are a clean heart and a pure conscience—God will not turn these away.

⁷Let the barriers of this flesh be broken as chains and shackles are loosed—that we will be able to worship Him in absolute truth.

⁸When counting your friends—although they may be few—give thanks to the Lord when you find they are true.

⁹The wise have learned not to chase after happiness because it is very elusive.

¹⁰The man who meanders through life with no defined purpose is like a piece of driftwood washed ashore.

¹¹Burdens feel heavier the longer we carry them—we will not be weighted down with them any longer if we lay them upon the Savior as He asks us to do.

¹²We have not been called to live our lives in armor-plated tanks or bulletproof vests—on the contrary,

¹³we live in delicate and translucent pottery so God's glory can shine through and His power is all the more obvious—there is no option but to trust Him for protection.

¹⁴Who is that man who has made the Lord his focus—who wakens in the early hours before the dawn with his mind stayed on Him?

15He is the man whose life has been swallowed up in purpose—who desires Him more than life itself.

16Teach me—help me to curb and control the appetites of this flesh—fleshly cravings able to cause harm to this temple of Your Holy Spirit.

17The outflow of the life of a Christian is manifested by a portion of the blessings he has received.

18Never—ever—think you are too insignificant for God to use—by doing so you severely underestimate His potential!

19Man has manufactured things like dynamite to come in small packages—God is infinitely more capable to make and use that which is small.

20In fact—His Word states that He loves to use the small things because it shows forth His great power even more clearly.

21Pain and suffering are a couple of unwanted traveling companions—being a child of God does not ensure that your walk will be free of them.

22As a matter of fact—they will slip in at various times—completely unbeknownst to you—and keep right in time—dogging your every step.

23Establish Your kingdom, O God, through the meek and lowly—the weak and unassuming—the simple and ordinary—may Your power be exalted today.

24The wise have discovered a painfully elementary truth they use to govern their actions—the right way is the hard way—the wrong way is the easy way.

25You will never know how far you have come if you do not periodically look back and see where you started from.

Psalm 76

Thoughts Of You Are All I Desire

1Am I in the habit of forgetting to think about You—failing to recount Your ways—maybe even losing my devotedness to You?

2I will redouble my efforts to keep You at the forefront of all my meditations.

³Your words move on me even in my sleep—I awake to consciousness and delight to hear Your whispers.

⁴Your Spirit incites me—it drives me with excitement to mull over Your closeness—to think that friendship with You is intimacy with my Creator.

⁵I make it my intention to fill every day with thoughts that center on Your majesty—filling up all the voids within my consciousness with an eternal awareness.

⁶I never need an excuse to dwell on Your goodness—it causes a bounce in my step and joy to spring up in my heart.

⁷I try never to waste even the smallest opportunity to proclaim Your greatness to those 'round about me.

⁸Annoyingly at times—my thoughts of You are distant—at other times they are scrambled like a plate of eggs.

⁹Sometimes I need to rein in my speculations like a cowboy would a wild mustang or an unruly stallion—or even an unbroken bronco.

¹⁰I am driven to draw closer to Your heart, O God, and that compels me to fill up my waking moments with reflections on You.

¹¹At various times I wrap my attention in monotony—then the Holy Spirit so graciously nudges my mind back into God consciousness with a sweet thought.

¹²When the blunt force of pain has clutched my body—my thoughts are quick to snap to Your attention—much like a wayward rubber band.

¹³I will gather my thoughts and fasten my mind upon His greatness —for He has done great things— and who is able to comprehend them all?

¹⁴Thoughts carom into my head off the backboard of other words spoken—the Holy Spirit then converts them into godly intellect and You, my God, are exalted above all.

¹⁵You instantly bless me—even more than a gambler hitting a mega jackpot.

¹⁶My exploration for godly messages is rewarded each instance I walk in the Spirit.

¹⁷The Holy Spirit is willing to help me recycle worldly ideas into godly thoughts—this makes it easier to keep my mind on You, my God.

Psalm 77

Exposed Weakness = Judgment

¹Looking down from Your throne, You see every one of us You have made—the masses of humanity—multitudes in Your likeness.

²From Your vantage point—through the eyes of God Almighty—You created each of us uniquely—distinctively individual in nature.

³Even if our external framework looks identical when we stand side by side, You see things inwardly—a stamping of Your conception too wonderful for man.

⁴Man's skill and technology cannot produce a machine that can peer inside his soul.

⁵You have reserved the marvel of this for You and You alone—You have given us strict warnings to not judge from the outward standpoint.

⁶You have exposed our weakness at this point—with scrutinies we make awkward and superficial judgments—neither do we care about what You see inwardly.

⁷Our sensitivity has become calloused—since we have failed to take into account Your leadings, we end up making stabs in the dark at shadows.

⁸You desire to lead us to a higher calling—to fine-tune us to Your Holy Spirit.

⁹Remove the knife of judgment from our grip—replace it with the shawl of compassion and the hand of friendship.

¹⁰Then you will replace the film of judgment that covers our eyes with the lens of grace and discernment—so we can clearly see Your will.

¹¹It is the inner depths that bring You either pleasure or pain—the offerings of the heart arise to bless You or curse You.

¹²May you sweep the depths of my soul clean, O God, so the joy of Your presence can fill and inhabit my innermost being.

¹³In the silence and the beauty of this hour—my spirit rises to share with Your majesty—an offering of praise and thanksgiving—the sweet longings of my soul.

¹⁴I am struck dumb—so I have no spoken words to offer You—now I simply commune with You and worship You in quietness—with pen and thought only—exalting You in utter sincerity.

Psalm 78

Your Word Exists For All

¹You declare Your Word with certainty—not with vagueness or skepticism—it is not elusive except perhaps to those who are insincere.

²It is available to all who pay attention—it gives guidance to those who obey and follow its guidelines.

³When a man's strength is weak and puny—that's when God is able to come through in a big way—He always excels in those situations.

⁴The angels of God have walked among us—we have seen their faces and they have even touched us as they have blessed our lives in an assortment of ways.

⁵Those who seek after God will only find Him if they have flung wide open the doors of their mind to the Holy Spirit—then invite Him in.

⁶A mind that is closed like a bank vault is unable to receive any teaching or instructions.

⁷Those who are searching for the Lord would do well to open their hearts at the same time—then the seeds of wisdom and righteousness can be planted for a great harvest.

⁸True worship in the presence of God exposes unworthiness—His mercy is able to wash it away as repentance surges out from a tender heart.

⁹The joy of the Father radiates each time a saint stands before Him free of self—drained and liberated to be filled with His glory.

¹⁰Who could blame You for not wanting to share Your glory with another?—for there is truly no other who begins to compare with Your Majesty.

¹¹I give my praise to no other—for You alone are worthy of it—I have reserved it for Your pleasure only.

¹²Each of God's mortal beings are stamped with a return due date—much like a library book that has been borrowed for a set period of time.

¹³Sin rebels against Your holiness, O God, and creates an immense chasm—the depths of which no man can measure.

Psalm 78 - Your Word Exists For All

¹⁴All eternity is watching as a lifetime of waiting—looking—and longing will soon culminate at the sound of a trumpet blast—like a buzzer signaling the end of a game.

¹⁵He hears the cry of the righteous as they intercede on behalf of their neighbors.

¹⁶Let the mighty power of Jesus intercede—causing the ways of the sinners to intersect the path of those who plant and water—prepare their hearts for acceptance.

¹⁷By the might of Your Word—You bring about harvest time—that is the thing with which You are pleased.

¹⁸The life force of God flows through my veins—it empowers me to be what I could not be on my own.

¹⁹Blessed is the man who has learned to use memories of the past to serve as the building blocks of his future—they serve to fortify and make him stronger.

²⁰The unwise have failed to use them profitably and thus they only serve to weaken and tear them down—there are lessons to be learned from good and bad memories.

²¹A truly godly life is only made possible through complete reliance on Him—this means leaving no stone unturned in seeking and finding His will.

²²We must never allow our problems and trials of this life to come between us and God—that will only block our access and obscure our view of Him.

²³God will change a heart of stone but only if it is yielded to Him.

²⁴My soul was lonely when I cried out—God came near and riveted me with His gaze.

²⁵You bless all men with the gift of life—though they may not recognize or accept it—the breath of God is life to all.

²⁶Like a bear after a winter's hibernation—my soul is ravenous for You, my God.

²⁷God's grace is available for the moment of need—not for the purpose of hoarding or stockpiling it for future use.

²⁸Faithfulness is not accurately seen through a single moment or event—it can only be measured by a life span.

²⁹Truth and fidelity—constancy and honor—these are Your foundational principles—You wrap them around Your heart and desire to see them displayed in Your servant.

30Great is Your faithfulness, O God, You rule with precision and order in all things—Your righteousness is unwavering—praise the Lord—O my soul—praise the Lord.

Psalm 79

You Fill Godly Hearts

1You reward those who seek after You with their whole hearts—their spirits are made alive—their ears are unstopped.

2You make their encounters with You real as Your presence passes before them—and opens the eyes of their spirits.

3They feast upon Your goodness as Your joy spills over and fills their vessels—as they walk in Your ways, You fill their paths with new light.

4You fill them with power for the coming day—inwardly You renew them with strength—You transform them and make them new in Your likeness.

5You clothe them in an array of praise—which protects them from the enemy—You give each of them a shield of faith as their guard.

6They are satisfied in Your presence, O God, filled to overflowing with good things.

7Your Word supplies them with fortification—it provides a barricade against any obstacles that come against them—it is a protective wall for them.

8You usher vitality into their beings as You draw them into Your very presence, O God; You dispatch a new energy and passion unto them, which keeps them filled.

9You wrap the smile of Your pleasure around them as a covering—it becomes their cloak of salvation—with it they are clothed in humility.

10Thoughts of You are all they desire—Your praise wells up in hearts quick to bless You in worship—Your nearness is a blessing to them.

11Their tongues can never cease exalting You—they worship in freedom—You have made Your worthiness evident through their lives.

¹²It is he who seeks the Lord with his whole heart who will never be disappointed—You will never turn him away destitute.

¹³Anyone who has a heart inclined toward his God is walking on the right path—his feet have stepped on holy ground.

¹⁴You will fill the desires of his heart—his pursuit of earthly things begins to wane as he becomes lost in a Holy Presence.

¹⁵Those who consume their lives in a search for the Holy One will drink deeply from His well of mercy and He will make them happy.

¹⁶God's children walk eagerly after Him with all their hearts—their feet will follow along in harmony because You will direct every step.

¹⁷In a quest for unspeakable glories with their Creator—their souls are unquenchable.

¹⁸The pursuit to find You, O God, to know You in Your fullness—to experience You in Your power—to relish Your presence and Your glory will consume their lives.

¹⁹All of these will culminate only after they have drawn their last earthly breath—and laid down this robe of flesh—then they will find completion to all their frail longings.

Psalm 80

God's Word Answers All

¹The godly man is humble without even knowing it—yet the fool seeks to know if he is and removes all doubt.

²God—the light of Your Word has pierced the blackest darkness of the night—it goes forth with blazing brilliance—it illuminates the path of those seeking You.

³You have transferred the light of the Word to our hearts—You have ordained us to reflect this light all around us.

⁴In days of old—God spoke through men in whom He placed His Spirit—in more recent times He cut to the chase and gave us a direct line through His Son, Jesus.

⁵The Word of God continues to speak through men today—those will-

ing to let the Holy Spirit guide them—to set aside their own desires and speak the hard words of truth.

6The call of the cross of Christ tolls the hour for complete surrender—total abandonment to our Lord and Master.

7Its bloodstained and nail-embedded wood glorified God in praise as it held His precious Son—for even such a brief moment in time.

8The exercise of the godly heart is the habitual devotion of praise and worship over even the smallest trials—the aerobics of the heavenlies.

9Those who go down the dark path may never return—shine Your light on them, O Lord, that they may see clearly and change their ways.

10When the cares and troubles of this life start to weigh me down—I let them rise on the wings of my praise.

11The first step in the journey to our salvation began with the babe in a manger—the Son of God was the first and the final step in that journey.

12The honor is mine to be Your son—adopted into royalty—or else I would have remained a pauper.

13Do you suppose you can ever catch God off-guard—is it possible to take Him by surprise—or does He get tired and take a nap?

14Is He oblivious to our summons for His help—does He daydream on the job—has His preoccupation with heaven caused Him to be indifferent to us on earth?

15Has there been any hour in which His mercies have fallen short—or His grace has dried up like a creek bed in the summer—can His love fizzle like a spent firecracker?

16Since when did the load become so heavy that He had to ask for assistance—can you name any handicap that has slowed Him down?

17Do disappointments dictate His future plans—is He aghast with surprise when calamity happens—are man's mishaps a hindrance to the Almighty?

18Have His resources come into short supply or His responsibilities caused Him to take a beating—where has His prosperity declined because of bad investments?

19What are the odds of finding Him out to lunch at a crucial time of need—do you ever get a busy signal when you call Him?

²⁰Does He speak with rambling jumbled words of confusion—are His thoughts incoherent as those of someone with a mental illness might be?

²¹Does the unknown shock Him or leave Him speechless—is He overwhelmed with accountability—can ordeals cause Him to have nightmares?

²²Does He lose His cool in the midst of chaotic situations—or will He come unglued at our ungodly decisions—is madness in His family genes?

²³Does poor eyesight hamper His powers of observation—is He incapable of seeing the beginning from the end—do difficult problems easily baffle or confound Him?

²⁴Do the mysteries of the universe unravel Him—do distressing dilemmas unnerve Him—do catastrophes bring him to His knees?

²⁵Has He ever given logic the day off—will He let foolishness reign in place of it—does He send good judgment on vacation—does He grant rationale a sabbatical?

²⁶Is He perplexed or swayed by our opinions of Him—do His judgments require counseling—are His policies under the advisement of a board—do the beliefs of His subjects alter His frame of mind?

²⁷The marvel of it all is that His Word will answer every question above—He is so much greater than any mind could ever dream of—all praise and glory be to His Majesty.

Psalm 81

You Are My Secret Place

¹The snare would have held me fast—trapped as in a vise—doomed to a lifetime of misery—but praise Your name—Your grace and mercy came by and released me.

²The wise servant will always leave markers along his journey that remind him of the goodness of the Lord—they give heed to times of nearness and blessing.

³The godly sow seeds of righteousness—they show them through

the good deeds they share with the needy—their baskets will be chocked full of blessings.

⁴He has called you to be a light and a voice in His land—He calls you with exceeding great power and might—will you hearken unto His voice that bids you to be His vessel?

⁵The secret abode of my soul holds the dwelling places where no one can go except my God and me—it is the spot where He and I are in the habit of meeting.

⁶A place of forsaken loneliness where I display the secrets of my heart —a place of isolation where He can have His way without interruption.

⁷In the hidden places of my heart, my shortcomings are ever before Him —I release them so that by His security and welfare—He can make untold victories mine.

⁸There He finds me empty and barren—He fills me with His substance—sweetness and knowledge —hope and song—He makes me new through praises and thanksgiving.

⁹I arise early in the morning and go to that place—He fills me with His Word—He tunes up the heartstrings of my soul so I can play beautiful music before Him.

¹⁰He sets the time for our meeting— I proceed with haste so I won't be late for His appointment—he rewards me with His presence.

¹¹His Shekinah glory fills the place where I am—I fill my tabernacle with praise for Him—He allows me to lift holy hands to His majesty and restores me with His strength.

¹²You are welcome in this place— Almighty God—I have heard the words of Your voice—excitement causes me to quiver as I listen intently.

¹³In the security and comfort of Your embrace—I find shelter in Your arms of love.

¹⁴You dismiss me from our secret place to walk the path You have set before me—but never from Your presence, which abides continually within.

Psalm 82

I Will Go All-Out For You

¹Contentment comes to those who adore God—to those who are not satisfied with just the edge of the Divine One.

²They clamor for the center and go all-out daily to get to His heart—they respect His presence and reverence His deity.

³The wicked have made their beds and refuse to change their ways—their enjoyment comes from the seeds of unrighteousness—they spurn the Almighty with their conduct.

⁴You will draw the one who is true and faithful to Your voice closer to You—the one who is steadfast in Your Word—then You will reveal Your glory to him.

⁵Heaven has come down and bathed him in jubilation—Your Word speaks truth unto his soul and imparts unclouded vision for the days ahead.

⁶My soul reaches for You, my God—in the midst of chaos as well as in the quiet hour—it stretches forth to grasp Your hand—to let You pull me near to Your side.

⁷Endeavoring to set aside all idleness—I strive to set my sights on one goal—that You might harvest me as a farmer reaps his crops at the proper time.

⁸Cherish the memories God leaves with you—the good ones become His smile upon you—the bad ones are reminders of His grace, while shoring up the failures of our past.

⁹Store the lessons learned down in your heart—value them like special gifts—like treasured mementos—memoirs of your journey with Him.

¹⁰Etch them into your mind as the Holy Spirit periodically refreshes them to your memory—so you can lead them out into the open during the days of trouble.

¹¹Write them on tablets of paper so the winds of time do not whisk them away as loose sand—accumulate them in your word processor for safekeeping.

¹²A wise man will not trust the frailties of the mind knowing that in time a photograph will fade—that etchings of stone can be washed smooth when exposed to the elements.

¹³He records the lessons of his past for the benefit of others—their memories will take on lives of their own—He will not fail to write down the words and visions of His God.

¹⁴The Almighty has quickened the following words to my spirit, and I was swift to follow His promptings.

¹⁵"The righteous acts of My saints have clothed them in clean fine linen, which they will wear to the wedding supper.

¹⁶I am Yahweh and from My perspective, the years of a man pass like the blink of an eye—or the beat of a heart—to some, I have multiplied their number of days.

¹⁷To the man who will trust in Me—I will surround his camp with My protection—I will make his ark to float in safety.

¹⁸I will cover the family of the righteous man with My security—I extend My mercy outward—even to those who are yet unrighteous.

¹⁹I will cover the man who completely trusts in Me and keep him safe—whose whole heart is resting in My bosom.

²⁰My angels will become his refuge—they will totally surround his property—their covering provides a canopy over his camp.

²¹They are quick to escort his praises into My presence—they continually fill My house with incense—their fragrance has a sweet smell that cheers Me.

²²I am pleased and will bless him with songs of joy—I delight to be his portion—his daily bread I send with gladness.

²³He has dedicated his camp unto My name—therefore My glory shall always be his source—I am pleased to have given him this vision because his heart is set on My ways.

²⁴I will not fail to bless the man whose longing for Me is deeper than the words he speaks—he will gaze upon My beauty and be satisfied."

That's what You made me for [a poem]

Precious Holy Spirit I lend myself to You,
that I may bring You honor in everything I do;
Lord, take my will and make it Yours until there's nothing more,
let all I am be lost in You that's what You made me for.

Psalm 83

Your Righteous Ones Are Light To The World

¹Almighty God is God of the extremes—He excels at the highest heights—the lowest depths—the farthest point yonder—the nearest spot possible;

²the blackest darkness—the brightest light—go ahead and pick out the polar extremes and He is there—but—He is also outstanding at the in-between positions.

³Let all who have understanding come to appreciate each new dawn—for some of them will never see another day—may they value it as long-lost riches.

⁴For those whose dawn is only the blackest of the night—I pray the light of Your presence, O God, will be the dawning of their new morning of comfort and hope.

⁵The Holy Spirit is the oil in my lamp, which will never run dry—He fills me daily with fresh oil.

⁶God's Word so aptly trims my wick so the light of His glory will blaze even more intensely—He promises it will never be extinguished.

⁷The Lord lights the lamps of the righteous—they will burn brightly until the day they enter His city—where the Lamb is the light and their lamps are no longer needed.

⁸Woe to the people of this world when the light of God is taken from it—how black will that darkness be—the lamps of the saints will shine only a short time longer.

⁹A soul becomes wise by learning to ask the right questions—then right answers are easier to come by.

¹⁰Uncluttered souls are free to pursue God to their hearts' content—and yet their hearts are never fully satisfied because they are relentlessly searching for more.

¹¹When you look for the enemies of your soul, don't just look at the obvious adversary—the distractions you are facing are also great opponents.

¹²The godly make it a practice of traveling light—too much baggage only weighs them down—this allows them to move on at a moment's notice.

¹³Who is like our Lord?—He makes walking through valleys and glens pleasant—while on the mountains He keeps a watchful eye out so you do not fall into a crevasse.

¹⁴The leadings of the Lord are eternal and show the way to everlasting life.

¹⁵Blessed is the man who has made the Lord his God—whose heart declares, "I have chosen the way of truth!"

¹⁶He who has found truth models it through integrity—without words—his actions shape these values to all he meets.

¹⁷Though fog and darkness shroud the truth—it will ever remain unchanged—as sure as the Father of Light.

¹⁸The wise man shies away from trouble—but the fool embraces it with open arms.

¹⁹Repentance turns weakness into strength—it turns godly sorrow into forgiveness.

²⁰Forgive my shallowness and lack of faith that I should ever be amazed by You—increase my faith so that I shall cease to be surprised by anything You do.

²¹The Holy Spirit takes me by the hand and leads me into heavenly places—those clefts of the Rock arranged by the Lord God Almighty.

²²It is there I am safe from the wrath of the tempter—his barbs of discouragement cannot reach me.

²³To the godly, the interruptions of the tempter are more than a nuisance—they come as weights to his soul unless he is able to cast them onto the Savior.

²⁴The righteous will persevere until they have reached the safety of God's promises—places of rest for their weary souls.

²⁵In those heavenly places You fill me with songs of joy—melodies of sweet praise for my Redeemer—rapture fills my heart with delight.

²⁶Who is able to comprehend His worthiness — to calculate His prominence?

²⁷Is it possible to keep tabs on His perfection—to compute His holiness—to estimate His character—to measure His virtue?

²⁸None of His creatures can!

Psalm 84

Each Day You Are My Praise

¹The heart of a servant is wise—it is quick to see the needs of others and then to reach out and supply them.

²When everyday people live out their faith through difficult times—the light of the gospel shines forth—then hope is born in the unbeliever.

³The godly hold no ties—no allegiances to temporal things—they have a common hope—a better assurance—their treasure is kept safely in the Master's house.

⁴All that I see belongs to You—the Mighty One—You are gracious and have blessed me abundantly above what I could imagine or deserve.

⁵For my life—You have given a ransom—the price was a gift of great worth to You—Your dearest and only Son for me—how can it be?

⁶The human heart often aches with the loss of a saint—but the spirit responds with pure elation as it joins all of heaven in a homecoming celebration for that child of God.

⁷Our soul longs to join that saint on the other side just over in the Promised Land.

⁸A heart on fire like the burning bush Moses saw is consumed by the holiness of Jehovah—consumed, but not extinguished—ensnared, yet sparked to disperse His glory.

⁹Even the deepest river has two banks upon which to rest and sides to support it.

¹⁰God paints each new day with vibrant pristine colors—His grace colors the daylight hours more grandly than a field of fresh flowers—when God is in it—is not even the dreary day beautiful?

¹¹The wise have learned to tame their tongues even though they seem to weigh a hundred pounds—for unleashing them may end up costing much more.

¹²In strengthening the hand of a friend, one can often find strength for himself—that way it becomes a double blessing.

¹³The life of the righteous is never lonely with the Lord by their side—He controls the raging river and

makes the walls of their enemies to crumble—their gates to collapse.

¹⁴Finding strength in your own flesh is the fastest way to fall—instead make the Lord your strong tower and you will have strength to stand—strength to spare.

¹⁵The downfall of many men has been their inattention to details—it has been the undoing of kings and rulers alike.

¹⁶The mercies of the Lord are extravagant—they reach far beyond our point of need—as if we could ever exhaust them within ten thousand lifetimes.

¹⁷This day—which stands boldly before me—I separate from the past and the future.

¹⁸What a gift You have given me—that of life—and I choose to dedicate every moment of it to You.

¹⁹You have taken away those who were my strength and encouragement so that You might become my source.

²⁰You banished them from my life so that You would be the Rock I lean upon—O praise Your glorious name—the name that is higher than the heavens above.

²¹Your jealousy, O Lord, has been my saving grace; it has shown me the true depths of Your love—You have exposed Your heart to me.

²²Let your heart guide your sacrifice as you give only the very best to your King—He will be proud of that.

²³My heart beats faithfully in anticipation of Your soon return, my Lord—that blessed hope promised long ago.

²⁴Never seeing yet fiercely believing —You are not only able to fulfill Your promised return—but You are in the nucleus of that process now.

²⁵When I think on each blessing You have sent my way—how could I begrudge You a single request You might make of me?

²⁶Holy Spirit—each day that I come to You with an open heart—You mine nuggets of truth for me from the depths of God's Word.

²⁷You probe me with scrutiny—paying heed to my deliberation—You forgive my ignorance with sympathy—for You know I am but dust.

²⁸You ordered my trail from the start, according to Your will—it is well marked with one-way signs—You desire that I not be confused about which direction to travel.

²⁹One day Your grace caught me at my lowest point and offered me a helping hand—it soon became my song of liberty—O praise Your name.

Psalm 85

When The Heart Of God Invades A Man...

¹When the heart of God invades a man, it will create an affection that won't go away—a craving that insists on pleasing Him—a closeness impossible to duplicate.

²He prepares an appetite for His Word—an urge for prayer—a yearning for godly passions—a fervor for His mission.

³This heart of God alters everything—it utterly rearranges a life—it uses—it chooses—it fine tunes—and it bruises.

⁴A sweet spirit replaces a spiteful disposition—His ways become our priorities—purity marches in and takes occupancy.

⁵It proofs and checks the motives—it polishes—it ignores—it cleans up—it restores.

⁶This invasion causes an about-face of ways—a changing of course—godly attractions in place of worldly desires.

⁷When the heart of God invades the heart of a man, it becomes the bridge he can cross over and into His infinite, yet loving presence—and a fulfilling relationship.

⁸It causes brokenness and surrender to infiltrate and expel the darkness—it softens the calloused spirit.

⁹It makes the will turn out to be submissively captive—it makes truth rise like a lily breaking the bonds of the earth—it ousts fear and doubt from the mind and heart.

¹⁰It touts confidence—it dismisses condemnation—it establishes the light of His Word—it introduces peace.

¹¹It saturates this man's heart with godly initiatives and causes him to reject hatred—His creativity penetrates to the core—He transplants new ideas—He injects inspiration.

¹²Hearing His voice becomes imperative—He causes a desire for communion to become central—He chisels His mark onto the door of this man's heart.

¹³When the heart of God invades a man's heart, it will be in sync with godly frequencies—He aligns His waves of glory and works them through the yielded heart.

Psalm 86

A Life Destined To Glorify His Greatness

¹When the pilings are knocked out from underneath your building—when the girders supporting your structure are washed away—how will you stand without His foundation as your base?

²He is my Rock and my Cornerstone—I have built upon His steadfastness—He has secured and sheltered my residence—I am safe because my soul is hidden with Him.

³The glory and marvels You hold for those who search for You are contained in the kernel of hope and faith they now treasure.

⁴Faith produces a divine outburst—courtesy of the hope that is within you—it is a flare-up of optimism that settles into a gritty pursuance of life in the world to come.

⁵Your plan is to occasionally allow an isolated glimpse—if we were permitted more than that it would negate our faith and make it useless.

⁶Is God more pleased with a martyr than with a willing heart and a sweet spirit?—a humble heart and a trustworthy spirit make His heart glad.

⁷Our past is able to hold the future hostage—it is quick to take it captive in exchange for a priceless payoff—a bribe of incalculable proportions.

⁸The believer brings his submitted life to God—in turn, he receives power to prevail—strength then becomes the byproduct of submission.

⁹It has been said in times past, "You are my portion"—now my heart burns within me as I desire You, my God, to be more than a portion to me.

¹⁰You are the Everlasting One—the Great I Am—my all in all—my completeness—when Your Spirit unites with mine, we are one in the bonds of unity.

¹¹Ribbons of praise adorn my garments—they are brightly decorated with worship—showing forth the glory of my God.

¹²Sequins of gratitude sparkle forth the gratefulness of a full heart—His love has made my heart full and it spills onto those around me.

[13]My testimonies turn out to be ornaments and garlands of tribute—You are honored as they validate and endorse Your pre-eminence and supremacy.

[14]Which man is willing to be used in simplicity, all for the sake of simply being used?

[15]To disregard recognition and fanfare—to shut out all aspirations—to forsake prestige and to even come to terms with obscurity.

[16]Therein lies the humble heart—the servant who pleases his God above all others—the one who scorns the acknowledgment of men but only seeks that of his Father.

[17]The breath of the Almighty resides in my being and gives me life—a life of praise and adoration destined to glorify His greatness.

[18]When I take the last step of this journey here below and You take my breath away with finality—I shall rest peacefully in Your presence;

[19]Then I will know my soul is exactly where it has always longed to be.

Psalm 87

He Lives For You And Me

[1]Some kings wear crowns of jewels—He wore a crown of thorns—some live a life of luxury—He walked a path of scorn.

[2]Their lives are for the present—He chose eternity—they live for no one but themselves—He lives for you and me.

[3]Plenty of the rich are fulfilled with the paydays of this life—they have taken no concern to store up for their eternal lives.

[4]The less-fortunate man pays no heed to the pleasures of this life—he is laying up treasures for the sweet by and by.

[5]When fatigue wrestled me to the ground—I cried out to the Lord and He gave me a timeout—His words revived and renewed my flesh in short order.

[6]"He who is ever attentive to My words—who is seeking Me with his whole heart—I will reveal the hidden mysteries of My throne—those things visible and invisible.

7 I invite him to lean hard upon Me and to press in close to My side.

8 I would challenge him to view Me as a close friend and not from a distance—to incline his ear unto Me and I will speak the things he needs to hear."

9 He whose hope is in the Lord is looking for an extension on his contract each time he lays down to sleep, confident that if it is not renewed he will be at home with his God.

10 You will use and continue to bless those You have chosen and called —You will allow nothing to go to waste—even the leftover broken pieces You will gather.

11 Accept my ritual of worship, O Lord, until my well-intentioned heart can once again dance with joy; until Your fountains of deep water burst through all my barriers.

12 You have become my well of living water in seasons of parched desert and desolation—I would have perished if You had not become my oasis.

13 I fasten my eyes upon You, Lord, like two pieces of material fastened by Velcro; never let my eyes stray from Your rules that hold me fast and keep me near You.

14 Holy Spirit, won't You fall on me— Holy Spirit come and set me free —Holy Spirit never cease to be— my praise and symphony.

15 You have opened my mind and funnel Your thoughts into it so that I might gain great insight into Your Majesty—speak, my Lord, and I will listen.

16 "I am God—the Lord Almighty— and there is none like me.

17 It is with excitement that I use my people as instruments of worship—I have endowed them with notes of praise—to be as the sounding board of a piano or harp

18 I have given them a freedom of expression and a desire to direct praise upward.

19 My intent from the beginning was to fashion those I have called so their cells would be infused with melodious song—they have the choice of where to forward that tune.

20 O how My heart longs for their praise to be lifted unto My heavens—giving all the glory to Me as your Creator.

21 See how My heart is cheered to hear your songs—to hear your symphonies of worship directed on high.

²²My orchestra is unlimited—the people of this world cannot contain it—nor can the entire universe equal its sum.

²³I have instruments of such depth and beauty that you could not imagine them if I gave you hundreds of millennia.

²⁴My heavenly bodies join with the worship of My people to create a masterpiece of gigantic proportions.

²⁵A fanfare that mortal ear has never heard resounds among the heavenlies and stirs the celestial beings to respond in unanimous expressions of worship.

²⁶I will be exalted supremely when all of heaven and earth join in unending devotion and when the hearts of my creation are focused on My glory."

Psalm 88

A psalm for Anna

¹I hear the ever-present footsteps of my Lord as I quiet the pounding of my heart and listen—they comfort me in my dark time and speak peace to my soul.

²His ever-abiding presence is always close—His whisper stills my storm—the raging storm in me—He walks with me in the dark places.

³He guides me by His hand as He places mine in His—His voice reassures me of His nearness—He has spoken to my fears and they have fled.

⁴I will ever trust Him—for He has become my burden bearer—He bids me to relinquish my heaviness to His care—O how I will praise Him for His love.

⁵The shadows have vanished—for He has brought me out of the dark places and set my feet upon a well-lit plain.

⁶I will ever rejoice in His goodness—His mercy has strengthened my backbone—His joy has made my heart new.

⁷In the midst of this life He has become my surety—my heart will sing new songs unto Him—He has secured my spot in heavenly places.

⁸My praises unto Him are my new source of strength—for He makes me glad.

⁹He has lifted up my soul in His presence—for He has supplied everything I need—O praise the Lord—O my soul.

Psalm 89

Your Face Is All I Need To See

¹My soul gazes hungrily into the surrounding atmosphere—it is looking for the light of Your glory—hoping to catch a glimpse of Your beauty—a display of Your essence.

²The dreams of my future must detour around the devastation of my past or they will collapse and crumble in its rubble.

³The Lord walks with me daily and there is never a dull moment—He lightens my spirit and makes it celebrate His company.

⁴Those who have trained themselves to cultivate a habit of heart worship and praise have discovered a deepening intimacy with the Lord—regardless of circumstances.

⁵A wise man knows that a few careless words can unravel a close friendship—and he is eager to choose his words carefully.

⁶Let me first be thankful for the new day You have set before me—for without it there would be no need for my daily bread.

⁷My soul is awakened through the caffeine of Your Word—it refreshes better than a morning cup of coffee.

⁸You validate an authentic disciple, and he serves as a reflection of his Savior—he mirrors godly traits to others anywhere he goes.

⁹Whoever severs the ties to unrighteousness has fulfilled the purpose of God—he has found it to be in his best interest to steer clear of sin.

¹⁰Nosiness leads a fool into sleazy paths—it has hooked his jaw and drags him along.

¹¹When the saint faces unexpected changes in his life—he looks to find blessings hiding inside—knowing that without change, growth is not possible.

¹²Let power and boldness consume me as You give me anointed dreams—ordain me to serve so that I might be sealed with "Holy to the Lord."

¹³God's love reaches further than our utmost imaginations—its scope is infinite in nature—unfathomable in reality—it most assuredly defies the logic of common sense.

¹⁴The Son shines ever so brightly on my mountaintops—they sparkle from His presence—His rays also penetrate to my deepest and darkest valleys.

¹⁵My soul has often sought refuge in the darkness of the night—sometimes in the uncertainties of the daylight it says to me, "Where could I go if not to You, my God?"

¹⁶Honor has become the bondservant of integrity and follows it all the days of its life.

¹⁷Your truth, O Lord, has covered me like a blanket—Your integrity has snared me.

¹⁸Praise flows from my heart because of Your continuous protection—even during the roughest seas You are always at the helm—I have no fear when Your presence is there.

¹⁹Your angels have gone ahead of me on my journey—they have prepared my path and made it safe—they are always watchful of my safety and well-being.

²⁰How I thank You for those mighty angels of the Most High God—they surround me with vigilance—they tender me with care at Your bidding.

²¹In the nighttime You give me light—Your presence has become my flashlight and makes my path bright.

²²My time of need is always before me—I shall never be overly concerned because I know the need supplier.

²³Thoughts of You are always with me—overshadowing my life—they exist in my daily walk as I dwell in Your company—whenever I stay in tune with Your frequency.

²⁴Sin is a magnet to the ungodly and they seem content to perish in unrighteousness—holiness draws the godly to the side of righteousness and sustains them.

²⁵I look through the gate of this new day and tenuously realize I have never been this way before—but, at the same time, I find peace and relief.

²⁶I hear Your voice—it speaks comfort and assurance—it says, "Never fear; for I will be with you each step of your journey and I have already gone before you."

²⁷My heart stands secure in that knowledge—it looks forward to each new delight You have in store—surprising new joys that await me.

²⁸When I rest at the close of the day, I will not be sorry that I chose to follow my Lord—His face is all I need to see.

Psalm 90

Made In Your Image

¹The fool has made a treaty with sin—but the righteous war daily against it.

²The godly see the hopeless and those in need as opportunities for His light to change lives.

³The fastest and surest way to receive a blessing is to be a blessing.

⁴An allowance of discontent is given to those who seek God with all their hearts—an uneasiness and dissatisfaction with life on this earth—a certain restlessness of spirit.

⁵A bond to this world is something the upright strives to shun—he knows worthwhile longings can never be satisfied this side of heaven.

⁶The truth and beauty of Christ can be witnessed in the face of a friend—through the kindness of his spoken words—through the thoughtfulness of his actions.

⁷The Lord has a plan for the life of each of His children—He has cut a specific pattern—like a seamstress making an article of clothing.

⁸His chosen design for us is special—He made us in His image—should we balk at going along with His perfect design for our lives—do we know better than our Creator?

⁹Throughout the ages, God has designed the ministering of angels to bless the downtrodden—these heavenly servants have guarded the innocent and displayed mercy to the less fortunate.

¹⁰You, O Lord, have ordered and directed my steps according to Your plan; sometimes You must direct them back when I have strayed from that pathway.

¹¹You have salvaged my soul from destruction—Your love has captured my heart—I will praise Your name forever.

¹²The wisdom of the resourceful has increased manifold because these souls have applied lessons from the past to the present.

¹³Your Word dominates my life—let it rule supreme until it becomes my DNA.

¹⁴I love You, O God, but not as much as I want to—not as much as I could or should.

¹⁵Enable me to love You to my fullest capacity—allow me to exceed that measure so I will be able to love—even as You love.

¹⁶Your Word reveals that when I can love You in this manner—then I will be able to love others the way You love me—teach me to love as if this might be my last day.

¹⁷Where can one find love with no strings attached—no holds barred—undeniably limitless and unconditional?—I have found such a love only in the arms of my Savior.

¹⁸Have you seen a man who is any happier than when he's walking close to the side of the Lord?—I didn't think so!

¹⁹The persevering man grows stronger as his spirit resists the howling winds that blow fiercely against his tree—his roots will reach deeper as they resist the opposing forces.

²⁰Reveal hidden strengths that lie dormant deep within my spirit—so I can praise You again for Your faithfulness—refresh me anew.

²¹This flesh has no power—I am made strong through the Spirit of my God—through His Spirit I can face a hundred foes and be victorious—a thousand and be triumphant.

²²How refreshing is the rest which comes from the Lord—a good night's sleep is better than a cool shower after a trip through a burning hot and dry desert.

²³He will not fail to bless those whose heart is pure—though they prefer to be anonymous—His favor rests upon the humble.

²⁴The Lord will not withhold His blessings upon those who walk uprightly before Him—His blessings are not merit based or contingent upon popular appeal or man's opinion.

²⁵I will enter His royal courts because He has called me friend—He has summoned me to come close—His friendship makes me glad—He has embraced me with open arms.

²⁶His kindness is full of warmth and holds no terror—He has attached to me the bond of His love—He

has permitted me to speak boldly to Him without fear of recourse.

²⁷There is never discord in His presence—He has made me familiar with His blessings.

²⁸All those who delight in Him are unhindered by fear and guilt—

and He delights also in them—His smile brings radiance into the room.

²⁹He has closed the door to all others—I am alone with Him—I am enamored by His presence—enthralled by His majesty—to Him be all glory and praise.

Psalm 91

Stir Me Until I Am Changed

¹It is my heart to honor You above all things—to establish praise in the midst of battle—to trust at all times.

²The kindness of the Lord has been heaped upon me—day after day His voice has revealed His goodness—O how His words have been my comfort.

³He assures me they will not cease coming forth until He withdraws the air that I breathe—for He is my all in all and I will praise His name forever.

⁴I have songs yet to sing—stories to tell—praises of His Majesty to lift on high—wonders to exalt—psalms to write.

⁵There will be more of all these to be heard when my voice is silent because God is worthy to be praised and praise for Him will come from yet another voice.

⁶As long as I have life within me I will praise my God, for no man knows when God will hand down His final judgment or when He will read His last sentence.

⁷Therefore, it would behoove man to walk reverently before God and in awe and humility of His splendor.

⁸One thing I am seeking, O God, is a continual awareness that You are always with me—through and in spite of any circumstances I face.

⁹The Holy Spirit, the love of God, and the beauty of Jesus are like the filling in a taco—we are merely the shell that holds it.

10 Purpose in pain can be unveiled as the child of God walks close to the Master—the mature believer is somehow able to turn life's burdens into fruit-bearing trials.

11 Your love, O God, is the strength of my life—the source of my well-being.

12 The bond of fellowship is strengthened each time brothers break bread together.

13 Ungodly people are swept away in a tide of materialism—the righteous stand secure while the river rages around them—knowing Christ is their Rock.

14 My life is filled with purpose—You have scheduled me for nothing except praise for my Redeemer—You wrote me into Your book for this reason.

15 Stir me, Holy Spirit, in the same manner that cream and sugar are blended into a cup of coffee—see that I am changed in the process.

16 Obedience to God's laws will show wisdom and understanding to those around you.

17 You have erased the sinfulness of my heart through the cost paid by Your Son—it was His sinless blood that settled my debt.

18 Each new day dawns with anticipation—that this could be the day that my Redeemer returns to take me home—O what excitement is emitted at that thought.

19 Those without God see their problems and are blinded by them—the children of faith do not dismiss their problems, but have concluded their God to be greater.

20 Are the natural eyes of man able to see clearly into the mind of the Lord and the ways of God—or are they capable of seeing there at all?

21 Is he able to peer over a wall and into the chambers of the Almighty —to monitor His ways and expose His private affairs?

22 Can his eyes look into His vaults and behold the places where wisdom is stored?

23 Would the caverns of the deep where knowledge is locked away be open for him to freely view at his leisure?

24 Will the scales that cover his mortal eyes prevent him from scrutinizing all the secrets of heaven and earth?

25 Should the mysteries of God's creation be available for his examination—if indeed he could even make them out?

26Can man's earthly eyes take in the Creator's storehouse of beauty—or would they fail him at the opening of the door?

27You, O God, are the mighty One—Your Word stands eternal and I praise Your name forever—replace these eyes with spiritual eyes and I shall see forever.

Psalm 92

In The Secret Place – He Is There

1A spirit-filled mind leads to the house of purity—everlasting freedom is its silent partner and supporter.

2Holy Spirit—I'm not filled with longing to go back to the places I have already been—but I so want to go to new places in God.

3Take me to the secret places of my Father—to the private quarters of His Kingdom—to experience His good pleasure is all I need—He has made me His treasured possession.

4To those intent on keeping His laws, the Lord is their righteousness—He rewards them with prosperity—they gain much from the untold riches of His Heavenly Kingdom.

5What a glorious morning—awakened by Your mercy—refreshed in Your presence.

6Each new daybreak signals a new mission—albeit on the same mission field—a new task awaits—or maybe I need to repeat an old one since I missed the mark last time.

7Cowardice was threatening to swamp my boat—waves of fear were tossing my little craft about like a cork upon the waters.

8You have cast me into the deep—You have removed me from the shore of safety—You have heard my cry over the tumult of the sea.

9Your Holy Spirit has thrown me a flotation device—my speck of faith has emerged as my life preserver—at my cry of desperation You reached out Your hand and saved me.

10Praise be to my God who heard my cry—out of this storm His voice rumbled forth, "Peace be still"—and suddenly all was calm.

¹¹My soul finds solace in You, my God—it hangs on to You like a small child to his mother's leg—like a drowning man to a piece of driftwood.

¹²Can the servant do his work while his hands and feet are shackled—is the ox able to plow while tethered to a pole?

¹³They who labor must be set free to do their best work—then they will bring rewards to their master and reap his praise.

¹⁴The laughter of God's children brings Him great joy—He is cheered at their merriment and is amused by their mirth.

¹⁵When God gives a vision He also furnishes provision along with it—He sets aside a special blessing for those who seek and find His storeroom of supplies.

¹⁶Failure is oftentimes a better instructor than success—the head is turned with pride when victory has its way—the letdown of defeat will repeatedly spur greater willpower.

¹⁷I have made my heart a sanctuary for Your love—it is a harbor where I can seek refuge and find safety—it is there Your love is opened to me like a flower in bloom.

¹⁸Put Your stamp of approval upon my heart—then praise will flow outward as I join my voice with the heavens.

¹⁹For the Lord God Himself is my treasure and my inheritance—He is my birthright, which is of inestimable value—I have need of nothing more.

²⁰He is my source of all things and I look to Him for my pleasure—my delight is wrapped up in Him—I have found His company preferable over man's.

²¹Awaken, O my soul, and hear the jubilant sounds of heaven's fanfare—its parade of pomp and grandeur can be compared to nothing man has ever heard or beheld.

²²Let my senses be quickened—let them come alive and revel in the glorious beauty of His Kingdom—at the resplendence of His gardens—His rivers of crystal clear water.

²³The luxury of all eternity has raptured me—its ornateness and elegance has made my spirit soar to new heights—You have drawn my spirit into worship.

²⁴Suddenly my gaze is riveted upon the brightness of His Majesty who is seated upon the throne—my eyes are quickly averted as they are unable to take it all in.

²⁵I have prostrated myself before His glory and I am unable to rise to my feet—praise for the Lamb is ceaseless and unbroken—it laps over me like the waves of the seashore.

²⁶He has stepped down from His throne and come to where I am—lifting me ever so gently until we are standing face to face—O the light and warmth of His face.

²⁷Leaning forward upon His breast I felt indescribable peace—His smile is pure and shines with tenderness—the gentleness of His eyes speaks volumes.

²⁸When He spoke to me, His voice was triumphant—instantly I knew each and every trial was worth it all.

²⁹My soul surrenders to His will even though it must tarry on this earth a while longer.

Psalm 93

His Ways Are Mysterious

¹What man who has drawn breath—has not stared into the scraggly face of old man trouble—or been accosted by his brother fear?

²Each and every one of my fears and my troubles has hightailed it out—because of Your Word they have taken flight like a bunch of robbers at the sight of law enforcement.

³O my God—I will praise You—when the daylight changes to darkness and the nighttime breaks into morning light—my thoughts are frequently before You.

⁴Praising God relieves stress—flexes your muscles—lifts the spirit—and conditions the heart.

⁵The blessings of the Lord bring complete joy—the wise have learned to store them up for times of drought—their joy also comes from distributing them liberally to others.

⁶The prayerful have studied the value of praise—they use it as an umbrella when the rain clouds of adversity come against them—it is their legacy.

⁷Man does not realize that at times God prefers to be undercover—He then allows His blessings to be labeled as "good fortune"—"a twist of fate"—or "a stroke of luck."

⁸His presence follows the committed heart—one that is steadfast and devoted.

⁹God lives in the heart of a man as well as at the end of his rationality—man's prudence cannot prove superior to God's wisdom on any level.

¹⁰Sing that sweet refrain that I love to hear—sing the sweetest name that I hold so dear—the name that brings salvation's plan—the sweet name of Jesus again.

¹¹The truly wise seek to be humble and the humble search for wisdom —when the two meet, a great man of God is found.

¹²When I recall the former days— those of my youth—I never imagined that the journey would have led so far—that the miles would have been so many.

¹³Only because of His faithfulness have I come this far—His hand has steadied my steps—because He has been my guide, my walk has been filled with peace of mind.

¹⁴The Lord has been my dearest companion and leader—when I would have gone to the left, His Spirit kept me on the straight path— blessed be His name.

¹⁵The path I'm now taking—You've walked that road before—it was for me that You trudged the course that I must take—so You could steer and maneuver me correctly.

¹⁶The way of the Lord is the most excellent way—it brings health to the body and healing for the soul.

¹⁷His ways are mysterious—they are outside of man's comprehension —incomprehensible as they are— He invites us to explore and hunt for them.

¹⁸In light of eternity—the life we live here on earth is not even comparable to one complete inhalation of breath—thus we must use the brevity of time we have wisely.

¹⁹The way of the righteous is led by enlightenment of the Holy Spirit —He clarifies their path and gives them a straight-ahead focus.

²⁰The wise have come to understand that God has given us all things— but we must not possess anything —for it all belongs to His glory and majesty.

²¹A man's heart was made for God and God alone—to be a shrine unto Him only—the fool has filled it with useless debris and left no room for the Creator.

²²I find You each time I make the effort to seek You—You are always there—patiently waiting.

²³Woven down through the middle of the garden of my heart is a deeply rooted desire to renounce and remove all things—that none would enter into it but You, my Lord.

Psalm 94

Surrender Your Worship

¹Those who honor God with their finances have positioned themselves to reap His abundant harvest of blessings—He will not fail to come to their aid in time of need.

²The well-adjusted soul has declined prosperity in exchange for the favor of blessings—knowing they have many facets and can be disguised by different faces.

³A fool tramples on purity and dances with glee at its demise—he has expelled remorse from his house and sorrow has gone with it.

⁴When the end had loomed seemingly larger than life—You were there with Your great mercy and grace.

⁵Your outstretched arm has reached low to lift me up and restore me in righteousness—Your Word has never failed to shine forth in truth.

⁶Shivers of delight attack and overtake me each time I think of how much You must love me—it is the amazing grace of my God that shouts His love from all eternity.

⁷O Lord, You have taken notice of each and every aspect of our day; our reliance upon You is backed by Your promise to be with us throughout all of our days.

⁸You have granted this day unto me as a gift—I choose to spend it wisely so that I might bring glory and honor unto my King.

⁹Teach me to worship Your holiness with reverence—not with lightness or disrespect—in order to please You with my gift of surrender.

¹⁰Can the pureness of the wine be savored if the cork is not removed from the bottle— how can the delicate scent of the perfume be shared if the bottle is never opened?

¹¹The fruitful servant has allowed the Holy Spirit to open him up to

Psalm 94 - Surrender Your Worship

those around him so that his spiritual prosperity will bless many others.

[12] Sweetness fills the room in which the Holy Spirit is present—His aroma fills every nook and cranny causing those abiding there to take notice.

[13] Blessed be Your name, O Lord, for You have caused me to find nuggets of gold amongst the rubbish of life.

[14] Facts pave the way to understanding—understanding goes ahead of wisdom—wisdom brings to light our inadequacies concerning the greatness of the Almighty.

[15] Today He said, "hear My words and be encouraged—don't fret about being a great seed planter in My Kingdom—these things you can't see and should not lose sleep over.

[16] I have many who are as the dandelion seedpod—their lives are ripe with seed and await My Holy Spirit to blow across them and scatter their seeds unto many places.

[17] I also have many who have been simply called to water—and nothing more.

[18] And what about the birds of the air whom I have instructed to pluck the seeds of the fruitful life—and plant them elsewhere at My bidding.

[19] I—the Lord Your God—dwell within you—you are My living temple—which should be devoted to Me alone—do not defile it in any way—for I am Holy."

[20] O God, I have tasted the deepness of Your love—what I relish most is knowing that it is everlasting.

[21] Your kind and tender mercies have watched over me—in fact, they are watching over me right now!

[22] The wisdom of Your counsel has led me according to Your will—Your desires are my motivation—they serve as my incentive to know You in fullness and power.

[23] The presence of the Lord gives rise to feelings of joy and that's where I want to be.

[24] I am fed by the truth of Your Word—my soul finds sustenance through Your faithfulness—I have never doubted its reliability for a moment.

[25] At Your summons I have tasted the pureness of Your river of gladness.

[26] If it were within the grasp of a man to attain perfection—then that would abolish the need for the Son of God—O how I praise Your name—for You have covered our sin.

Psalm 95

You Bring Forth A Song Of Praise

[1] Praise is the expression of your faith springing into action—proclaiming God will complete what He is in the process of doing—it is confidence in His plan.

[2] Success is bound up in the belief that His joy becomes your strength—much like Samson's hair was the symbol of his.

[3] The enemy knows you are doomed if you quit praising in the early phases—don't give him this satisfaction.

[4] The secret lies in the ability to praise God even when all you have in front of you is a small beginning —God is the master of the trivial start.

[5] Any assignment is easier when you are energized by His joy—praise will change the very surroundings you find yourself in—go out eagerly and make a difference.

[6] The saint has learned that praise will not change your problems—but it will have a huge influence on your attitude.

[7] You set up my spirit with a heart of worship and a song of praise—the Holy Spirit has overshadowed me since my conception and has fashioned a great work within me.

[8] While on this journey of faith, the traveler must expect—and will surely encounter many trials—spiritual growth requires it.

[9] The answer to fear is resistance—after enough opposition to it, you will be able to watch it hightail out of the camp—it has lost its hold on you.

[10] The attacks of the enemy have peppered seasoned saints—but the salt of the Word has preserved them.

[11] The nightingale sings a lovely song —next time you hear it, listen closely and see if you can tell from where it comes—it is a song borrowed from the heavenly courts.

[12] Outward beauty is a consequence of inherited genes that cannot be altered—it is temporary in nature.

[13] Inward beauty is a result of absorbing spiritual truth—it is uncovered through prayer and study and lasts forever.

¹⁴The garden of God's grace thrives with well-cultivated fruits of the Spirit—just taste and see that they are good.

¹⁵The Lord sends sunshine on my plants and initiates their growth—He rains upon my dry grasses—they flourish in their proper time of year.

¹⁶When I become parched, He waters the dryness of my soul—His favor allows me to throw off my jacket and dance for joy in the warmth of His rain.

¹⁷His presence came from who knows where—it matters not but He was there—He came to me when I was low—and pointed out the way to go.

¹⁸God—You see straight into my heart—right past the window shades of fear—the barricades of insecurity—even past the drapes of doubt.

¹⁹You have searched me and heard my thirsting soul cry out for You—only You know the insatiable hunger that cannot be quenched apart from You.

²⁰My will must be lost in Yours to the point that I will gladly do those things I do not enjoy—content to know that You are pleased with my service.

Psalm 96

Your Praises Dance!

¹The discerning have observed that quitting is the only thing required for failure—failing is a step in the learning process and can be achieved as easily as doing nothing.

²Those who follow hard after God have found His peace to be so much more than an absence of conflict—it has become a great sense of well being that completely fills them.

³I will praise You within the framework in which You have placed me—knowing quite clearly I am governed by the regulations and limits of this life.

⁴When You are pleased to pass me through to the other side I shall be free to worship You with utter abandon—unfettered by the restrictions that I am bound by now.

Psalm 96 - Your Praises Dance!

⁵My heart is full of praises for You, my God—my mouth speaks forth Your goodness—my language will speak freely in proclaiming Your excellence.

⁶Your praises dance across my tongue—my heart joins in union—then my voice adds melody that is somehow pleasing to my God—O praise His matchless name.

⁷You have blessed me with honor—You have rested Your anointing upon me and dignified me with praise.

⁸This day You have rewarded my faithfulness to You with duty—that which I have not sought after—You have sanctioned my diligence and set me in places You desired.

⁹In reverence, yet with anxiousness, I come before You—knowing that where You have placed me requires a godly wisdom—that is what I seek after.

¹⁰The prayer of my heart is that You alone would reign supreme in my heart and life—You, O Lord, have been gracious to me; nothing good have You withheld from me.

¹¹Who is he that lingers in the presence of Jehovah, whose thoughts are on Him night and day?—It is he who has doggedly pursued Him all the days of his life.

¹²Blessed are they who have put their trust steadfastly in the Lord—they have found a Savior who is long-suffering and merciful.

¹³Spirit of the Living God—be my witness—the very words I speak—the commanding force of my life so others might know You.

¹⁴I tag along after You like a young boy follows his older brother—because he finds security in his presence.

¹⁵The love of God works through His saints in order to heal wounded hearts—the righteous are His hands to a hurting world.

¹⁶He leads those who seek after Him down corridors of praise—they are jubilant to be following His counsel.

¹⁷Your promise to make Your dwelling place among us has been my confidence—You are the God of my heart.

¹⁸In God's hands desperation can lead to your destiny—for the best results, place the anguish of your soul into His hands and follow His lead.

¹⁹The road of ease does not pass through the life of the godly—He makes sure of that.

20Without difficulty there would be no battle—we would not taste the bliss of victory.

21Those who have learned to accept aging with dignity are wiser still—they realize it is God's plan and little can be done about it.

22Caring acts are low-budget items that lead to high-yielding profits—to be valued more than a nest egg of pure gold.

23The fiscally responsible person has learned to get along well with delayed gratification.

24In times of gloom He lifts my spirits—His nearness bolsters my morale.

25Smite the stubbornness of my heart with a swift blow—cripple it by the strength of Your might—lead it away captive to the dungeon.

26Anyone who searches can find complete forgiveness in the depths of His love—do not take it lightly for it is a costly thing.

27Your laws, O Lord, are not grievous nor are they unattainable; You have placed them within our grasp—we must hold them tightly or the enemy may snatch them away.

28Let us find the fortitude to follow Your Word wholeheartedly—for fear that we forsake Your blessings and forfeit a lifetime of good favor.

Psalm 97

A Martyr's Testimony

1The saints of the Lord have seen grief and distress—troubles have plagued them—but with His hand upon them they have not been overwhelmed.

2Sorrows are multiplied so their eyes might always behold the King of Glory.

3They find relief through His ultimate example—they see triumph because He has walked the way of sorrow before them.

4His eyes have beheld the beauty of their sacrifices—He has written them in His journal and is saving them for the day of their redemption—O praise His glorious name.

5Each of His children have a cross to carry—matching their strengths and character—they look to the

Savior for courage to carry their crosses gracefully and with honor.

⁶You, O Lord, have blinded their eyes to the glory of their crosses but it has become evident to those around them.

⁷Allow the light of their testimony to illuminate the way so that it will draw sinners into the fold to find mercy and grace.

⁸The magnificent cross of Christ has borne all our sorrows even to the last one—how can we do less than bear our share of that cross?

⁹Unto our sorrow and grief You have multiplied joy and peace.

¹⁰Give those suffering saints strength in the midst of their trials—open their eyes to eternal joys that await them.

¹¹You are leading the way to that everlasting home on high, which You have adorned with their lives of praise and sacrifice.

¹²You have called Your followers to lay down their lives—whether in the spiritual realm or the natural.

¹³Your blessing rests upon them as they are willing to lay down the most precious gift You have given them—their lives in sacrifice.

¹⁴Must I walk this pathway alone, no, never!—He has promised to always walk with me and when I am unable to walk, He will pick me up and carry me home.

Psalm 98

Worship All His Fullness

¹The warmth of Your love and glory fill the earth and spill over into man's heart.

²Bestow upon me a circumcised heart so that I might love You passionately and without reservation—and devote to You a lifetime of serving.

³Serve the Lord joyfully and with gladness during the times of abundance—for who can possibly know when it will be gone—with thanksgiving offer Him praise daily.

⁴The brightness of His countenance brings light unto my soul and causes the shades of nighttime to take flight.

Psalm 98 - Worship All His Fullness

⁵Wisdom can assist in the happy fulfillment of life—peace of mind is a choice you must willfully make—contentment is an inside job and must be established in the heart.

⁶Even the roar of a caged lion can strike terror deep in the heart of a man—knowing there is but a thin line of safety between the two of them.

⁷You settle my mind and calm my soul when my thoughts are fixed on You—Your Spirit soothes my anxiety immediately.

⁸Through His promises, He makes the godly strong—He has promised divine grace whenever our human efforts fall short.

⁹I will gather my thoughts as a hen collects her chicks—so You may keep them under Your jurisdiction and authority.

¹⁰The wonder and glory of the presence of God Almighty is resident in the life of the believer—it has infiltrated and seized the private heart with conviction.

¹¹Holy Spirit, give us a taste of the unseen so that we will clamor for more; then it will consume our remaining days with passion.

¹²The Lord has been the lifting of my spirit—He has brightened my eyes —His Spirit gives confidence to my voice.

¹³He keeps His watchful eyes over me —His hand is upon me—to accompany me at all times and to align my steps in a straight course.

¹⁴Yet my heart is urging me to climb higher and to walk the lofty road that is far above the customary way. Not that I would know You, but that I can know You more.

¹⁵My lifelong urge has been to seek Your face—often I have either squelched it or put it on the back burner—fortunately Your grace has not deserted me.

¹⁶The mercies of the Lord invite me into His house—they have paid the price of admission for my ticket.

¹⁷Whoever clings to the things of this world creates a barrier to the Most High—I ask for You to open my blind eyes to Your presence so I may see You in and around me.

¹⁸Meekness does not equal weakness—actually it is quite the opposite and results in strength—a quiet and unassuming gentleness —in other words humility in reserve.

¹⁹The godly strive for meekness and find it when looking to the Master's example.

[20]The obedient and blessed servant of the Lord is a friend to sinners and a lighthouse to those who have gone astray.

[21]Sinful men can then find faith if the eyes of their souls look upon God—He applies salvation as a result of that faith.

[22]A warrior is only allowed his tender moments off the battlefield—otherwise he must be focused and stouthearted.

[23]You have sealed my mouth in Your presence—my ears You have opened wide.

[24]There is no sound as sweet as the voice of my Lord—symphonies pale in contrast.

[25]You have exposed my heart to Your love—it is out in the open and laid bare to Your workings—Your goodness has covered it with a wrapper.

[26]I look to You with satisfaction and worship all Your fullness.

[27]You have removed the curse that sin and sickness put on my life—now I am absolutely liberated to praise Your name forever.

[28]My heart has sorrowfully followed to the foot of the cross—it now rejoices in the empty tomb and my risen Lord.

[29]Praise the Lord, O my soul, my Redeemer lives evermore; He has risen victorious—cutting off all His enemies.

[30]He has filled my spirit with life and made me to prosper with praise—misery has fled and joy has replaced it.

[31]Pure peace arises and reigns in my heart at His Word—He has ransomed my soul and has at long last vindicated my faith.

Psalm 99

Yes, Lord, I Am Yours

[1]Your voice came into my being long before I was conceived—I answered Your call then and I have been Yours ever since.

[2]Your speech issued forth and spoke words to my spirit—I said, "Yes, Lord, I am Yours," as I bowed to You in humble submission.

[3]And now I seek to know You in greater ways—with methods un-

orthodox to this human body—those not suited for mortals.

⁴Which ingredient prevents a man from reaching his true potential in God?

⁵Can a man persuade God of his sincerity or his deep longing for Him since He already knows that?—the blockage exists only in the persuasion of his mind.

⁶Although I am mandated to walk this earthly road of the common man—to live the simple life of a pilgrim—my dwelling place is found in the Holy One of all creation.

⁷Lead me captive into Your flock—pierce my heart with Your awl and then I will forever be marked as Yours.

⁸Your Word stands forever, O Lord—as a monument to truth—it was the lifeblood of those who proclaimed it.

⁹You spoke the Word and men of God carried it forward—those who heard Your voice and were not afraid to publicly make it known.

¹⁰They have left a lasting legacy for the remainder of the world to trust in.

¹¹The Word of God is mighty and who can know its true power?—it leads to salvation for many but to death and destruction for more.

¹²By the light of Your Word and the transformation of Your Spirit, You have radically altered my life from its former state of sinfulness.

¹³Your Word, O God, is the handwriting on the wall—Your Spirit must act as our interpreter if we are to make any sense of it.

¹⁴Your Word has aroused the appetite of my spirit—like the aroma of grilling steaks, which can cause the mouth to water and the appetite to be whetted.

¹⁵The honeycomb of Your Word has nourished my craving—its sweet drippings have brought renewed vigor and stamina to my soul.

¹⁶The spiritual course of a godly man will be determined by the setting of the compass of his heart—it must be turned God-ward.

¹⁷God's presence does not walk among man's feelings—His abode is only in truth and certainty.

¹⁸The life of faith becomes clear after realizing it is not how much you believe—what matters most is who you believe in.

19 God's Spirit will take liberties with those who have yielded themselves unto righteousness—they will hear His voice through the noise of the crowd.

20 The parachute of the Almighty has landed within their borders to which there is no other access—He secures their domain with blessings because of their praise.

21 Praise the name of the Lord, my God—the Lord Almighty is His name.

22 Are they to be penalized who cannot make their voice heard—who are unable to cry out to You in their desperation?

23 Your ear is attuned to their thoughts—You even hear their silent cries—You will not scold those who opt to speak with You through voiceless contemplations.

24 His hand uplifts and supports the downtrodden—He lifts them from their despair—He cheers up their countenance in the midst of misfortune.

25 The godly are not exempt from the enemy's attack—the power of the Word will shield them from it when they apply it properly.

26 No matter how dark the day may become—in due time the sun will shine again.

27 When I measured my strength I found it was not equal to the task—then I cried to the Lord and He gave me a helping hand.

28 The prayer of a child is precious to the Father—their faith is pure and unadulterated.

29 The wisdom of a grown man is not equal to that of a four-year-old child and his grandmother—unless he has learned to keep his mouth shut.

30 The silence of his wisdom must console him—his God is his strength and he has found grace through Him.

31 The Word of God is precious and brings quiet confidence—may I never let any of His words fall to the ground.

32 God's blessings come in a variety of different flavors—like ice cream at the local parlor.

33 A wise saint will not fail to witness His goodness, knowing that not every blessing may be to their liking; sometimes even a deplorable flavor will soothe a sore tooth.

34 As a young child might despise his vegetables unless a loving parent persuades him of their importance—so the wise have learned likewise with God's blessings.

35 God's Word displays the wisdom of forgiveness—it is able to change your life from bitter to better—sometimes it is the extremely bitter pill that is lifesaving.

36 It is the saint as well as the sinner who receives illness from the hand of the Lord.

37 The godly know it is merely a period of testing and trial—pity the sinner who has no idea whatsoever.

38 Poor health brings on prime time for the adversary of mortal man—he knows to work his wiles when you are at your weakest point.

39 Today my soul is weighed down and I am unable to lift it up to You, my God.

40 Release Your waves of encouragement so they sweep over me like the waves of the sea—wash my spirit clean and afresh.

41 The child of God has learned this secret—whenever he feels down—he just looks up and You restore him.

42 God's faithfulness parallels traditional wedding vows—in sickness and in health—for better and for worse—His faithfulness stands true.

43 Who do I have besides You, my Lord?—even if all forsake me You still remain—You are the star I set my compass on—the lighthouse that guides me safely to shore.

44 When I sat down and reflected on my life since my birth—I did not fail to include the best or the worst times You have granted me;

45 Still I was unable to discover even one isolated incident when I did not need You as my Lord—Your hand upon me strengthened my spirit.

46 If Your strength had not been my support and sustenance, what would my life have amounted to?

47 Your grace and mercy have preceded me all the days of my life and have overcast me with favor—when I had lost all to the light of sin—Your grace became my mirror.

48 Under the wings of the Almighty I will rest and find a place of safety—under His care I will flourish and be blessed.

49 When I looked for a way of escape—a place to skirt around my problem—He said to me—"not so fast!

50 Have you forgotten so quickly My Word to you—that I will be with you in all circumstances—no matter what comes your way?"

51 The soul needs and actually blossoms from encouragement in the same manner the body requires oxygen for life.

52 You have set a guard over the resting place of Your saints—Your might has made it secure.

53 From the mountain heights with its purified air and early morning dew come glorious flowers and breathtaking views.

54 Down in the valleys deep and at the canyon floor with its silent beauty come glorious flowers and early morning dew.

55 Although the flowers on the mountain heights and the deep valleys are both similar in many respects, we must see each from different points of view to truly value them.

56 Lord, how good Your Word has become to me as I poured out my soul to You—You are granting Your servant his deepest longing.

57 My sights are set on being counted in that number—when the righteous stand before You robed in white.

58 You have called and anointed the willing with a fresh encounter—their total surrender is accorded Your blessing.

59 You have acted on my behalf and who can hinder Your salvation?—let it rise up mightily against my enemies—for my enemies have become Your enemies.

60 Your Spirit of power has penetrated the wall of separation between my soul and spirit—now I am filled with Your goodness and delight.

61 I live for the glory of my King—He fills my vessel with life and I will praise His glorious name forever and ever.

Psalm 100

Your Justice Upon America...Foretold

1 Weep and wail, America, for what is about to come upon you—because you have failed to take heed of My words and My warnings, you will soon incur much affliction.

2 The crown you so proudly wore on your head has fallen to the ground and another has picked it up and

put it on.

³O that you would have regarded the numerous examples I left before you—but you were headstrong—too obstinate to learn from those who have previously fallen.

⁴I had marked out a plan for you—one of prosperity—one which was designed for a glorious destiny—but you have turned aside to follow other agendas.

⁵Your good deeds have become a stench in My nostrils because your unrighteousness has covered them.

⁶See how your eyes have become glazed with materialism—self-indulgence lines your streets—restraint has left the country.

⁷When you stop up your ears—it doesn't alter My Word or change My mind—it only puts you in the same arena as the generations who preceded you.

⁸Because of the righteous amongst you, My mercy and grace has shielded you from persecution, financial ruin, and devastation like other countries have experienced.

⁹Your barns have not been empty and lacking—yet the winds of adversity that howl at your doors are soon to be set loose and you will experience things you have never seen.

¹⁰The dam that has been holding back the floodwaters of unrighteousness is soon to be breached—the seeds of iniquity are set to be unleashed in a furious fashion.

¹¹Why have you failed to hunger after righteousness like I created you to do?

¹²Your land is soaked with the blood of many who have cried out to Me—I have heard their cries and will demand payment and judgment for the innocent unborn.

¹³You think I have turned My head because you have allowed debauchery to run rampant across your nation—lewdness and depravity are becoming unrestrained.

¹⁴Your morality has plummeted to new lows—I see corruption and dishonesty at every turn—fraud and deception have become your byword.

¹⁵My Word, which was once the bedrock of your foundation, has been removed and replaced by another message—your arrogance has turned your head to this travesty.

¹⁶Which of you can pinpoint My lack of mercy—or show where My compassion has been in short supply?

¹⁷If you could indeed charge Me with anything it would only be that I have given you far more chances than you deserve—more warnings than a father gives his errant child.

¹⁸You have been riding high on the crest of the wave like a surfer at high tide—all the while giving little or no thought to My miraculous provisions for you.

¹⁹In your waywardness you have forgotten Me—I no longer receive your thanks for My protection—you take pride in your own abilities to protect yourself.

²⁰Can you not see the dark storm-laden clouds rolling across the sky as the thunder rumbles its voice to make known the approaching storm?

²¹The lightning that zigzags across the heavens—along with the shrieking of the gale force winds—heralds the looming turbulence.

²²What will it take for you to cry out to Me—to acknowledge Me as your God?

²³When your land is ravaged with pestilence—will you seek My face again?

²⁴If I close up My heavens like a curtain drawn at the final act of a play—and famine is starving your land—will you curse Me or praise Me?

²⁵How will you continue to worship the almighty dollar when I take it from your grasp and put it into the hand of another?

²⁶You have become a slave to other peoples—they own you because you have failed to honor Me and put Me first—with contempt you have disregarded My commandments.

²⁷Where will your trust be when I strip all of your securities and possessions from you—when your markets collapse—when your wealth is shriveled up like a piece of dried fruit—when your property is put in the hands of those who did not purchase it?

²⁸I am about to exact punishment on this nation—not because I am a God of vengeance but because My Word demands it and My justice has foretold it.

Psalm 101

My Soul Is Covered By Your Glory

¹Although the subject of our faith may never appear while we search for it—nevertheless it remains forever.

²It may be veiled with clouds as the stars—or even the tallest mountain peaks on a darkened night—yet they still stay put in their place while hidden from our view.

³My Lord abides in the dark clouds—His presence surely abides in the shadow.

⁴He comes out into the open when I call Him—when I seek Him early in the morning His presence shines ever so clear.

⁵I awoke early to the glory of the Lord—shining in through the window of my soul.

⁶It was like glorious sunlight that had scattered the darkness of night—it filled the room with peace and joy.

⁷Day after day You renew my strength—You remarkably multiply the small amount I begin each day with.

⁸You start me out fresh and new each morning—I begin each new day with a clean slate—O how I glorify You for this gift.

⁹I find all my strength in the Lord—His ways make me strong and through Him I am able to do the impossible—is there anything too challenging for Him?

¹⁰Whenever the sins of my past threaten to overcome me—I follow that crimson stream to the foot of the cross and receive my pardon there.

¹¹Infirmities are torments from the enemy—daggers intended for the soul—they pierce the flesh with a poison tip.

¹²The intensity of the candle's flame is equivalent to the brightness of light it emits.

¹³The only confidence the saint holds concerning tomorrow is that no matter what comes his way—he will be with his God—what a blessed assurance that is.

¹⁴God's Word is a roadmap and a guide to holy living.

¹⁵Who are they that desire to be blameless and holy—undefiled by sin—pure in all their ways—untarnished by the corrosion of this world?

Psalm 101 - My Soul Is Covered By Your Glory

[16] You will teach them to walk in truth and righteousness—to be scrupulous in all their ways—forsaking disgraceful behavior and clinging only to compassionate living.

[17] As a bowl becomes a container to hold and mix things together—so let my soul hold the good things of my God.

[18] Pour into me the necessary ingredients to become that consecrated bread—a most excellent sacrifice unto the Lord.

[19] Let any praise and honor that might come my way be redirected to the Father—who is all glorious and worthy of our highest regard.

[20] Those who sing joyfully are His ministering spirits—they are content to worship Him—oblivious of the quality of their voice—knowing the Father Himself is satisfied.

[21] A dozen of the most generous benevolent thoughts—does not go even a fraction of the distance that one simple act of kindness travels.

[22] You hold the power to bless others within your own two hands—use it wisely and the Father will reward you handsomely on that day of judgment.

[23] The strength of a strong man is tested by his endurance—the wisdom of the astute is tested by the Lord.

[24] I press in to the gloriousness of new life and fresh spirit—He has increased my daily allotment so that I receive more than my minimum daily allowance.

[25] His Spirit leads my soul through the fog into a small clearing just up ahead—there He expounds the necessary truth for the moment unto me.

[26] When the burdens get greater—His grace is greater still—nothing passes my way that escapes His notice or care.

[27] The affection of His love surrounds me like a warmhearted hug.

[28] My ambition is never to settle for less than what my God has in mind for me.

[29] I look forward to seeing the face of my Lord when I walk across that final bridge between life and death.

Psalm 102

My Afflictions – For Your Glory

¹What do I love more than to please my God?—at this moment, nothing.

²The purpose of our testing and hardships is often hidden behind a smokescreen—sometimes not to be discovered until years later—or maybe never in this present life.

³He has set me before the hill called adversity and bid me to climb it—when I looked up at it my heart grew faint.

⁴The path leading upward was lined with jagged rocks—briars barricaded its entrance—a pool of water coming out of its side collected at the base.

⁵Knowing the way was steep and long—I drank deeply from the water—because I would soon need it for refreshing.

⁶Knowing He would lead the way was my comfort—His words, "Follow Me" were all I needed to do just that—other times we walked side by side and hand in hand.

⁷Although my journey has not reached the summit yet—He is still with me daily—for He promised to never leave me alone.

⁸There is none like You, my God—if I could search galaxies—eons of space and time—all known and unknown existence—I could still find none to compare with You.

⁹Those who truly hunger after the deep things of God will never be satisfied with crumbs—they will settle for only the meat of the Word and the water of the Spirit.

¹⁰Let me make Your heart glad, O God—with loving words and a cheery countenance—then my worship will bring cheerfulness to You, my Lord.

¹¹The bell of life tolls daily for every man—yet no man knows which day it will cease—and the bell of death will clang.

¹²My praise for You, my God, will never cease as long as the bell of life tolls for me—as sure as the breath of God is resident within me.

¹³The trial You surrounded me with was my prison—today You have set me free—You have opened the door—You have pardoned and released me.

[14] Do not let my discharge bring any amount of smugness to my soul—but I will rejoice in Your goodness and praise You for Your favor.

[15] You have spoken a clear word unto my spirit—we are called to obedience—not necessarily the pleasure or enjoyment of it—it is not for us to understand.

[16] Though my understanding has been darkened—You have shined the light of Your love into my heart—Your Spirit has encouraged my soul with peace and assurance.

[17] The night was long but the dawn broke through—bringing light to my world—He has stayed with me through it all.

[18] Let me rejoice—if perchance any of His afflictions are laid upon me—for He has already endured every one of mine—and with gladness, too.

[19] The enemy of our souls is aroused to wrath when we have chosen to follow the Forsaken One and lay down our all—otherwise he is not concerned in the least bit.

[20] In the same way a fingerprint identifies a person—the Holy Spirit has become my soul print and IDs me as His.

[21] Sometimes He must grab me by the nape of the neck to restrain me from going off on my own headstrong way—but He always does it in kindness.

[22] Must I reach out and take up my cross in order to follow You?—the choice is mine to make—You have left it up to me—but to follow You I will do on my own accord.

[23] The common lot of man is not the things our crosses are made of—no—it is that very thing that tugs at our souls and our consciences that demands denial.

Rise Up Now Within Me (a poem)

Holy Spirit, light the way – point us to the Father
open up these eyes of clay – 'til we see no other.
Burn a new and fierce desire – fill these hearts with passion
be our all-consuming fire – 'til the lost are saved.
Rise up now within me – I must not hold back
do the work through me that You must do.
Moving forth in power – taking full control
'til I've yielded body, mind, and soul.

Psalm 103

I Have Beheld Your Love

¹The wise man's purpose in praying is not an attempt to change the mind of God—instead he uses it as a meeting place—a place of conversing with the Almighty.

²The sinful man's tongue rolls along like the lava flow of a volcano—he is bent on destruction—who is able to turn him from his evil path?

³Wise saints have encountered a life-changing truth—what others sometimes mean for evil, God can and does use for good—as in the story of Joseph and his brothers.

⁴Patience is the only successful remedy against tribulation—it is in your perseverance that you will find a measure of relief.

⁵Even if I could—I don't believe I would—change a stroke of His design—He has fashioned me—in complexity—and covers me with love divine.

⁶My Lord has walked the common ground of all mankind and tasted all our griefs—He has sampled each of our frustrations—for our benefit.

⁷His compassion has been increased because of this journey—His understanding of our heartaches has been made a reality.

⁸He who lives far above the earth has no objection to walking among His people—down in their midst—for He knows they are unable to reach up to Him.

⁹I have beheld His glory—the sweetness of His presence—His voice has touched my ear—His Spirit has caressed my spirit.

¹⁰The love of God helps me walk righteously before Him—to be blameless and pure—not because of the purity of my heart—but because of the cleansing blood of His Son.

¹¹The ground upon which I walk was formed by the will of my God—and it pleased Him to place me here within this sphere to carry out His purposes.

¹²As we walk along down here, trials consume us daily—when we pass from this life into His everlasting presence—all will be forgotten except the beholding of His beauty.

Psalm 103 - I Have Beheld Your Love

¹³Death is waiting to shake hands and embrace each living being—only the Father knows the time for this appointment.

¹⁴There is no dodging it—so make all your amends prior to its arrival—say what needs to be said to those you need to say it to—forgive all men and hold no grudges.

¹⁵God speaks and His glory covers the earth—His Word fills it with righteousness through the people He has placed on it.

¹⁶The spoken words of the godly activate His power and authority with conviction.

¹⁷God's mercy and grace never go on vacation—neither should our forgiveness of the shortcomings of others.

¹⁸The fool is sure his cup is full and running over because he is trying to fill it upside down—he is pleased with this accomplishment.

¹⁹The foolish man fills his mouth with meaningless words and empty promises—he rattles off glib-sounding assurances—uncaring of whether he can fulfill them or not.

²⁰Even the wise man has been known to make well-intentioned pledges that he never keeps—rash words that sounded good at the time.

²¹But You, O Lord, are full of promises—some pleasant and some disastrous—which upon examination we find that time and truth have dealt You a perfect record.

²²Your Word cannot fail like we do—that which You make known is truth and in time Your truthfulness will be revealed.

²³It is not Your nature to withhold good things from those who walk honorably before You—so the godly man knows anything You withhold cannot be good for him.

²⁴Those who choose a path of abstinence from worldly desires are on the path to an uncluttered spirit—the freedom to seek after God and His will in prayer follows that.

²⁵If it were not for the desert places—how could we take pleasure in the joyousness of God's rivers and lakes—His beauty that abounds in all of His creation?

²⁶See how feeble and decrepit this body has become—yet it still loves to praise Your name in delighted worship.

²⁷My spirit rises up past the frailties of this flesh to give You glorious praise.

²⁸Each breath I draw refuses to cease its praise to my Creator—You always make me aware of Your greatness—my surroundings give witness of Your Majesty.

²⁹When my mental faculties fade—or even cease altogether—You alone know my heart—and that takes precedence over my mind—in that I will take refuge.

Psalm 104

I Will Praise You All Of My Days

¹Those who satisfy themselves with pleasing God will find their greatest pleasures fulfilled—they will feast on a life packed with good things.

²My heart has praised You—my mind has worshipped You—now my lips follow suit in loving adoration to You, my God.

³You advance my days like an odometer on a car—my life is a work in progress.

⁴The days of my life no longer drift by lazily—like clouds of Your heavens blown along by gentle breezes on a warm spring day.

⁵When I number my days they seem miniscule in light of eternity—they click by faster than a baseball card in the spokes of a bicycle tire.

⁶My days are hurtling past with the speed of an avalanche down a mountainside.

⁷I rise early in the morning with a grateful heart—knowing He has blessed me with another day to praise His Excellence.

⁸A new perspective has seized me—I treasure this day as it may be my last—urgency grips me tightly as I consider His purpose for me.

⁹He has established me to be His oasis for those needing the living water of life.

¹⁰When I come to that dry barren place in the desert—praise wells up within me and bursts forth as tears of joy—rivers of life begin to flow.

¹¹I will praise the Lord—for He has caused rivers to run in my dry places—He irrigates my barrenness.

¹²Exalt Him in your dry place and be refreshed—praise the Lord in your situation and He will turn it into a blessing.

¹³You, O Lord, have allowed our songs to reach the gates of heaven—they have overflowed into its courtyard—as they rise our praises are carried into Your throne room.

¹⁴Our songs have been far-reaching—they have encircled the world and covered it with the blessing of Your name.

¹⁵The song of praise is the song of the supernatural—it banishes the power of despair.

Psalm 105

Let Praises Ring Out For Our King!

¹Let all His saints praise Him wherever He has called them—He is fervently looking for their praise.

²Praise cannot keep silent—it brings forth power—it voices the glory of our God—it becomes a vehicle delivering freedom and hope.

³He illuminates precious words from His book for His saints in the daytime—in the night He sings songs of peace as their lullaby.

⁴Last night my soul was singing the song of the redeemed—O how I love to sing that—again and again—O how I love to give praise to my God.

⁵Let every praise express my duty—every gaze behold Your beauty—let all my days bring Hallelujahs—as I sing unto my King.

⁶Just as the newness of the morning brings freshness to that day—I am never disappointed with the clarity Your presence brings.

⁷Who is able to hold the Almighty hostage—or what power can force His hand—is there anyone able to contain His might and omnipotence?

⁸Unless You fill me with Your Spirit and replenish me daily from Your storehouse of strength—unless You pour into my pitcher fresh water of life—I can go on no more.

⁹Daily You water my garden with cleansing rain—You place fresh lettuce in my basket—may I never complain about the turnips and rutabagas You put there.

¹⁰A word from the Lord is like an appetizer before a gourmet meal—it whets the appetite.

¹¹The kingdom of God is available to work mightily in the hearts of those who have made up their minds to follow Him.

¹²Desperate times call for desperate measures—invest in the God of hope, trust, and live confidently.

¹³Even the inanimate objects of Your creation have been known to sing Your praises—I have heard it with my own ears.

¹⁴Come let us rejoice—lifting our praise unto Christ the King—come let us rejoice—exalting His holy name.

¹⁵The godly rejoice as they follow their Lord because they are leaving a blueprint for the next generation—to honor God.

¹⁶With their voices they sing—You alone are my high place—my security.

¹⁷Your patience, O God, is a testimony to Your mercy—for with kindness and longsuffering You have dealt with me—You gently correct me and straighten my path.

¹⁸Before You uttered one single "let there be"—I was in Your plans—before the planets played "ring around the rosie"—You knew my course.

¹⁹How great are Your plans—Your thoughts are incomprehensible to all mortals—Your actions are all charted in righteousness—truth is Your straightedge.

²⁰My soul has peeked through the skylight of Your Word and has seen the portals of heaven—clear to the throne of God.

²¹I find rich joy in the deepest reaches of my soul—because You abide there.

²²It is in this place that cares are absent—it is here that You teach me the ways of Your Spirit—Your peace is present to uplift me.

²³Contentment has provided the winds of tranquility for my sail and nourishment for my bones—Your bounty sustains me—I'm absorbed by the peace of Your presence.

²⁴Holy Spirit—You are the essence of my God—don't ever leave me—for I never want to live without You.

²⁵O that I may never forget one iota of all Your many blessings—that thoughts of them would continuously hover within my mind.

²⁶I will allow remembrances of Your blessings to accompany me daily—to walk closely to me—to lead me by the hand into avenues of worshipping my God.

Psalm 105 - Let Praises Ring Out For Our King!

27 Your Word has been my teacher since my birth—it established my feet on even ground while I was learning to walk—and teaches me to walk uprightly.

28 Expand my capabilities that I may also learn to run—You are teaching me to run with diligence—Your strength gives me the stamina to endure.

29 I sing—You are my strength, O God —hide me away—in Your pavilion, Lord—that's where I'll stay.

30 You crown my heart with all sorts of blessings—I need no crown for my head—jewels are fleeting but joy is everlasting.

31 Take time to hush those anxious and rebellious thoughts—those that would bring you down—those that are full of doubt and confusion.

32 Allow them no room to reside within your dwelling—divert them by means of other channels —let your mind dwell only upon the power of the Father.

33 Looking steadfastly into the eyes of the Risen One will never allow defeat to come near—much less to attack and strip victory from our hands.

34 Hush and be silent before Him—revel in His majesty—He will calm your anxious heart.

35 The rain falling against my window pane brings thoughts of how His mercy so freely showers the life of the believer and brings eternal goodness.

36 The rain of His Spirit soaks the clods of my soul—when hope is absent those clods become unyielding and hard like granite.

37 Pulverize those clods of hopelessness so that seeds of peace and joy may germinate into a bounty of belief—then I shall rejoice in Your faithfulness.

38 The rain of the Spirit cleanses the atmosphere of my soul—thereby purifying and washing away the iniquities of my sin.

Psalm 106

His Favor Rests Upon Those Who Praise

¹"To those who choose to travel the road of praise upon their daily walks—I will grant them the right to run on the highway of righteousness.

²I have blessed My people with abundant opportunities to worship—and they have made the most of them in order to lift high My praise.

³Their praises have shaken the rafters and overflowed into the upper chambers of My house because they desire My blessings—they seek My face night and day.

⁴They have pushed aside other duties and obligations to afford time for Me—they have ditched other wants and desires to petition My mercy for their lands.

⁵Their obedience to My Word is made evident by their requests—the hearts of those seeking My mercies have been made clean through repentance—humility is leading them on My straight path.

⁶Their praise will transport them swiftly into My presence—I will cause them to walk uprightly—I will hold their lives blameless before Me.

⁷I will also hold them above reproach because they have exalted Me above all gods—the praise of their lips exemplifies their hearts of worship—and with that I am pleased.

⁸My favor will be upon them continually and I will bless all that they do—as they spring up in My strength—all of their works will glorify Me.

⁹My way is simple and easy to understand—I will always choose praise over sacrifice—I hold your worship from the heart even higher than your works.

¹⁰Bow your heart in reverence before Me—I am there whenever you praise Me because I inhabit each and every one of your praises.

¹¹I—the Lord your God—am truly a jealous God and I insist there be none besides Me—put Me first and never be disappointed—for that is My rightful place."

Psalm 107

Your Wisdom Gives Life To Those Who Listen

¹Wisdom has shown me it is better to die with dignity and joy than to live unhappy and unfulfilled.

²When the godly face their greatest frustrations—they take a step in faith and find a bridge to support them.

³Bitterness cripples the heart of a fool and his lameness follows him all the days of his life—it is a cancer to his soul.

⁴The truly wise man has allowed faith to rule his inner struggles—he stands on God's Word confidently and has forbidden fear from coming onto his property.

⁵It is not the wise man who has listened to the voice of fear and been driven into hiding—his imaginations have caused him to lose his God focus.

⁶The finest gold contains impurities which only the most intense heat and prolonged searching will bring out—Holy Spirit refine me so I will be fit for the Master.

⁷Trouble soon becomes the saint's classroom—it is often a place where God works His benefits on their behalf.

⁸God's deliverance is the enemy's destruction—His hand of favor upon the godly will be their protection.

⁹A single moment by itself does not contain the whole of victory—just as a single battle does not determine the entire outcome of the war.

¹⁰The child of God holds Him as the nucleus of his life and uses the godly moments of his day as the atoms built around the nucleus.

¹¹The heart of the wise has not yielded to pride but has slain it by the Word of God—yet Lucifer's sin has a discouraging way of resurrecting and must be crucified daily.

¹²The man who exhausts all of God's blessings in this life ceases to be.

¹³A heart at peace has been touched by the finger of the Almighty—it has been anointed with composure and will not fret.

¹⁴The godly person will stay "in the next county" away from anger—thereby staying close to the heart of the Lord.

¹⁵The best way to bring the light of the gospel to others is to first be attired in it yourself—that way it turns into a shared blessing.

¹⁶A spiteful person heaps disaster upon others—a concerned man shows kindness to the less fortunate.

¹⁷Pretense only masks reality—truth exposes both in time.

¹⁸The law of sin has hijacked the sinner and held him captive—he is powerless to fight back and ceases to struggle any further.

¹⁹Do not curse the poor in your heart—for they have enough troubles of their own—lest someone wealthier than you looks on you with disdain and curses you out loud.

²⁰Without love man will quickly perish—he is no better than a bird with two crippled wings.

²¹Whoever has placed his faith in the Lord has given each and every one of his troubles an expiration date of today.

²²Good news travels fast—but bad news travels even faster—it is a banquet table set for gossips and their friends.

²³The righteous pursue the Lord with integrity—but the ways of the wicked are wrapped in the evil desires of the depraved.

²⁴Wisdom is a foreign tongue to the fool—to the ungodly it is a different language—it is the vocabulary of the Almighty—He pronounced it and gave its meaning.

²⁵A blind eye to sin is a blessing from the Lord—it prevents a man from straying and preserves his life.

²⁶Blessed are they who have learned to offer a deaf ear to words of hindrance against their soul—those utterances that are provoking to their spirit.

²⁷A servant gives no heed to the opinion of his neighbor—nor does he care what his fellow worker says—his ear is open only for the reassurance of his master.

²⁸Sin owns the man who is slave to it—although he longs to be free he cannot shake the bonds of it.

²⁹Pour out your heart—share its love daily with all around you—then there will be room for more to be poured into you.

Psalm 108

He Supports My Life

¹Be with me, O Lord, as I walk this wearisome journey—I am blessed that You have given me another mile—praise to Your unrivaled name.

²You have already apportioned strength for this day—it is mine to reach out and claim—You have already allocated to me my quota.

³Your wisdom has taken into account my daily needs—and You have set aside in Your storehouse provisions for each and every one of them.

⁴My shopping cart is empty—yet the aisles of Your storehouse are overflowing—You beckon me to receive so You may meet each need.

⁵Holy Spirit—what a wonder You are—You have met me in my hour of need and sustained me.

⁶I am poor and in great need of Your goodness—satisfy the desires of my heart and I will ever praise the name of my God.

⁷Whoever desires revival above all else must walk in the plainly marked paths of God—He sweeps His people into His presence every time they sincerely call upon His name.

⁸O that You would show Yourself through me this day—what more could I possibly ask?—let my face reflect the glory of my Lord.

⁹The fire of my heart rages for You, my God—it burns hot and is fueled by Your Spirit and Your Word.

¹⁰Every step of my way is in Your plan—You alone know the direction I should be traveling since You have already charted my course.

¹¹Today I will seek You with all of my heart—You have bestowed upon me the gift of life for another day—what greater blessing could I seek?

¹²With this breath will I praise You and not another—You gave it to me with purpose.

¹³Although You have not lined the path I walk with roses and the stones I traverse are rough and jagged—the terrain I am climbing is steep—and this cup I drink is bitter;

¹⁴Even so—the praise that comes forth refuses to be harsh—the breath You give me is holy and I must release it with reverence.

¹⁵Spirit of the Living God—melt my heart like a candle under a flame—mold me the same way a potter lovingly shapes the lifeless clay with his hands.

¹⁶Let the spoken words of my life reflect and translate the workings of my spirit—all that is within me shall praise His name.

¹⁷The dawning of this new day brings a heightened sense of rapture—a different sense of wonder and delight lay before me.

¹⁸Could it be—could this be the day I cross the Jordan in that glorious chariot You will send to pick me up?

¹⁹Or even better—perhaps this day holds the return of my Lord—when I will see those eastern skies part and His glory revealed at last.

²⁰He will draw us up to Him faster than metal shavings to a magnet—and then all our hopes will instantly become realities.

²¹Praise — praise — praise to the Father above — praise — praise — praise to the Father of love—for His mercies endure and His love is secure—yes, His love is as deep as the sea.

²²The Father has left us a valuable commodity—as sojourners of this earthly realm—His ever-abiding peace—ours for the taking—His abundant power follows that.

²³What sorrow have you suffered that He has not already seen and tasted—and what grief has come upon you except what He has shouldered?

²⁴His Word compels us to come unto Him for our relief—to lean hard upon His might and draw upon His strength—your grief will be brief when you make Him the Chief.

²⁵It is my soul that longs for You, O Lord—more than a drowning man longs for the next breath—for without that, he has no hope of life—and neither do I.

²⁶My love for You, my God, goes deep—may it go deeper still—Your strength is my reservoir in the dry places.

²⁷You are my strength, O God—when the day is young—You are my strength, O God—when the day is done—You are my strength all through the night.

²⁸Even in death nothing will silence my praise—my soul will live on in eternal praise.

²⁹For the child of God, death holds no terror—His called ones are only passing through the doorway of life into life everlasting.

³⁰When the breath of this life has ceased and grown silent—there will be other avenues of praise more glorious than this—my soul and spirit will never cease to praise Him for eternity.

³¹The angels of the Most High have been my companions in this earthly life and they shall continue to be until they present me before His throne.

³²They have dutifully carried out the directives of my God—they have snatched me out of the way of harm on many occasions—shielding me from peril has been their task.

³³Come and walk with me down the pathways of my God into His presence—let us point out His everlasting goodness and take comfort in His amazing grace.

Psalm 109

He Is The God Of All Tomorrows

¹Awake my slumbering soul—rejoice in His goodness—glory in His majesty—stretch out before the Lord and lift His name high.

²Come let us praise Him—elevate His holiness—applaud His greatness—shout aloud His holy praises—exalt Him in highest honor.

³Let our praises filter through the heavens—rising like a warm summer breeze.

⁴How can the natural light profit a man in his room if he refuses to open the shades on his windows and doors and let it in?

⁵Does his soul languish in darkness if he fails to let the light of the Spirit come in?

⁶The light of God's Word has pierced the darkness of this world—it is available to all men who will seek after it and open the windows of their soul to it.

⁷You, O Lord—have turned a new page in my book—a new chapter is ready to begin—You are its author and You have signed its title page.

Psalm 109 - He Is The God Of All Tomorrows

⁸May all who read from it glorify my God—let His majesty be praised forever—He has illustrated it with His glory—the colors are shades of His mercy and grace.

⁹His story is interwoven with my life and written across the pages of my book—it is a sweet story of redemption—its plot line runs deep.

¹⁰My spirit talks with my God during the night hours as my conscious mind is at rest—quite often it is not informed of these confidential exchanges.

¹¹They meet behind closed doors to discuss things of grandeur and magnificence—and those matters that might bring my carnal mind into alignment with His purpose.

¹²The godly man has submitted his mind to the Spirit in order that they will be in one accord—the Spirit makes it steadfast in power and peace—and nothing can shake it.

¹³I hold Your truths dear to my heart so I will not be led astray—they are my righteous protector.

¹⁴Within my arsenal I have the sword of the Spirit as my guardian and defender—to keep me from sinning against You—my God.

¹⁵The heart of the Master is smitten when His disciples choose to ignore His commands—when they turn a deaf ear to His words.

¹⁶You are my worship—the praise on my lips—my heart will adore You for eternity—my worship is more than a song I sing—my praise unto You is my offering.

¹⁷I rise early in the morning to meet with my God—He has never failed to show up—it is my finest hour unto Him—it is a godly hour.

¹⁸My eyes do not have to travel far in order to see You—for You surround me with Your presence.

¹⁹You have placed all of my tomorrows in front of me—no matter how few remain—and bid me not to look unto them.

²⁰Today—this present day—is what I must focus on—You have not given me an advance on any of my tomorrows.

²¹Sometimes the tomorrow we so eagerly sought and looked forward to has dawned even more bleakly than yesterday.

²²The bright promises we enthusiastically looked for were held beneath the rain clouds of today—and in that we find no joy.

²³But through all this—my God remains unchanged—I am encouraged to cast myself upon His certainty with my life.

²⁴Come what may He remains—forever to be exalted.

Psalm 110

Walk The Path Of Righteousness For His Glory

¹As you chat with those around—they observe your frame of mind and closely watch your conduct—this becomes your life's message and sermon to them.

²God's desire is for the walk to agree with the talk—with that He is well pleased.

³My Father's tender smile bathes me in light all day long.

⁴Who is he that makes sure he matches his every step in time with that of the Holy Spirit?—he is a wise and obedient son.

⁵The wise are convinced they are going somewhere and not just out for a stroll.

⁶The Father reveals His Will as you step out and obey Him in faith—it is a step-by-step process—He plants His purposes in your heart and awaits your commitment.

⁷Even the ticking of the clock reveals His disclosures—He makes His words known to the one who listens.

⁸"Listen to Me—I will call forth praise unto My name—praises due Me—then blessings will shower strength and power and fall upon you from My hand.

⁹Speak unto me, Holy Spirit—speak to me the words of God—I must listen so intently—teach me the words of God.

¹⁰Going forward into battle—marching forward unafraid—truth has gone out right before me—it will be my shield and shade.

¹¹The righteous and the unrighteous have one thing in common—the Almighty God is the creator of both.

¹²He who is a friend of God has chosen to seek after His righteousness—he searches after it persistently and with great determination.

¹³Although he never knows it—humility fuels his pursuit for the Divine.

¹⁴The ungodly have foolishly shed righteousness—they have thrown it to the ground and trampled on it—they have no intent of ever retrieving it.

¹⁵My God comforts me at all times—in my despair and in my joyful times—his concern is always over me like an umbrella.

16 The totality of man's knowledge cannot even scratch the surface of God's greatness—His Majesty has hidden His secrets for a later time.

17 When the saint has learned to enjoy each moment delivered to his doorstep—he has truly learned to relish life for the moment.

18 Today He asked if I would follow Him—I said, "Lord—You know I will follow You anywhere—even unto death."

19 He waited patiently for me to join Him—then He led me down the lane—straight onto the pathway of pure joy and life everlasting.

20 I asked Him for a meek and quiet spirit—instead He gave me a plate of joy like a river with a side dish of mercy.

21 I requested purity of heart—He gave me a bowl of gentleness along with a spoonful of unspeakable love.

22 He drew me to Him and we walked the path of righteousness—His delight was in my astonishment—the light of His love exposed beauty at every turn.

23 He laid His peace upon me like a warm blanket on a cold night—and fulfilled all my longings in an instant.

24 He will fill and use a yielded vessel for His glory—He will guide it until it will speak His story.

25 He said, "blessed is the prophet who drinks from My fountain—he has tasted waters directly from the source and His words are true.

26 Even if you seek for it like at an archaeological dig and it takes centuries to unearth the truth—he will never be put to shame—it will not be revealed until the right time.

27 Though they are despised for their words in this life—they will be rewarded for their obedience to My voice.

28 They have blessed Me with their service—and they shall receive manifold blessings when they come into My Kingdom.

29 How wonderful for those who receive My words and are moved to action—they have implemented My true purpose for their lives.

30 You pray to Me for miracles—but I say they walk among you—they are even in your midst—pray I will open the eyes of your heart—so you will see them come to pass."

Psalm 111

He Awaits Your Praise!

¹All you people of the Most High—who sits enthroned in the heavens—He awaits your praise—lift up your voice and exalt Him.

²Cry aloud with Hosannas—let your Hallelujahs ring out in chorus—praise the Lord all you people.

³Stand before Him with uplifted hands—with hearts full of praise—with feet that cannot stand still.

⁴Have you forgotten how to worship Him—how to lift high His holy name—how to pierce the heavenlies with javelins of praise?

⁵Cut loose your bands—those straps that hold back your arms and tie your feet—those restraints that bind your tongue and hold your heart captive.

⁶Clap your hands unto Him with wild enthusiasm—throw open the bowels of joy—for He alone is worthy of all praise.

⁷Let us enthrone Him on this earth even as He is enthroned in the heavens—He has chosen to reign in your heart—so never fail to display His righteousness.

⁸Is there any other name to be praised more than His?—no—and ten thousand times no—it is only through His name that salvation comes.

⁹Praise His name—Jehovah—El Shaddai—praise His name in the congregation—for He is everlasting—His name is the glory that covers us.

¹⁰The splendor of His holiness has come to dwell among us and abides within us—it fills the place where we dwell—He is holy and there is none like Him.

¹¹I will ever praise Him—from the moment I rise—'til I lay down my head.

Psalm 112

No One Knows The Day Or The Hour...

¹Many false cries and warnings have been sounded throughout time immortal heralding the Messiah's return—these have only highlighted the foolishness of man.

²Those specific dates and times chosen have only served to mock God and His Word—causing the unbeliever to scoff and be clothed in cynicism and distrust.

³Within His Word God has mercifully given us the season for the return of His Son—withholding the day and time—reserved only unto Him.

⁴Do not allow your zeal to make rash statements that expose your ignorance and discredit your Maker.

⁵At the Father's appointed time Jeshua shall sweep the earth—gathering those who are ready and waiting—watch for Him daily—for no man knows the day or the hour.

⁶Rest confidently in God's Word—be assured that His Word is truth—know that He is the Lord your God and He cannot lie.

⁷Do not permit your definition of soon to come in opposition to His—for with Him a thousand years is as a day and a day is as a thousand years.

⁸Rejoice that your redemption is drawing nearer—nearer than the day you first believed—do not fret about when He will appear—just stand ready at all times.

⁹With eyes of faith look up—for your Redeemer is set to return—much like a runner at the starting blocks of a race—He awaits the signal of His Father.

¹⁰Lift up your eyes and see what He is doing—throw up your hands with gladness—give Him a wave offering—exalt Him in His temple on all occasions.

¹¹Cry out to Him with a heart of thanksgiving—bless His name with all that is within you—do not withhold your praise for His greatness or He will find it elsewhere.

¹²His glory demands your reverence and wholehearted worship—He dotes on your praises—be made complete in your adoration of His majesty.

Psalm 113 - You Give Grace To The Humble

¹³Never cease to look for His coming—enjoy His presence as you stand in His sanctuary—extol His wisdom and majesty—speak it loudly with confidence.

¹⁴Let the praises of your heart rise to the throne—let them mingle with your tears as they join the angelic host and all the saints of heaven.

¹⁵Lift your voice in triumph declaring the righteousness of the Almighty — Jehovah Jireh — the God of all eternity.

¹⁶You have gathered in His house to bless His name—praise Him with exuberance—exalting His eternal majesty.

¹⁷Praise the Lord Most High all his people—the Great I Am that overshadows you with His covering—His glory is your banner—it is He who is crowned by your praise.

¹⁸Acclaim His name forevermore—for He is worthy of exaltation for all eternity—worship Him with your highest regards—cherish His splendor.

Psalm 113

You Give Grace To The Humble

¹O Lord, deliver us from the deceitfulness of complacency, may it never enter our homes or lie in wait at our doors; rebuke the swagger of smugness from our walks.

²The feet of the Lord's servant bring light and joy into each room they enter—they are counselors of peace and their mission is righteousness.

³Blessed are those who are called of the Lord and their place of service is backstage—they are quite content to be behind the scenes—theirs is the backup role.

⁴They have learned to find pleasure in the few days of their meaningful life—and they are wiser than the wisest man to have ever lived on earth.

⁵Contentment has kissed them full on the lips—they have found satisfaction in the rudimentary things of life—their true pleasure is made complete in pleasing their Creator.

⁶Dismay about the brevity of life does not worry them—nor are they bothered that their lives are but a drop in the ocean—they actually find pleasure in being that drop.

⁷A life of luxury was not their ultimate goal—indulgence has not made their hearts leap for joy—rejoicing has not been their honeymoon.

⁸The simple things have kept them company throughout their daily lives—they are satisfied with little and do not sweat the small stuff.

⁹They were not deserters to the common folk and they were no strangers to the laborer—they bonded well with the peasants and the public.

¹⁰At times a lack of self-assurance brought annoyance knocking at their front doors—shame accompanied their lack of boldness—timidity looked over their shoulders.

¹¹Peace of mind became their friend when the few things they were able to do—they did to the best of their ability.

¹²They were not upset when mirth and merriment chose not to be close companions.

¹³Prudence was esteemed as their principle—caution was highly regarded—reasoning and vigilance was their good example.

¹⁴Their blessing came knowing their Maker found good pleasure in them.

Psalm 114

The Depths Of My Soul Are Stirred

¹The Lord undergirds me with strength and gives me hope for a new day.

²He starts my day with a clean slate—He affords me a fresh start—along with new mercies—His provisions are before me.

³To awake in Your presence, O God, is precious indeed; I will ever praise You from the breaking of each new day until the finish of that same day.

⁴Thoughts of You are ever before me—they have preceded my first waking moments—they burst

Psalm 114 - The Depths Of My Soul Are Stirred

upon my consciousness with singing—You are worthy of non-stop praise.

⁵At Your insistence I delight to roll my troubles upon You—for I do not have the strength to lift them up to You.

⁶Suddenly my load becomes immensely lighter—I am able to straighten up—I no longer walk stooped over.

⁷You have made my steps lighter—I look forward to the coming day instead of fearing it with dread—You strip away my anxieties as I move out in anticipation.

⁸My face is toward Your glory—the light of Your Word has shined on my path and comes against the enemy with power and precision.

⁹Keep my heart bent in the direction of Your will—let it swallow my will—may Your preferences always be my inclination.

¹⁰I will lift my soul unto You, my God; the praises of this heart I will pour out before You, O Lord—spilling over the rim of my vessel.

¹¹You have heard my groanings—the utterances I cannot express with words—You even hear my deepest sighs.

¹²How can I wrap my thoughts around You since You cannot be contained—can Your greatness be recounted?—its detail defies verification—describing it fails miserably.

¹³Yet I will focus my thoughts upon You—I will direct them toward You—for You are everywhere I go.

¹⁴The depths of my soul are stirred with gratefulness for Your love—You delight in my praises—it is my extreme pleasure to exalt Your majesty with them.

¹⁵I have no other worth but to bring worship and praise to my King—the King of all ages—the Ruler of eternity.

¹⁶Your love has singled me out and given me purpose—to administer unto You a life of devotion along with a heart of thanksgiving—these I willingly surrender.

¹⁷I will sing His song continuously—it is the song of the redeemed—of the Lamb who sits upon the throne—it shall always be my sacrifice of praise.

¹⁸The redeemed of the Lord will bring glory—alongside honor and praise unto Him—it will be revealed in all that they do.

¹⁹He has branded their hearts with joy and everlasting peace—they will find rest.

[20] They delight to go out—oblivious of the terrors of darkness that surround them—their assurance has beheld the greatness of the One within them—and they are unafraid.

[21] The redeemed of the Lord will stand up and proudly say—blessed be the name of the Lord—blessed be the name of the Lord—for He is my light and my strength.

Psalm 115

My Desire = Your Good Pleasure

[1] A sensible man will not keep to himself the praise that he should pass along to another—by pocketing the good words that should go to others, he forfeits a blessing.

[2] He will not sidestep ways to encourage his fellow man—for he knows that he himself often longs to be encouraged and lifted up.

[3] The sacrifice of a grateful heart often goes unseen except through the eyes of the Master—His watchful eye does not miss those denials done in secret.

[4] He has allowed the faithful to go through a season of testing and to come forth as a field of wheat—standing glorious and victorious at harvest time.

[5] Who is the man who has lived and not dreamed of a life devoid of troubles or trials—one that is free of all tribulations?

[6] If we were to live a life without any heartache—how would we be able to praise properly?—we would be missing out on that hope and longing we now have.

[7] O how quickly my spirit leapt within me when it received witness of the answer it had searched for—my joyful heart knew no bounds as it worshipped in praise.

[8] Happiness is contagious—so let it rub off on all those around you—infect them with a dose of your joy.

[9] A good and faithful wife should be treasured more than her weight in solid gold—her worth is much higher than wealth and fortune.

[10] He holds my hand and leads me through the dark places—I close my eyes and trust Him in faith.

Psalm 115 - My Desire = Your Good Pleasure

11His arm is around me—He holds me close so that I will not stray from His side.

12He quiets my mind and closes my eyes in sleep so that I might receive rest for the coming day.

13O Lord, my heart is an open book before You—there is nothing hidden from Your view—You know all my longings and desires—they are reserved especially for You.

14Hope rises in the souls of the godly—it stands at attention and salutes His Majesty every time it recalls the faithfulness of their God.

15My soul awakens to the sweetness of Your Spirit, my God—You have been my sustaining joy.

16Dreams of the righteous have led to the discovery of hidden secrets—sometimes they uncover truths known only to God.

17Even as these mortal bodies break down—the glory of God will shine more brightly through the character of the righteous.

18When disease comes knocking on the door of the godly—they are willing only to surrender their bodies—they refuse it access to their spirits.

19He exchanged the stripes upon His body for my healing—it became the hem of His garment for me.

20Death has proven itself a formidable foe and is no respecter of persons—it touches all from the greatest who ever lived to the least—a curse since the beginning.

21Never let it be said they died before their time—or they were just in the wrong place at the wrong time—or their time was cut short.

22God has given each of His creatures a predestined number of heartbeats—and only He knows that number—it cannot be altered or changed against His will.

23Neither time nor circumstance brings death to the forefront—it comes by His design and purpose and the conclusion of the number of allotted breaths He has promised.

24Treasure each one and use it for His glory—the only thing of lasting worth.

25Do not waste them frivolously—for once they are gone they can never be retrieved—do not fritter them away with no regard for eternity.

26O that I might hear Your voice—for I have made You my choice—now let my soul rejoice over You.

27For You, O Lord, will lead my soul into peace—I have made You my choice and I will not be turned away.

28 The desire of this heart is to know Your good pleasure—teach me what it is that pleases You the most and I will do that unrelentingly.

29 The gateway to my mind has been overlaid with Your Word—it fills the tunnel to my vision—my ear canal is made receptive listening for Your voice.

30 I will worship—I will bow down—singing praises unto Christ the Everlasting King.

Psalm 116

My Soul Sings You A Love Song

1 The Lord teaches me to sing joyfully because I have heard the keynote of my God—He has become the tonic pitch of my song.

2 I will worship—I will bow down—singing praises unto Christ the King.

3 My heart is a musical instrument of worship unto You—it is the means by which the melodies of my soul are set free unto my God.

4 The songs of my soul are a fitting expression of my love for Him—a channel of my ministry unto His Excellence.

5 He rejoices in those who have dedicated their songs of devotion unto Him—He is pleased and His smile is upon them.

6 He made my hands to be instruments of worship—sometimes to clap my praises unto Him—sometimes to wave in exaltation of His goodness.

7 Even my fingers dance before Him upon my keyboard—I exalt Him with my worship and He—in turn—has used it to bless many others.

8 I will also raise my arms in worship to my heavenly Father—they are the branches of my tree upon which He places His fruit.

9 God rocks my praise—no part of me will keep silent—for He is worthy of all honor—my adoration refuses to remain unspoken.

10 I will hail You and heap up my praises for Your excellence—they will mount up with a powerful crescendo.

11 When I call out—You are there to summon the forces of the heaven-

lies to be my backing—they immediately thwart the powers of darkness with light.

¹²Your favor has been my defense—my protection and my armor—Your Word has become my security and my vindication.

¹³The thirst of a godly man drives him to the foot of the cross—scattering any smug half-heartedness—as the rays of morning sun chase away the shadows of darkness.

¹⁴I have tasted a helping of Your glory at the onset of my day and I hunger for more of it all day long.

¹⁵I have felt the surging of Your power within my being—it refreshingly splashes over my soul and brings fullness of joy.

¹⁶My soul says—I will arise and go unto my Father—for He has called me by name—now He asks that I come unto Him.

¹⁷I will stand before His Majesty and bathe my soul in His presence—allowing His anointing to baptize me with glory—I will always praise His name.

Psalm 117

How Big Do You Believe I Am?

¹"Let he who is apt to feel weak—look up—and receive strength from Me—for I am your God.

²Reach out and receive My salvation—you think I do not hear you but My ear has gathered your every word—I have not let even one of your thoughts pass by.

³You think I do not see you but I do—My eyes are upon you—even at this very moment—I see where you are—but more importantly—I see the depths of your heart.

⁴I see your inhibitions—those things that seem to plague you day after day—I am really longing for you to bring them to Me—leave them in My care.

⁵Why carry unnecessary weight on your shoulders—is it because you think I am unable to carry it—or because you think I am unwilling?

⁶It is I who formed the galaxies—My command created the universe—I am able to carry the weight of the heavenlies—now what was it you thought I was not capable of?

⁷You have no idea the strength I possess—My might you cannot fathom—yet you stumble along under such heavy loads—under the pretense you do not want to bother Me.

⁸Is it that—or maybe that you really do not believe as you want to believe?

⁹Seek Me for that need you are harboring—do not think there is anything too trivial or great for My competence.

¹⁰I am speaking this word specifically for you—hopefully you are listening.

¹¹Put all things aside right now (you do know what now means, don't you?) and come to Me—I am waiting—will you come?"

Psalm 118

My Judgment Upon The Nations

¹"Cry aloud all you who are My people—say many prayers for the nations—those peoples of the earth who have ignored Me in spite of their desperation.

²A deadly disease has come against the nations and wounded the peoples within them—My judgment is set against them.

³I can clearly see the nations teetering on the brink of disaster—they have chosen their own ways and scorned the path I approved for them.

⁴They reach out to gain strength in one another but they will only succeed in pushing each other down—like a string of dominoes set up to be toppled.

⁵Why have they set their kingdoms against Me?—because they have allowed the evil one to lead them.

⁶Lift up your voice, My children, while there is yet time—for soon I will bring My fire against all the ungodly.

⁷Righteousness is fleeing the earth—I am withdrawing My messengers of light—soon total darkness will blanket the entire planet.

⁸My patience and longsuffering have been exhausted—it is time for My glory to rise from the face of the deep—it shall return unto Me.

⁹What I have said before I will say again—My Spirit will not always strive with man.

¹⁰The sound of My punishment will soon cover the nations of the earth as I repay the enemies that have come against My Kingdom.

¹¹Their security was in their magnificent ships—they paid no heed to My call for justice—they trampled My paths of mercy with carelessness and indifference.

¹²I have left them high and dry—I have dry-docked their ships—they are beyond repair and unsalvageable—fit only for destruction.

¹³They set up their will against Mine—challenging Me in all their ways—but now I will put down My foot against all of them—declaring them to be unsuitable.

¹⁴I will not destroy the righteous along with the wicked because their hearts have been set on Me.

¹⁵My favor will rescue them from everlasting damnation—My reward will be dispensed with good pleasure.

¹⁶Whoever is caught up in the material pursuits of this life will not enjoy the pleasures of heaven because they have rejected My message.

¹⁷This I have foretold from the beginning—now rise up My children and come to Me—there you will dwell in safety."

Psalm 119

All Creation Sees And Hears His Majesty

¹The whole earth has heard His voice—all of His creation has trembled at the sound of it—when it speaks, the waters convulse and the light cannot stand still.

²All of God's peoples have witnessed the majesty of what He has made and are without excuse—only a fool would stand and blaspheme His might.

³When I look at all Your starry host and gaze upon the beauty of Your creation I can only shake my head in wonder—my soul cries out—there is no other god like You?

⁴Seek the Lord in earnest—with gladness of heart and freedom of will

—lest your misery force you to seek His face—then what have you gained?

⁵Let Your love, O God, flow unto me like a river—refresh my spirit with songs so that it quiets and soothes my mind with music—You will not keep Your love from me.

⁶You have made Your home far beyond the reaches of the universe—beyond the places where time and space make their lodging.

⁷Even then You are at home in the hearts of mortal man—to be their God and supporter—companion and friend.

⁸These God-honoring saints have learned to live their lives in such a manner that they will die before their convictions do.

⁹The Word of the Lord reveals His thoughts to that man who constantly seeks Him.

¹⁰To the downtrodden even a smile—along with an encouraging word—can be greater than winning the Megabucks jackpot.

¹¹People who are godly and full of His Spirit emit the scent of His presence wherever they go—their actions exude His glory and unwittingly touch others in the process.

¹²Sin desires to tag along in the lives of those who will allow it—as for me—I have sent it packing so that it cannot pester me any longer.

¹³Even during my nightly trips Your thoughts go with me—You never leave me alone because I have determined to keep You close—my night hours overflow with joy.

¹⁴You have planted the righteous and the godly throughout the land—as a holy seed to ensure new generations of believers.

¹⁵Blessed is the man who walks with conviction before His God—his roots shall go down deep as the roots of an oak—no small gale will cause him to budge.

¹⁶O Lord, my God—You are the beat of my heart—I will not pretend to understand Your ways—of this I am sure—You have been the beat of my heart since the first one.

¹⁷My heart beats wildly for You—I feel Your presence and I've fallen head over heels in love with You.

¹⁸Let us walk faithfully to the end of the road—though our vision is clouded and the end cannot be seen clearly—we will push on with perseverance.

¹⁹The words of my God raise the spirits of those who walk discreetly

—those who tread upon paths of peace and mercy will find solace and will not be upset by gloom.

20When the words of a man's heart come to worship, they bring sweet adoration unto the King—uplifting both the giver and the receiver.

21Let the quietness of your faith bring exaltation unto the One who is greater—then it will surely lead to renewal and intercession with the love of your heart.

22God vastly outshines our wildest fantasy—do not be lulled into being content with mediocrity—forsake your past triumphs and strive for new goals.

23Let your hope be based on the everlasting truth of God—the bedrock of all eternity.

24His promise is just beyond the reach of our physical grasp—but with the hands of faith we have already reached out and taken hold of it.

25The submissive soul has discovered that each act of obedience is an opening of the windows of Heaven —whereupon he has been flooded with radiant light.

26Know this and listen closely—take note today of My words—"I have not grown weary of hearing your cries—My ear will never grow tired of listening to your petitions.

27Have you—my children—become weary of crying out to Me—has your faith weakened so that you no longer believe I hear?

28Let your voice grow strong as your praise soars unto the heavens—do not keep your worship to yourself or I will solicit it from other avenues.

29I will anoint those who release their wills unto Me—I will grant the godly who dwell on My virtues power to walk in truth—and My mark will abide upon their lives."

Psalm 120

Down That Road Of Unending Praise

¹My soul delights in Your presence, O God—it finds contentment in Your nearness.

²Preserve my heart by the salt of Your Word—so it would season my spirit in truth and purity while giving essence to my words.

³I have spoken my prayers into Your ear, O Lord—and my worship I will sing unto You with gladness of heart.

⁴You have banished the ungodly from Your presence—may I never be like one of them—send Your Holy Spirit to comfort the godly in the wee hours of the morning.

⁵I will begin each new day with a fresh offering from the fruit of my heart—my lips will join in thanksgiving for Your bounty.

⁶Is anyone angry—anyone disgruntled?—go ahead and speak your complaint to the earth and it will testify against you.

⁷Even though the earth is rocking and shaking—the ground is quaking—and turmoil abounds on all sides—God remains firm forever—He is not fazed by these in the least.

⁸The Word of the Lord directs my steps and also corrects my missteps.

⁹My soul lives in peace because it has apprehended who You are—You are the Great I AM and I will proclaim your sovereignty forever.

¹⁰Distraction commandeers my thoughts—I have herded them together like sheep in a pen—will they ever quit mulling around—will they stand still at all?

¹¹The enemy of your soul seeks to heap disruptions upon you in order to interrupt your quiet time with the Lord—he strives to drive a wedge into your concentration.

¹²Why allow him to succeed?—do not fret—do not bother your thoughts a moment longer—once the distraction has passed, quietly return to His peace without further ado.

¹³I will come into Your presence, O God, so I can replenish my strength—daily I must draw upon Your might lest I be wearied and weakened.

14Prepare me to walk a new path—a victorious path of worship—one where the brightness of Your presence shines overhead.

15Lead me down that road of unending praise—open my eyes to Your Majesty—my ears to Your sweet expressions—my mind to Your Word—so that I might not stumble.

16The worship that comes forth from this vessel is my utmost unto You—I will praise You to the best of my ability.

17There are no carved figurines for me to pay heed to or focus my gaze steadfastly upon—I refuse my adorations access to any object—there is no other god besides You.

18I will not put up with any idols becoming the center of my attention—nor will the carvings of man captivate the throne of my heart.

19Sweep me into Your presence, O God—as a janitor moves dirt from the floor to his dustpan.

20Let me be enamored by the shroud of Your glory — caught up by Your all-encompassing love — drawn into Your embrace.

21I eagerly look for that day when all of mankind—when all of God's creation will acknowledge His greatness and majesty.

22O that He would freely receive all the acclaim that is due Him—He deserves all the glory—for there is none like Him.

23Let Him hasten the day when all of His beings—both in heaven and under the heavens—bow before Him in reverence—bringing to Him their tribute of praise.

24His majesty should—and will—be proclaimed from the highest heavens and from the lowest depths—let all His creatures rejoice and abound with praise.

25The Lord God—the Mighty One—He is ruler over heaven and earth—over all principalities and dominions—lift up your voice with praise all His people.

26If it wasn't for You, my God—this journey would not have been worthwhile—because of Your strength my faith has carried me further than my feet ever could have.

27The work of Your Kingdom is paraded daily through the righteous living of the saints of the Most High One.

Psalm 121

My Heart Gladly Welcomes You

¹O Lord—here You are knocking at my heart's door—peering over its wall—checking out its defenses.

²Looking out the peephole I quickly swing the door open—throwing my arms open wide as I welcome You with a loving embrace.

³My soul has rejoiced in the early morning hours—and yes—it has rejoiced all throughout the day.

⁴You have lifted it up, O Lord, and cradled it in Your hands just like You lift up my branches that hang low—those that droop and touch the ground.

⁵The prayers of the saints have added much traffic upon that heavenly highway—it is paved with their requests and washed by their tears.

⁶I have stood in the stream of God's grace—it has washed my past away—all the way downstream—now I sing the song of the overcomer.

⁷His mercy will touch those hurting places and anoint them with healing salve—His love will heal your scars and remove chains of bondage.

⁸He showers me with treats all day long—blessings sometimes too awkward to mention—nevertheless I will praise Him for all His favors.

⁹Just look around and you can see the signature of my God—His handiwork abounds all over the earth.

¹⁰He crushes the mighty man who revels in his own strength—He exalts and gives power to the weak and defenseless each time they look unto Him.

¹¹My soul has found a temporary place of rest in You, O Lord—it is longing for that day of eternal rest—when peace and joy will reign forever.

¹²Blessed be the Lord who answers my prayers before they are even on my tongue.

¹³I raise my hands high in praise and my misfortunes fly up to the throne of the Almighty One—immediately You make my heart lighter.

¹⁴He will not suffer me to bear more struggles than I am willing to carry.

15 The prayer of a righteous man is for victory in the midst of trials rather than deliverance from them.

16 Pour out your prayers before Him like you pour out water from a pitcher.

17 The kindness of a man's heart will overflow in goodness to others—he will not count the cost—nor will he expect repayment.

18 Do not forsake the Lord your God—His faithfulness has never left you stranded—the promises of the Lord have never left you in the lurch.

19 Do not neglect to serve Him the remainder of your days—in return He will crown you with everlasting life in the presence of His saints.

20 Purify your hearts by the blood of the Lamb—He will put away uncleanness from your daily living as a trash collector disposes of your garbage.

21 Bring to the King of Kings your offerings—those of thanksgiving and sacrifice—worship Him with gladness—let your songs of praise be sprinkled with liveliness.

22 The wise man has verified that the safest place to be is in the will of God.

23 When the gentle breeze of the Holy Spirit blows across the wind chimes of my soul—it plays beautiful music.

24 Even when I depart the face of the earth—my God still knows my location—my address is in His book.

25 And when I settle with the dust of the earth—His presence then abides with my soul—for He will never leave me alone.

Psalm 122

Test Me…And I Will Come Forth In Shining Splendor

1 The delight of my soul is in service to my King—the joy He brings leads to eternal liberty—His contentment with my work fills me with pleasure.

2 My strength for the day has gone—I feel like a rundown battery—Your touch uplifts me and I am renewed.

3 You add vigor to my weakness—

rest on top of weariness—stability to my unsteady gait—alertness for my tiredness—comfort to chase away the aching.

⁴I look for You, my God—You are my hope—You have made my expectations to flourish like the opening of a lily.

⁵The window of my soul remains open unto You—send Your light in to banish all shadows—brighten my room with righteousness.

⁶When virtue trumps carnality it is because integrity is leading the way.

⁷Whenever moral frailty gets the upper hand on justice and purity it only leads to ruin—foolishness often leads to foul play.

⁸The believer's faith goes ahead of him—it rises in strong opposition to unbelief—casting it down in defiance.

⁹It stands strong in the midst of great trial—reaching to higher levels than humanly possible.

¹⁰Grasping hold of divine powers—I wield my faith as a dynamic weapon to be put to the test.

¹¹Inspiring strength in the face of shards of doubt—this faith is a saving grace to the godly and a strong testament to their God.

¹²When the righteous put this faith to the test, it will come forth in shining splendor—strong and resilient—confident in the Almighty.

Psalm 123

Who Can Behold The Light Of His Glory?

¹Who is it that can fill his mind with God's greatness—who can fully comprehend His comings and goings—and who is able to discern His beginnings?

²Only the one who has the mind of the Lord resident within is able to sense even the tiniest of all the mysteries of His greatness—though he should not gloat about it.

³Your vastness cannot be measured nor Your greatness described—in the arena of time, centuries are to You as grains of sand in an hour glass or those upon the seashore.

⁴The light of Your glory outshines the

brightness of the sun—no mortal can behold it.

⁵A prophet's voice can be heard at times in tender tones—for he has penetrated the inner veil and gazed upon the beauty of the Holy One.

⁶He has heard the voice of the Most High and has taken note of His words—the dictates of His mouth—and the wisdom of His understanding.

⁷At times the prophet's voice is harsh and reprimanding—he is simply subservient to his Master and is compelled to lay forth His message.

⁸The Lord sits in His chamber—clothed in infinite patience—hemmed in by eternity—He waits to speak words of wisdom to all who boldly knock on His door and draw near.

⁹His heart is eagerly waiting to find those desiring to see His glory and taste of His goodness—He will offer them blessings because they delight to praise His name forever.

¹⁰Inadequacy is the stronghold of the righteous man—it is common for him to have an excess of his own shortcomings.

¹¹He disregards his own self-worth as weakness but finds strength in the power of his God—his dependence on Him is intensified when he views his own meagerness.

¹²Peace of mind becomes his abode—his heart rests easy knowing he will never be more capable than his Creator—his place is one of praise and support for his King.

¹³Let the prophet's voice persist in ringing out in spite of man's unfaithfulness—he has obeyed the Spirit's call and will honor God's gift with his life—let God be praised.

Psalm 124

Salvation Comes To Those Who Seek You

¹The godly serve as a viewfinder through which the world sees the love and benevolence of a caring God—they share a healthy look into the other side of eternity.

²Where does this hope I so desperately cling to come from—is it because of who I am or what I've done?

³That could not be further from the truth—but let me tell you about my Jesus—it's all about who He is and what He has done that gives rise to my hope.

⁴God's love was so great for your heart and mine—in fact He could not bear the thought that anything would separate our souls from Him—so He gave His only Son.

⁵Where could we find a love greater than this—that our heavenly Father led His beloved Son to the foot of a barbaric cross—then asked Him to take our place?

⁶Today—my God—You will lead my feet along an unfamiliar path—my footsteps You will guide by the knowledge of Your Word.

⁷I will put my trust in the Lord and not in worthless hunks of wood and metal—then my mind will remain fixed only upon Him.

⁸Come and look with me into the mind of the Spirit—He has shown me such great things of truth and beauty—He will not neglect the small things, as well.

⁹He has revealed that murmurings and complaints are not His will—His good will is to do that which He has shown us with gladness of heart.

¹⁰His Word will stabilize those who are unsteady—He will level the uneven places and give you a firm footing.

¹¹Walk with confidence and do not hold back—what He has shown you He will not withhold.

¹²O God, let passion for Your will pour out of me like perspiration from a long-distance runner—may it be released like beads of sweat off the forehead.

¹³You have smiled upon us today—we have received ample strength to walk the glory road—we have had to lean upon You in our times of frailty.

¹⁴The Word of the Lord has opened the doors of wisdom to the godly—You fill their minds with truth—nuggets from God's great storehouse.

¹⁵A wise man closes each door with grace because he never knows when he may be required to walk back through that door.

¹⁶Our thoughts ride on the wings of our words—the currents of the heavenlies carry them to appropriate places—scattering them as seed from the sower.

¹⁷You, O God, cherish those who seek Your face—You furnish peace to those whose hope is in Your name—who cry out to You in confidence and expectation.

¹⁸Salvation has come unto hearts that seek Him—upon them He will establish righteousness so that they might be called sons of the Lord Most High.

¹⁹He scours the earth to find a man who is willing to commit to His purpose—to be filled by His Spirit and power—to give up all for the sake of His glory.

²⁰When the famine of Your wonders comes—and scarcities of Your marvelous deeds surround us—when You fail to dumbfound us with the unspeakable.

²¹I will praise You in the absence of Your wonders—let miracles cease—yet I will praise You forever—I stand unwavering in my vow to praise You for who You are.

Psalm 125

You Bring The Hidden Ones Into The Light

¹"Where are the righteous ones—those I have called for a purpose?

²They have gone into hiding and their light is unseen—yet I will expose and uncover their light in My own time—for My own purpose.

³They will shine forth as brightly as a beacon—giving light to those far away—I have chosen them to light My path and to bring many to safety.

⁴I have put My breath in them—My Spirit is their light—they will step forward in victory—and triumph shall be their middle name.

⁵Although they tremble now—they

shall come out in boldness and in My strength—for their hearts are fixed on Me.

⁶Those I have chosen I know well and they have heard My voice—obedience to My Word has lined their hearts like the shelves to a supermarket on grand opening day.

⁷I will honor them in days to come because they have not defiled My Word—they are the delight of My heart and have made Me their choice over all other things."

Psalm 126

His Blessings Are New Every Morning

¹Follow the road that your Savior has walked—follow it clear to the end—He has left markers to guide every step—follow the narrow way through to the end.

²My soul greets the morning with a smile and shakes hands with a thankful heart for another day blessed by His presence.

³It rises up to bless His name and speaks to my God with utmost reverence—with tender thanks I will render unto my King a heart full of honor.

⁴He holds my reward in His hands—I wait patiently for it—He will be pleased to cover me with blessings in His good time.

⁵How is it possible to ever reach the other shore unless you somehow cross the river?

⁶The distant shore beckons—how my heart is yearning to go there—will it be soon?—He will transport me safely to the other side.

⁷Sometimes when I am exposed to Your wonders I get a rush of joy and shivers up and down my spine—especially when I swell with pride knowing that You are my God.

⁸Those who choose to follow the Master have clothed themselves daily with salvation—they have put on justice as their undergarment.

⁹They have dressed themselves in true righteousness as one might pull up a pair of pants—integrity has become their shirt.

¹⁰Man was not meant to know the vast secrets of the Almighty—to

be made privy to His innermost thoughts—to comprehend the unfathomable workings of His mind.

[11] He never intended man's mortality to behold such wonders—nor did He intend mankind to unravel all the mysteries of His universe in a lifetime.

[12] My God has apportioned unto me strength for today—He has measured out my portion—praise His name for all His blessings.

[13] He extends them to me day after day—throughout this toilsome life—like so many pearls on a string.

[14] Your strength, O God—has marched into my morning—much like a soldier in battlefield formation—it renews me with fresh power to stand against the enemy.

[15] You—my God—come to the aid of those who look for You—those who are willing to call upon Your name—the desperate make You their desire.

[16] So let Your glory fall upon me—let it fill me through and through—not simply for my benefit—but for Your all-consuming purpose.

[17] You have nullified the power of the enemy—You have made it ineffective in me because of Your Word—it has cancelled out the penalty of my sin.

[18] When I have exhausted my supply of strength at the end of the day—You take the night hours and re-supply my stamina so that I awake refreshed in Your good Spirit.

[19] My soul takes pleasure in Your goodness and trembles at Your Word—it is You I exalt and give glory unto—O praise the Lord—praise Him for His dominance.

[20] I will praise my God for His renown—He gives far more than He takes—His blessings are for those who seek Him with all their hearts.

[21] In the stillness of the night hours He watches over me—in darkness my soul finds rest in Him alone.

[22] At the midnight hour He comes to my bed and comforts me—His voice brings rest for my weariness.

[23] He speaks in hushed tones and whispers my name so that I know He is near.

[24] He covers me with sleep until the dawn of the morning—then awakens me with gratefulness and singing.

[25] My soul sings forth a beautiful song for His hand of protection—it lifts unto Him melodies of praise for life itself.

[26] The joy bells of my heart join with my voice of praise with worship to His majesty.

Psalm 127

The Godly Will Shine

¹Blessed are they through whom God has shown His light to the world beyond what they can possibly see—His Spirit has reflected it far past the realm of their natural vision.

²God hears the motives of the heart—they speak much louder than words ever could.

³If God hears the ungodly—how much more does He hear those who are inclined toward Him?

⁴Why take life for granted—do you know whether your next breath will come?—go ahead and praise the Creator—praise the Father of life now while you can.

⁵I will praise You, my God—while I can, I will praise You—for You have sustained me with joy since my youth—gladness has led me by the hand since my childhood.

⁶I spend my days in contentment because You, my God, have satisfied me with lavish mercies—Your gospel of grace has consumed my life.

⁷You have connected my heart to Yours with love bonds—like the lines of a ship attached to the tugboat that guides it along—these are what keep me close to You.

⁸You knew my heart before I was born—my destiny—my desires—You knew I would answer your call before the world was formed—how amazing that is.

⁹Your righteousness dwells in those who have made You their mainstay—daily You dispense justice—truth is Your staff by which You rule the earth.

¹⁰You have spread joy from Your stockpile generously across my countenance—much like jelly upon a peanut butter sandwich.

¹¹You liberally apply peace like a lotion—and radiance brightens my appearance.

¹²You have released my disappointment and cleared up my whole demeanor—as when a purifying rainstorm cleanses the air.

¹³What causes the godly to shine in the midst of rain clouds?—they have learned to shed hardship like a dieter has learned to shed troublesome pounds.

¹⁴The Word of God is a receptacle into which I plug my spirit—it gives power to my mind and energizes my heart.

¹⁵Praising God is no troublesome matter—it is the joy of my life as well as the grounding of my soul—the liberated freedom of my spirit.

¹⁶The prayer of my heart is that You, my God, would take me over—day by day—hour by hour—minute by minute—piece by piece;

¹⁷Do this in the same way a Monopoly player wins the game by acquiring one property after another—until he has all of them.

¹⁸Narrow my thoughts until You have shrunk them to one desire—You—and nothing else is left—lock me away inside Your will—with no chance of liberation.

¹⁹The Lord fills me with His goodness—otherwise nothing of value resides in me.

²⁰Feelings or circumstances do not lead the life of the unwavering man—his faith anchors him securely to the Rock.

²¹Sin pours unrighteousness upon those who embrace it—just like water is poured from a pitcher—it fills the glass to the full—and so does sin.

²²He leads my soul along the good way—His hand steadies my steps and I walk in confidence.

²³Let the Word of the Lord become your daily bread and it will nourish and sustain your spirit—it will show the way you should go.

²⁴He delights in me each time I place my trust and confidence in Him.

²⁵Do not turn away from the Lord in your times of exhaustion—instead turn all the more unto Him for strength and peace of mind—let Him be your support.

²⁶He has placed the veiled joys of heaven within the hearts of the searching ones—His call once tugged at their heartstrings—now it leads in full procession up His royal path.

Psalm 128

You Deserve Our Very Best

¹If we continue to walk devotedly we will come to that joy sitting in front of us—it is currently out of sight—just over the crest of the hill—maybe right around the next corner.

²Faith stands aside—amused—as it watches the struggles of self-sufficiency try to stand on its own two feet.

³Any vision devoid of God—is not of God—He must be the only means of bringing it about.

⁴Faith is blind to the natural things—and as such must be operated solely in the spiritual arena—there are other times our Lord gives us wisdom and a sound mind to use.

⁵Quite often faith negates human wisdom and strikes a death blow to reasoning and logic—it steps to a higher level and marches to a different drum beat.

⁶Blessed are they who have walked that course—who have flung caution to the wind—who have let go of their securities and crutches.

⁷They do not fear rebuke or scorn—their confidence is in the Lord and His promises.

⁸My voice will continue to praise the name of my God—my heart will worship in truthfulness and in reverence.

⁹I will bow before Him—so others will say they know at least one person who seeks the Lord in truth.

¹⁰My heart will testify—my words will join with truth—I will declare to Him alone all majesty and greatness—I will never cease to seek Him as long as I have breath.

¹¹Trust takes no pleasure in the past—the yesterdays no longer hold any promise.

¹²Hope is wrapped in the shell of tomorrow and delights in it—the future of today—which contains the mysteries of God.

¹³The Spirit of the Lord has invaded our hearts and fills them with peace.

¹⁴He has selected the godly to live a life of sacrifice—worship—and usefulness—unto their King.

¹⁵The gemstone of a man is seen in a heart devoted to the Almighty God—a heart driven to the discovery of His plans and purposes.

16 Give God your very best—He wants all you have and all of you—do not make Him settle for your crumbs—your leftovers will not please Him.

17 You are a full measure of joy to Him when you do not withhold your best—offer Him your finest gifts with a willing heart.

18 Shake loose the praise you have for Him—do not hang onto it tightly as a belt stretched around the waist—set it free to accomplish that very thing He designed it for.

19 Crushing trials may come against the wise man—nevertheless his discipline of thankfulness has cushioned him—for he has laid up a great treasure.

20 The peace of God allows us to trample the footsteps of the enemy in triumph.

21 To walk in truth is the mark of success that abides upon the life of the child of God.

22 How can you give away that which you have not received?—Ask Him to fill your pantry with good things—do not be stingy with your wares.

23 He measures the hearts of His saints and finds them full—not only to the brim—but overflowing the top—with passion running down the sides.

24 He leads their hearts from victory to victory—they do not even stop to consider it—He causes their enemies to come out into the open where they soon meet their demise.

25 You alone, O Lord, are my guiding force—You lead me down righteous paths while shielding me from the ungodly.

26 Your eyes have seen all of my ways—none have been hidden from Your sight—in kindness and love You direct all of my steps—at Your command I turn right or left.

27 The desires of my heart lie deep within—but they are not kept secret from You—the words of my mouth come from those desires—and are ever open before You.

28 Your love calls out to those who desire You in limitless ways—Your presence abides in every corner of the earth—it pervades the face of the deep.

29 The words of the godly are life unto them—they are Spirit and life to all who hear them—especially those who pay close heed to them.

30 God honors the strength of His servant as He calls him to difficult service—only He knows the rigors and demands of His calling—He is quick to give grace in times of need.

Psalm 129

Your Love Surrounds Me

¹"Because I love you I have surrounded you with many soldiers—they are an extension of My right arm and form your protection.

²I will use the warriors from amongst you to clear the battlefield—their prayers are a stronghold and a weapon of defense against the enemy.

³Your life is hidden within My hand because you have desired Me supremely and I have purposed to do this."

⁴O Lord—you have cared for me since birth—spoon-feeding me in my infancy—then teaching me to feed on my own.

⁵I have grown up with Your Word and it has become my daily bread—it has provided all the sustenance I need.

⁶Let me be caught away in a tide of Your glory—swept up in its cleansing stream so that its undertow might carry me straight to the throne.

⁷He allows His glory to fall like showers of rain upon the just—and they return unto Him as a surging river.

⁸The purifying Word of God bathes me daily—washing away my impurities—scrubbing away the pollution of the world that has tainted my soul.

⁹His daily presence ignites the hope of heaven within my heart—it lifts my head up to see the glorious view—instead of the weariness of my feet.

¹⁰My prayer, O God—is that my thoughts would forever be vigilant toward You—let them look for You like a bird dog after his prey.

¹¹Nudge my thoughts when they lose their focus on You, O Lord.

¹²When the burdens grow greater—teach me—yes, help me not to shrink back from all You have purposed for me.

¹³I will walk in faithfulness to Your Word—recalling all of Your promises but never recanting my commitment to You, my God.

¹⁴To the saint Your presence is transforming power—to the ungodly it is nothing more than a doormat to tread upon.

¹⁵Your presence is a light in the room that illuminates every dark corner—where shadows have to take flight.

¹⁶It exposes evil and brings it into light—it shines brightness upon righteousness and brings warmth to the heart.

¹⁷My thoughts of You—my Lord—run rampant and free—like a young goat on a hillside—frolicking and kicking up its heels in the breeze.

¹⁸Holy Spirit—You are the anchor of my soul—keep me tethered by a very short rope so I will not drift from the center of my joy.

Psalm 130

A Passionate Heart Is Above All

¹Why does the wicked man seem to prosper and the sinner flourish?—only because the sin within has not sprouted its own seeds of self destruction.

²For many, the pain called change is a bridge to growth—knowledge is only a handrail.

³Do not let your mind wander too far from the truth—it is evident all around us—it waits for you to reach up and salute it sharply.

⁴What if that homeless one you met was God in disguise—would you now want to befriend that person?

⁵Or your fellow man, who was having a bad day, lashed out at you—would you still speak unkindly to him if you knew it was a test from the Almighty?

⁶Remember—His ways are above ours—His works are often in the unconventional realm—so take every opportunity to praise Him—let each circumstance glorify Him.

⁷You, O Lord—occupy the depths of my being—Your presence dwells there continually—the peace You bring is my constant comfort.

⁸The paths of my God are up the mountains of glory—they are lined with the flowers of praise

and the fruit trees of righteousness.

⁹The righteous man has been satisfied in his incompleteness of knowledge—for he knows his earthly knowledge will never be fully realized.

¹⁰His call unto me leads deeper—below the surface—His Word is my root structure and it is well established in the vine.

¹¹I call out to You, O Lord—save me from myself—lest I am destroyed by condemnation—it is merely a spear offered by the enemy.

¹²You heard my cry and came hastily to liberate me—Your mercy has pardoned me.

¹³He chooses and sets apart the humble—His Spirit has recognized them as such—they are overlooked and cast down by the worldly ones.

¹⁴Their commitment to excellence has caught His eye—He has taken notice of their deepest longings and is pleased.

¹⁵God gives a heart of knowledge and understanding to those who seek to please Him—to all whose desires are pure.

¹⁶O God—You fill the whole earth with Your glory—and the heavens are covered with Your likeness—the presence of omnipotent Jehovah.

¹⁷Even as Your Spirit covers the earth, it is searching for an eager heart —one that is fervent to be filled— one that is passionate with desire for Your intimacy.

¹⁸He enables my voice to be a sweet and mighty sound unto His ear— with power it shall rattle the windows of heaven—with authority it will ring out His praise.

¹⁹He has promised, "to those who lift high My name—who exalt Me unashamedly—to them I will give a lion's share of My blessing.

²⁰I have commanded that your witness be more powerful than an eloquent sermon—speak volumes without saying a word—let it be made strong through the absence of sin."

²¹The mind of God knows a man's heart long before his actions can reveal it—before his heart shows its true colors.

²²A man with an unteachable spirit is bound by ignorance—he is destined to learn nothing—Lord, create within me a teachable heart and a willing spirit.

23Lift me up when I have fallen—pick me up so I might stand—place me right into the hollow of Your great and mighty hand.

24Keep me safe from foes around me—banish fear and all alarm—now I'm blessed within the safety of Your everlasting arms.

Psalm 131

Take Charge Of My Thoughts, O God

1Each time my thoughts are directionless and inconsistent—when they drift away from Your ways—I am vexed that I have somehow fallen short and let You down.

2Why does my mind want to go places without my permission—like a wandering child who constantly wants to go out and play?

3I shame it in front of You, my God, and ask for Your help in controlling it.

4Take charge of my thoughts—as one might take the hand of a child and lead him on a correct path—make the desires of my mind line up with the desires of Your heart.

5The seeds of doubt and discouragement are from below—courtesy of the enemy of my soul—Your light, O God—always shines encouragement on me from above.

6Condemnation is the devil's acid—it eats away at the spirit of a man just like muriatic acid would on concrete or stone.

7My soul will ever praise You when my mind has let me down—when my memory has faded and life has turned upside down.

8You place within me Your Holy Spirit, who sustains me—He will stir me each time my mental faculties fail—my spirit will respond with a heart of praise to my God.

9Let me endeavor to narrow my thoughts into a focused beam upon the Lover of my soul—let Him infiltrate my mindset.

10And should my voice grow silent—speak into my soul words of wisdom and my voice will once again verify righteousness—making known all that You have intended.

11The godly do not concern themselves with the course they take—they walk closely with the Master and are confident in His leading.

¹²The shining splendor of the Lord Most High has pierced the darkness with brilliance and distinction in order to shine into the hearts of those who seek Him wholeheartedly.

¹³Days without end—O Ancient of Days—that is Your name and who You are—Your righteousness began before time was set in motion.

¹⁴You established Your Word and the worlds out of truth—I have only caught a glimpse of them both—You have spread them past the horizon in a jaw-dropping display.

Psalm 132

I Will Glory In Your Power

¹It is the wise man who refrains from speaking words he does not want others to remember or repeat—he has learned how to stifle his tongue with grace.

²Hindsight has proven you can seldom keep people from shooting at you—prudence instructs you not to hand them the ammunition to do it with.

³When you are in the den of lions—never look them in the eyes—you might see how big their teeth are and lose all hope.

⁴Let go of your search for mastery—it only brings momentary pleasure—instead search for the Master with the same intensity and find genuine fulfillment.

⁵I strive for all words coming from my mouth—sentiments flowing from the fountains of my heart—thoughts off the top of my head—to bring God glory.

⁶If the Holy Spirit does not move upon them—let them be slain and crucified—never to rise again—pour Your anointing on the words that issue forth from within me.

⁷You afford peace to the settled mind and contentment to the committed soul.

⁸The words of my God are sweeter than the most magnificent music heard on earth—they bring instruction and nourishment—they sustain my soul when the tide is low.

⁹His seal of approval has endorsed my life—He championed my cause—He vouched for me to

Psalm 132 - I Will Glory In Your Power

those who opposed me—His endorsement has been my reward.

10 He has marked my report card with truth and accuracy—His evaluation is certainty—with forthrightness He has given me a fitting value.

11 I lift the cup of my soul unto You, O Lord—fill it with the sweetness of Your love—full it to the brim so that even when jostled—it can only spill out sweetness.

12 All those who walk in righteousness have been clothed in splendor—His robe is a priestly robe—not made of burlap but rather of luxurious velvet.

13 They will learn to walk the way of royalty—with regal stride they bear the mark of the Priestly One.

14 When they encounter unrighteousness—they throw it off quickly so it will not stain their imperial robes.

15 How costly is this garment of splendor?—there is no cost except to the One who purchased it—and to think He offers it free of charge—how awesome is the love of God!

16 Often the voice of my God has come to me in a hushed and holy whisper—yet it is of no avail unless I have quieted my mind to hear it.

17 Teach me, Lord, to have a serene and tranquil spirit—let Your peace and quietness reign supreme within my soul.

18 Holy Spirit—be that brigade that drives away the interference surrounding me—turn the chaos into tranquility.

19 You alone, O Lord, are my strength—You do not despise or look upon my weakness with disgust—You have made me and You find glory in it.

20 I will glory in Your power, my God, and praise Your righteousness all the day long—I am in Your never-ending debt.

21 A starlit night begins each and every one of my days—You have planned and marked my course with a certainty as sure as that.

22 You have seen to it that my days are filled with chances to praise Your greatness.

23 Regret has shamed me and would have held me captive over missed opportunities to draw closer to You if Your mercy had not rescued me.

24 I will praise You all the more in my latter days—for should they not be greater than the former days?

Psalm 133 - Hope For Our Helplessness

²⁵Your compassion has looked upon my weaknesses with pity and understanding.

²⁶The difficulty of my journey has not been lost to You—You have documented my weariness well—it has provided occasions to rest upon Your bosom.

Psalm 133

Hope For Our Helplessness

¹We are Your people—created by the hand of the Most High—truly a delicate and fragile people.

²You did not form us from the granite rock of the earth—but rather from the soil of the ground.

³You did not found our nature on strongholds—but upon weakness and dependency.

⁴You have given us good reason to rely on Your strength—we are completely without recourse and entirely at Your mercy.

⁵Your established Your Word upon truth and beauty—strength and power.

⁶Omnipotence has been Your footing—Your dominion has reigned supreme for all eternity—time without end stands at Your right hand.

⁷Sovereignty has become Your right arm—all authority has surrendered to You—who of all people is able to reason with Your wisdom?

⁸You have left our vulnerabilities exposed — they have become our soft underbellies — uncovering our helplessness.

⁹Wisdom is able to teach us reliance on Your might—but only if our pride will tolerate it—as we trust in You, teach us to set aside our conceit and vanity.

¹⁰You created mankind for closeness with his Creator—whether or not he takes advantage of this desire is up to his free will.

¹¹As for me—I am cashing in all my chips for my God—I willingly exchange my life for one roll of His dice;

¹²Days full of purpose with the Great I AM are far superior to a game of chance.

¹³Direct us, O Lord—in areas of Your Spirit—let us clearly see the futility of our feelings—for they are more fragile—and even less reliable—than fine spun glass.

¹⁴Ground us upon the certainty of Your Word—only in that alone can we hope to find safety and security from all that would buffet us and strength for our helplessness.

Psalm 134

You Guide Our Days 'Til Eternity

¹Your love, O Lord—has lifted me higher—it has raised my soul unto a heavenly place—the glories of Your grace have bathed and washed it clean.

²I rejoice in the splendor of each new day—I look unflinchingly into the face of it to see the face of my God.

³You stir Your wonders of might and majesty deep within me like a cook stirs a pot of stew on the stove.

⁴I no longer consume energy planning my day—You have mapped it out for me.

⁵Although I do not know where it leads—my strong confidence is in Your guidance—praise the Lord—O my soul—praise the Lord.

⁶The stillness of the daybreak wraps me like a warm blanket on a frosty morning—yes, even the silence speaks to me—Your words rouse my spirit.

⁷Your blessed quietness brings rest to my mind—it becomes a clear channel that I use to direct my thoughts toward You.

⁸O the wonder of it all—when I am lost within Your presence—all of heaven and earth seem to flee and I am left alone with the awesomeness of You—my God.

⁹Could it really be that You have looked upon me with such love and compassion—that the Almighty has reached down to touch my soul?

¹⁰How embarrassed I am that the great King would even look upon me—and with such wondrous love—greater than any mortal man has known.

Psalm 134 - You Guide Our Days 'Til Eternity

¹¹I will praise Him—yes I will praise Him—for He has made me the delight of His heart—O praise His righteousness and honor.

¹²Lord—You know my heart even when my lips speak otherwise—let the motives of my heart line up with the words of my mouth—and may they both be honoring unto You.

¹³Are the godly perfect—or do we have flaws and fractures to deal with?—as creatures of clay we are imperfect and flawed and have limited capabilities.

¹⁴We have allowed the Holy Spirit to live in those areas between the cracks and fractures of our souls—He has become the glue that holds them together.

¹⁵The anguish of life disappears when He turns it into a song of jubilant praise.

¹⁶The light of my new home shines brightly upon my heart—the glory of it I have seen afar off—it shines upon the trail I must take to reach my new home.

¹⁷Blessed are they who are not offended by the love of the Father—that marvelous hope He has sown like good seed upon their garden.

¹⁸Blessed are they who are greedy for the voice of God—they pass through life listening for Him on any occasion—how they hunger for His Word and righteousness.

¹⁹Restore lushness to my barren thoughts whenever they wander from Your goodness—refresh my mind with the reservoir of Your joy.

²⁰Your Word, O God—speaks to me even in judgment—it corrects and shows me the error of my ways—it leads me into understanding.

²¹At times the prophecy of a man can be judged false rather quickly—other times it may not be revealed until the Day of Judgment.

²²The prophet is not quick to pass judgment—nor is he swift to pass on a word he has received unless it has been sanctioned by the Holy Spirit.

²³I have seen the shadow of His hand as a result of the light of His glory—what a divine joy to know He is nearby.

²⁴Day and night His presence hems me in—hiding me within the folds of His garment—He wraps me in peace and safety—why would I want to leave His safety at any time?

²⁵He is passing by—though you cannot see Him—pausing—He waits for you to call out to Him—go ahead—for He is tender and forgiving.

²⁶His grace is simply amazing—do not shove it to the side or tread it with disgust—He has set aside this opening so that you might step forward and walk through it.

²⁷Do not continue to reject God or He may tell you that you are on your own—then what will you do?

²⁸God sometimes uses others to fertilize your garden—to cultivate your plantings—to water your roots—but you must allow it—they are the gardeners of His wisdom.

²⁹"I, the Lord your God, will hide My face to those who refuse to acknowledge Me—to those who profess Me with their actions I will be a light in their darkness."

Psalm 135

He Is Pleased With A Sincere Offering

¹Nonsense flows from the lips of a fool—a wise man carefully measures his words.

²It is the simple-minded person who hangs on to the notion that he is of no use to God—that has become one of the most successful wiles of the enemy.

³The wise have discovered that God loves them in spite of their quirks and inabilities—their futilities and inadequacies are no barriers against His love.

⁴Who has never received one blessing from the hand of God?—those who happen to forget the gift of life are quickly trapped by their own foolish thinking.

⁵Always direct your thoughts toward God—whether in your leanest or your fattest of times—He is worthy of praise at all times—so pour out your heartfelt praise to Him.

⁶Acknowledge His greatness—that is one sure way to get His attention—He loves to hear your accolades.

⁷The cross of Christ serves as much more than a mere safety net—it stands as a bulwark of salvation for all mankind who would venture beneath its shadow.

Psalm 135 - He Is Pleased With A Sincere Offering

⁸The blood of Christ—the Lamb of God—did more than blot away the sins of man—it purges them completely for those who have received it on the doorposts of their hearts.

⁹God's great faithfulness surpasses anything man could hope to imagine—we have failed to see its limits—the eyes of our hearts have not beheld its vastness.

¹⁰Blessed are they who have found the fullness of their God—because they seek Him unceasingly He has granted them their portion—He has served them with abundant grace.

¹¹Give favor to the steps of Your servants, O God—so they might walk in Your ways all of their days—and pass on the faith of their hearts to those around them.

¹²He has set His royal canopy over the heads of those who walk in the ways of the Lord—their lives of simplicity pale with His plans for them in His everlasting kingdom.

¹³They have allowed their lives of faith to guide their footsteps—casting aside lives of ease and earthly reward—they have responded to a heavenly call.

¹⁴Futility has nipped at their heels—but they plod on resolutely—You have given their souls encouragement through Your heavenly light.

¹⁵You have called them upward to a life of glory seeing they have forsaken all to follow You—where their hearts will never want for gladness again.

¹⁶The security of the godly is not found in their righteous works—but solely in the faithfulness of their God and His amazing grace.

¹⁷It is not with a beautiful voice that I offer a love song to my God—I am lacking this instrument that I might vocalize well for Him—I have only a heart of worship to offer.

¹⁸Yet I know He will be pleased with my offering—for it comes with eagerness and not reluctance—I am intent on turning my heart unto His will so He will be overjoyed.

¹⁹And when my heart and flesh grow weak—my God will support and sustain me—my spirit will grow stronger still as He becomes my subsidy.

Psalm 136

You Speak Boldly In The Quietness Of My Soul

¹Today He awakened me with a fresh stirring in my soul—a new resurgence of the close presence of my God—and how it did quicken my spirit.

²He stilled and quieted my soul before Him—He sedated my spirit with His glory and brought it into alliance with His.

³Then with trembling voice I spoke this question to Him—why doesn't my voice lift high Your praises more often—why at times is it hushed in silence?

⁴His reply did not linger—it brought immediate comfort to my soul and had no chastisement in it—it sent reassurance my way and placed a quiet confidence within me.

⁵Nonetheless, His Word came with boldness—it did not hold back His response—He said, "can you hear the rowdy shouts of your spirit as it exalts Me in the dance?

⁶Have you ever seen it fling aside all its dignity, kick up its heels, and cut loose across the ballroom floor of heaven?

⁷Are you able to make out the deepest longings of your soul as it cries unto Me—have you heard it rooting and cheering my praises while you go about your daily job?

⁸Were you eavesdropping when your body talked with Me in the stillness of the night in language you could not possibly comprehend?

⁹Tell Me when you have overheard it exclaiming My greatness unto the heavenly hosts?—my how it filled the heavenlies with praise.

¹⁰Obviously you are unable to hear when your strength speaks to Me with an elated voice and exalts My worthiness—it sings My virtues aloud when it is feeling weak.

¹¹Can you listen in while your mind is at rest—can you hear those occasions when it rouses the angels of My Kingdom to rally around and join it as it expounds My loftiness?

¹²Are you able to fathom that your mind divulges your praises unto Me while you sleep?—you express your worship unto Me even during your subconscious times.

¹³Have you ever watched your soul come before Me in humbleness simply to bear witness of My renown and honor?

¹⁴Has your spirit given you insight into its communion with Me—and shown you some of our closest encounters—when it was enraptured before My presence?

¹⁵I, the Lord your God, know all these things and many more—which I will make known in the days to come.

¹⁶Remain in Me—stay on course—and I will constantly inhabit each of your praises—I will lift up those who choose to honor Me."

Psalm 137

You Have Written Your Love Upon My Heart

¹Today I will set my mind upon seeking the Lord—it will be my goal to bring Him pleasure through all I say and do—to know Him in close fellowship.

²My soul gets its stamina from Him—His reassurance is my booster—He breathes new life into my spirit the weaker my humanity grows—in frailty I will praise Him.

³I am like the flower—here today—tomorrow I will be in His garden—He has transplanted me into His Kingdom.

⁴The radiance of the godly will shine like the stars in heaven—He has scattered them across His neighborhood—causing them to give off light wherever He has placed them.

⁵The howling winds of the storm still prevail—but He has tucked me inside His cave—which is hewn from the Rock of Ages.

⁶He is my light and my comfort in its darkness—His hand shields its entrance so I will feel no alarm.

⁷New meaning and understanding come to those who search Your Word daily—to those who are guided by Your Holy Spirit.

⁸The Lord has lifted up my soul—He has encouraged me to take another step—His Word shows me the right way to go.

⁹He redeems my ways and removes the dark clouds that obscure His handiwork—His worthiness swallows up my desires.

¹⁰My thoughts of Him are better than the shouted words of man—He directs them on a heavenward path and anoints them with purpose.

¹¹He honors the thoughts and intents of the godly—they please Him and achieve His purpose in their lives—He bears witness that what they have done is worthwhile.

¹²Sit quietly in His presence and be strengthened by it—wait in the silence and listen for His still small voice.

¹³This time of communion with your God weakens the strongholds of the enemy—it causes the very foundations of the powers of darkness to shake and begin to crumble.

¹⁴The whole earth is radiant with His glory—indeed the universe is alive with His presence—it exposes the evil deeds of darkness—which try to flee His revealing light.

¹⁵His glory fills those places I have set aside with honor for His majesty.

¹⁶You have made the godly stand out as a mark of Your grace—a flagpole of Your mercy.

¹⁷We may be crude and ungainly as a flagstaff—nevertheless we are the bearers of Your Gospel—the banner of Your truth.

¹⁸To those who have yielded their hearts to Him—His pardon has flowed over their sins like the mighty Niagara—it has washed them into the sea of God's forgetfulness.

¹⁹The blood of Calvary's Lamb has more than whited out our sins and transgressions—it has removed them—as if they were never there—O praise the Lamb of Glory.

²⁰This amazing grace provides full remittance—if we will only ask for it.

²¹He has dealt in love with our pitiful mistakes and willingly grants us forgiveness.

²²My God—the Mighty One—the Alpha and Omega—has lovingly sandwiched us between His eternal arms.

²³What He has started He will complete with splendor and majesty—what has He begun that He will not finish?

²⁴He writes His words upon the hearts of the godly—He places them there for us to read in times of sorrow and despair—an antidote against all fear.

Psalm 138

His Continual Presence Becomes My Pledge

¹When I came to that desolate place I could not find You—I was unable to see You because my eyes were closed from weeping.

²Then You opened my eyes and dried my tears—You spoke unto my condition and I gained courage to go on.

³The narrow path demands a focused view whereas the broad path eliminates the need for restraint—it curtails the urgency for caution.

⁴Forever I will lift my voice—proclaiming that You, my God, have been my choice—I will praise You and rejoice with never-ending gladness.

⁵The light of His love shines upon our many trials—not with a pot of gold at the end of the rainbow—but with a rainbow of grace to counter each test.

⁶He applies the many colors of His rainbow against the many hard times that come our way—He has covered them one and all.

⁷Death holds no terror for the slave who has not been freed from his master—it has also become a haven for those riddled by disease.

⁸My life has been filled with good cheer but never more so than now—I will keep Your words to me private but not Your deeds—I will let them ring out with my praises.

⁹Holy Spirit come—come in strength and power—Holy Spirit come—come and light the way.

¹⁰I have seen the light of Your glory shining upon the faces of Your older saints—it is a light unto all who pass by them.

¹¹To some it may be like the twinkling of the stars upon a darkened sky—to others it may be more like the brilliance of the full moon against a cloudless sky.

¹²They have honored You with their lives unto the very end and the luminance of Your Spirit has reflected off the face of their souls.

¹³Your purpose, O God—has been fully realized within their lives and You have blessed their faithfulness both now and for eternity.

¹⁴They have bloomed like glorious flowers for a season—then Your wings of mercy will carry them to their eternal resting place with grace.

15 I have unfulfilled dreams that I place at Your feet—You have promised each one will come to fruition in Your time—at Your command they shall all come to pass.

16 When I awake upon my bed—long before the sun has undertaken the task of covering my side of the earth—You are already there.

17 You have been at my side throughout the watches of the night—as attentive to my safety and comfort as a mother beside her sick baby.

18 When I sleep You send Your angels to stand guard over me—if I am stirring during the night You are there at my side.

19 At the whisper of Your name You draw even closer—this is too marvelous for me to know—that the Creator of this world would care for me—O praise Your name.

20 It is during the stillness of the night that You refresh my soul—Your presence revitalizes my mind and body—like the dew upon the grasses of the earth.

21 Early in the morning—even before the light of day—You examine me—much like a physician goes over his patient with a fine-toothed comb.

22 You bring to light my shortcomings—though they never surprise You—throughout the day You test and try me in order to know my heart and where its pleasures are found.

23 My Lord—my God—today I look for You to be the teacher of my class—the scout master of my troop—the head at my table—the chief of my tribe.

24 O, that You would be all I have ever needed and longed for—be both my greatest fulfilled and unfulfilled desire—You are my utmost satisfaction.

25 Even if the adversities of the Almighty fall heavy upon me—my heart will still trust Him—when His reasons remain hidden—His continual presence becomes my pledge.

26 I consecrate my weaknesses unto You—so You can plug Your power into my vessel and shine Your light through me.

27 The light of God's Word leads straight to the heart of the godly—exposing His desires to those who follow His statutes.

28 The righteous man awaits his heavenly dispatch with eager anticipation because his eyes of faith have not grown dim.

Psalm 139

If I Should Die Before I Wake...

¹I will lie down in quiet repose—yielding myself unto peaceful slumber.

²And if I should not awake in this mortal flesh then I will be content knowing He has finished His work in me.

³He will then awaken me with joy on the other shore—prepared for eternal life everlasting in His presence—so do not cry tears of sadness for me when I am gone.

⁴I know the sleep of the godly is sweet—but how much more is that rest in the Rock of Ages—the Lover of my soul?

⁵When I lay upon that bed of death may my Creator be blessed by my final words of praise unto Him—let my ending thoughts be focused on His greatness.

⁶As a cup of coffee is good unto the last drop—so let my life glorify Him in my closing moments—so that I may be like a dishcloth completely wrung out.

⁷His thoughts have been my companion and His Word my strength—His blessing upon my life has come through a span of music and words He has poured out through me.

⁸Now I yield my life—body—soul—spirit—and mind unto His will so He will receive all glory and honor due Him.

⁹Serving Him has been a pleasure above all pleasures—without measure—leading unto eternal treasure.

Psalm 140

The Tenets Of Godly Wisdom

¹The wise man refuses to give his worries a voice—he puts them in a garbage bag and leaves them on the curb for the trash collector.

²Never blame the weatherman for his forecast—he just reports what he

sees—One much higher than he controls the elements and directs them with precision.

³The words of a foolish man are quick to tear down—they are like a handsaw with a dull and rusty blade—serving no useful purpose.

⁴Words from the godly are weighed carefully—they are used to instigate hope and to spur on belief—they are like salve to a wound—they build up and do not destroy.

⁵The fool takes great delight in irritating others—he finds much pleasure in the discomfort of others—caring not whether he causes ill will.

⁶How wise are they who choose to focus on things of the Spirit that unite us rather than the petty issues that only serve to divide!

⁷Everyday trials are common threads that unite us—the Lord makes us into the garment of righteousness through them.

⁸The man with understanding has learned that victory is often the result of multiplied failures—he declines to let the past take his focus off the future.

⁹While arrogance and conceit create a center of attention for the enemy to delight in—love will find a way to draw the Holy Spirit near to your heart.

¹⁰Those who spend time with knowledgeable people will become like them—but whoever hangs around unsavory characters will be in for a migraine.

¹¹The pressures of trouble place immense demands on your faith—all the while revealing the true depth of it.

¹²The righteous are able to exchange resentment for rejoicing because they have found grace that will move them outside of suffering.

¹³Kindness is the currency of heaven and those who use it heap big dividends—those who receive it are blessed in turn.

¹⁴Each kind deed—word—or thought is a step in the journey that leads to everlasting life for His saints—before long those steps have amounted to miles.

¹⁵Truthfulness and integrity are the windows through which we can peer into the souls of the godly.

¹⁶When a ray of gloom is cast toward the righteous they are able to deflect it by becoming pillars of happiness.

¹⁷Humor soothes a weary soul the same way ointment relieves a burn.

¹⁸The foolish man's gold will perish with him—his treasures will vanish because he has hoarded them.

¹⁹The wise will be doubly blessed because they have learned to share their belongings with a generous heart.

²⁰They who have nothing left but God will find they still have more than enough.

²¹The provision of food for these earthly bodies is a byproduct of God's goodness and blessing.

²²How can the bee feast from the nectar of the flower unless the flower has opened its petals?—so it is with Your Word, O God—to those who hunger after You.

²³As a steak is seared to seal the juices in—burn Your Word within my soul, O God—so it will produce tastiness and full flavor.

²⁴Wisdom teaches a man to gain a close familiarity with his problems so they will not become his downfall—they will become the teacher and he will be the student.

²⁵He will accept troubles as a pesky family member and then introduce them to the Rock upon which he leans—his trust will be rewarded with victory.

²⁶He who trusts the Lord his God is freed from many anxieties—he does not multiply his sorrows many times by rehearsing them beforehand.

²⁷Do not waste your strength on worry—it only saps your energy and accomplishes nothing—trust in the Lord's might—and by His power you will find strength to spare.

²⁸Malice is the drug of choice to the vindictive soul—it has chosen to harbor animosity and forsake forgiveness.

²⁹The blessing of the Lord accompanies every gift of a generous heart—He is quick to cause it to multiply many times over—unbeknownst to the giver.

³⁰Basking in the sun is of limited appeal—basking in the presence of the Son is of eternal significance.

³¹Be vigilant and sober—do not glance back too often to view your footprints—for by doing so you may run into an obstacle in front of you.

³²God blesses the godly with a forgetful mind—they are quick to forget injustices and insults that have been done to them.

33A hasty decision—who can undo it?—the Lord has been known to turn it out for good in the lives of those who have a heart turned to Him.

34Who can put a number on life's aggravations—who can count that cost?—to the untrusting heart the price may be one of ulcers.

35Do not waste time on regret—for who can change what is done?—take a little time for planning and you will not be as apt to stumble and fall.

36The actions of a fool will trip him up—they will expose his ignorance without him saying a word.

37A joyful heart has become the laughter of heaven—even while here on earth it will clang the bells of mirth.

38He halts the steps of His faithful ones so they will ponder His desires and not slip past His care.

39Aches and pains are God's way of reminding us of how glorious heaven will be.

Psalm 141

You Fill My Temple With Glory

1The children of heaven have come to earth to sing the songs of Zion—with the voices of angels they sing heaven's praises.

2My God—what does it take to know Your power—in the depths of my soul—in the closest distance from Your heart to mine?

3Show me the answer to this—my deepest desire—then I will be filled with the fullness of Your presence.

4The brightness of Your glory shines across my path—pointing my soul upward.

5This shining path—which stretches upward and leads to the heart of my God—shines all the more the longer I travel it.

6I have had sweet communion with my God in the garden of my heart—it is there that we visit and speak the depths of our hearts to each other.

7None of my concerns ever put Him off—while He confers to me the measure of His heart—the pas-

Psalm 141 - You Fill My Temple With Glory

sions of mine spill over into the recesses of His heart.

8 With divine foresight He watches over my soul—with great deliberation His Spirit has raised mine to new heights—His watchfulness has protected me with great care.

9 Who is there like my God—who can glean joy out of the midst of sorrow—and peace from deep inside troubles?—He alone can direct life to come forth from death.

10 By His command He causes galaxies to form—molecules to come together in alignment with His purpose.

11 Although my God dwells in—and is at home among the multitudes of stars He created—He is equally at home and loves to inhabit the lower regions—which He made.

12 He has chosen to take up residence within those who have opened the door and welcomed Him with open arms.

13 His truth is my strength—His Word is my lookout—for He guards my habitation at all times —He has made me His inheritance.

14 I will look beyond the afflictions of this present life—clear past the things I can see—all the way to the light of glory.

15 His hand has placed me upon that solid Rock—which cannot be moved through all eternity and beyond.

16 In His search to find a heart abandoned only unto Him—He will move all of heaven and earth if necessary—to accomplish His purpose.

17 He covers my soul with the shade of night—there it finds a respite from the heat of the day—from the tedium of sorrow that scorches it.

18 His peace sets my mind at ease— He anoints me with new freedoms while He bathes me in His glories.

19 The Lord has set me on a high place —He has carried me up the mountains when the fogs of the valley have surrounded me—when the heavy mists encompass me.

20 He takes me into a mountain clearing—there my soul will rejoice in His greatness and marvel in the beauty of His creation.

21 I will lift my spirit in adoration to His majesty—blessed be the name of my God.

22 He has clothed me with righteousness and called me to a higher purpose.

²³I lift my face to You, my God—I have found Your ways to be delightful—they are the paths my feet long to take.

²⁴How can my countenance help but shine with gratefulness—You fill my temple with glory—Your presence is the missing link.

²⁵My God—You are my greatest desire—the throbbing of my heart—unto my final breath I will exalt You.

²⁶His Spirit has caused me to rise up in desperation—to throw off sleep—like a bull throws a rider off his back.

²⁷He has made me to walk the lonely path so that I will never lose sight of things eternal—He has walked the forsaken way before me.

Psalm 142

The Heavenlies Testify To Your Truth

¹The truth of the Almighty marches on—through darkness and light—it is not shackled by desperation—nor impeded by brick walls—it is not stopped by gates of iron.

²It marches on in the hearts of man and travels from here to yon—it is shared through the light of actions and deeds—at times it does not even need spoken words.

³Teach me to listen—so I can hear Your voice—slow the rushing of my words and the multitude of my petitions.

⁴Today in the quietness I give You such as I have—my heart—my life—my soul.

⁵I will let my spirit speak to You of the visions of my heart—the unformulated depths of my soul—the jumbled chaos of my mind—the reserved thoughts of my intellect.

⁶Then I will speak unto You with truth and honesty—all that lies hidden from view—the hidden thoughts and secrets of my heart—let them heap blessings upon You, O God.

⁷Lead me this day, Heavenly Father—show me Your precious truth—Your deeds have crusaded across the universe with precision.

⁸The way of greatness has been Your path for all eternity—You have

known no other—You do not walk as a man—You do not stumble in Your steps.

⁹All who have peered through the eye of a telescope have seen Your wonders displayed in the heavenlies—they have caught a glimpse of Your paths into other worlds.

¹⁰Even when I read about the galaxies that abound beyond our world—I am awestruck—surely the universe is not a big enough canvas on which to display Your true greatness.

¹¹The extent of the works of Your hands has left us in starry-eyed wonder—how can we contemplate even a fraction of Your enormity?

¹²The telltale signs of Your greatness are enlarged each time we view the vastness of Your creation—my soul can scarcely take it all in.

¹³My mind was not prepared for the revelation of Your majesty—so You allowed my soul to dwell upon its awesomeness—surely I was humbled and brought low by it all.

¹⁴Even my mind's eye was not made privy to all of Your glories—they scatter so far abroad that these earthly eyes have not even skimmed the surface of all Your creation.

¹⁵You have filled our world to capacity with evidences of Your immenseness—Your far-reaching grandeurs have dazzled our eyes—giving only a taste of what is to come.

¹⁶Which camera is able to capture that true heavenly "Kodak moment"—do not all lenses fall short of portraying God's greatness?

¹⁷I will lift my soul in joyous delight knowing that no earthly rapture can convey Your glories—nor adequately reveal Your true worth.

¹⁸How I praise You, my God, and magnify Your name—You have blessed my soul beyond description—my spirit dances before You with lightness of step.

¹⁹My faith has reached high—toward the stars in the heavens of my soul—some glimmer dimly while others shine so brightly.

²⁰You, O Lord—have placed them there to be markers along my journey—they are the shining authority of Your will and purpose—guiding lights that show Your truth.

²¹Truth has been a testament of Your Word and will govern and rule in the lives of all who yield themselves to it.

Psalm 143

My Soul Worships You In The Safety Of Your Arms

¹The angels of the Most High attend to the needs of those who trust in Him because He is pleased by the faith of His children.

²Any time we see the fangs of the enemy and hear the snarling of his growl—we can trust in our Good Shepherd who shows us our safety.

³His arms of protection have kept the wolf at bay—His conquering voice has caused him to flee—His Word speaks forth reassurance that all is well.

⁴He rules mightily throughout the heavens above—He also rules the earth below—there is no place where His arm is short and His might is not seen or felt.

⁵By His Word He has vindicated the righteous—by His judgment He pleads their case—His justice has set them free in liberty.

⁶What can I bring before Him—what can I offer Him that will be pleasing—how can I give Him joy?

⁷I will bring Him my finest sacrifice of praise—my most sincere heart of thanksgiving—with that He will surely not turn me away.

⁸My worship to Him will rise upward like the daily offerings—like the scent of a burning campfire—it will be pleasing to my God.

⁹I will worship You, my Lord—my Savior and my God—there is none other that compares with You.

¹⁰You have added the fat of health unto my bones so that I may praise You all my days—so that my voice will never grow silent in exhaustion.

¹¹Do not let my heart forget its victories—let my mind quickly recall Your miraculous feats—those that display the strength of Your hands and the power of Your right arm.

¹²I have believed Your truth—my heart will sing Your praises—my mind will refresh itself with the wonders of Your love.

¹³Let the inner parts of my soul be filled with Your glory—no areas be left unmoved.

¹⁴I will play sweetly upon the organ—dedicating the hands that play it and the heart from which harmonious worship emanates—in reverence and holiness I will exalt Him.

¹⁵Let the desires of my heart and the prayers from my lips come before You—not as noise—but rather as a sweet song and a pleasant aroma.

¹⁶The stillness of the morning carries my worship to You, my God—as my eyes are wet with tears and my soul ponders Your greatness—Your words have blessed my soul.

¹⁷My God—it is Your voice that falls so sweetly on my ear—the voice that draws my heart to Yours—the sound that strikes my heart strings with beautiful music.

¹⁸I will listen intently for it—like a lost seaman listens for the foghorn and welcomes it with his life—he will follow it all the way to a place of safety.

¹⁹He shelters me in the palm of His hand and there is room to spare.

²⁰My God is greater than the most extreme hopelessness to be found—greater than the depths of disparity.

²¹There are hidden springs within my soul reserved for me by my Creator—many streams flow from their abundance.

²²Along this path I walk are various plantings—all of which get their nourishment from this life-giving water.

²³Blessings are received freely by those who walk in the chosen way—their lives are resolute and with direction.

²⁴Those who are wise have learned how to receive a blessing as well as how to be one—they are happy to give others their occasion to shine forth.

Where life shall reign forever [a poem]

O hope of God my glorious light – the joy of life not squandered
My eyes behold few precious sights with much more to be pondered

When faith stands on that distant shore and nothing else can sever
The peace and joy of God Himself – where life shall reign forever

Psalm 144

You Are My Father

[1] You have been the God of my fathers throughout the ages—since before my birth.

[2] Your hand was quick to guide them whenever they called out to You—each and every time they followed Your commands.

[3] All who sought You found You accessible—You even showed light to those who went their own way—the wooing of Your Spirit drew them unto You.

[4] Sometimes their days were marked with futility—their strength was not Your equal—the wisdom they possessed was not always well used.

[5] You bathed their days with sunshine and rain—Your bounty was their blessing.

[6] You bid all who followed Your ways to come closer—many were satisfied with seeing You from a distance—they didn't crave You like You desired.

[7] You, O Lord, have begotten me—to add to their lineage—to bring about a passion You have desired—I am but a branch You have grafted in.

[8] Let me be that one You are searching for—with diligent heart and steadfast soul—the kindred spirit drawn closer than life itself.

[9] You, my God, are all I could ever need—You are my joy and sweetness—You are more satisfying than a chocolate malted shake or a Hershey candy bar.

[10] Your Word is my food—the meat and potatoes of my life—the nourishment I need.

[11] You are my Father—without You I have no life—my heart will ever praise You—You are the fulfillment of my greatest desire.

[12] I will bless Your name each time I recall Your goodness—every time I reach an understanding of Your greatness.

[13] Let my praises be uplifting—by my praise You are exalted—I honor You with my life—for what else do I have to offer?

[14] Flush my mind free of contaminants so it will be pure and clean before You.

[15] The steps of a feeble man are shored up by his friend—his life is made rich by his benefactor—his spirit is encouraged in the land.

Psalm 145

Thank You For My Sufferings

¹I will thank You for the trials standing before me—for I know I will find You in the middle of them.

²When my spiritual eyes are opened—burdens become blessings in disguise—benefits uncovered.

³My God adds peace to my demeanor in the midst of all my afflictions—He relaxes my countenance in spite of them—He has made them to become my joy.

⁴He has not made my thorn in the flesh to depart—instead—He has caused it to become a rainbow unto me—a daily reminder of His love and grace.

⁵Thanksgiving in the midst of suffering is the epitome of our highest praise unto the Master.

⁶I will yet praise Him through all of my trials—He has determined them to be building blocks of my faith—they become opportunities to trust Him more.

⁷Should His saints refuse adversity?—never—they should accept it cheerfully and offer it unto God as their sacrifice of worship—then they will be drawn close to Him.

⁸O Lord, You have risen a conquering champion over the rubble and ruins of my life—You stand triumphant over the offense and pride that would have condemned me.

⁹How I praise You for Your love and Your mercies—they are great and numerous—too many to behold.

¹⁰All day long Your presence sequesters me—in the night You cheer up my spirit—I need You, Father, and long to be the expression of Your glory.

¹¹You have given me a heaping serving of peace so I can rejoice in Your goodness.

¹²Let the spirit of submission and praise be victorious in me so that this would be my finest hour—then You, my God, will be exalted above all.

¹³When my faith is able to see past the eyes of this natural man—then I can clearly see Your glory.

¹⁴My soul will arise and I will bless Your name—both now and forevermore—praise the Lord—O my soul—as I exalt Your righteousness with reverence.

Psalm 146

Remind Us Of Your Awesome Power, O God

¹O God—please become the distance between me and that yonder mountain—stand in between for me—for I do not have the strength to climb it.

²When I almost collapsed—You were there to give me smelling salts—so that I might be able to go on.

³So often it is the small things that trip us up because we feel sufficient in ourselves—we only seek Your power for the large things.

⁴It is the same power of the mighty ocean wave that sweeps over the tiniest grains of sand we confidently walk on—that smashes against the boulder of human insufficiency.

⁵Your power, my God, is mightier than the breath that fills our lungs —although You are in that also.

⁶If I gently blow upon a cold and frosted window pane I can witness Your presence—it is my personal reminder of how close You are.

⁷You receive praise from the ends of the universe—all You have called by name from far and near will praise Your majesty throughout Your Kingdom.

⁸Even the stars and planets You have named—they are Your creations and cannot hold back their praises for Your greatness.

⁹I will praise You all the more—because Your Spirit dwells within my being—praise the Lord—do not be quiet, O my soul.

¹⁰In our eyes this earth upon which we walk is bigger than we can imagine—but in Your eyes it is no larger than a grain of sand at the bottom of the oceans.

¹¹For who is able to measure Your universe—or with what measure can we gauge Your power?

¹²How deep is the love of God—if it is not greater than the worst depravity of mankind—how could He ask us to love our enemies?

¹³There would be no hope for the atrocities of a man's soul if it were not for such a love that my God has shown—it can obliterate the vileness of a repentant heart.

¹⁴You place the righteous in one another's paths so that we may be encouraged and strengthened in our daily walks.

15You allow our paths to cross with those of sinners so we might be a magnet of truth and a light of Your Word unto them.

16The powers of darkness are only for a while longer—they have been ordained for a set time and will not prevail a minute past.

17What is able to strip away those powers of evil—who is able to thwart and stop them in their tracks?—only the King of Kings—He is able!

18We have seen the powers of our God made manifest—they have circled the earth in majesty and triumph—He has displayed His glory from one end to the other.

19It is the prayers of His saints that have aroused His mighty power—they have caused Him to sweep the earth with radiance—they beckon His hosts to come in victory.

20When the brilliance of His light comes it will cause the darkness to scatter with finality—banished to its everlasting destination to be constrained there forever.

21The place of God's abode is peace and love—He furnishes His home with joy everlasting—His heavens continue to declare His magnificence all around His Kingdom.

22The pure in heart are filled with a full measure of His love—they have learned to receive it with thanksgiving.

Psalm 147

Your Light In Our Hearts Shines Through Our Worship

1How I will praise You, my God—not only will my words give voice to You in praise—but the longings of my heart will follow suit.

2You, O Lord—have heard the utterances of the deep places of my soul and have crowned me with power from on high—heavenly ministering has attended me.

3Time slips away to the place You keep it stored when I am lost in Your presence—it disappears quickly like the final moments of a sunset.

4When I sought You I found You to be no further than the whisper of Your name—Your nearness was closer than the breath upon my lips.

⁵Your voice was silent unto me in order that I might humble myself before You—to listen intently and to pray.

⁶Teach me to be comfortable in Your quietude—to know that all is well and that heaven rules supreme over all—it is the reward of the faithful.

⁷My soul meets with God in the beauty of His silence—when my spirit meets His—then I will adore Him in worship.

⁸In awe and reverence I have gathered my soul before Him in pure untainted stillness—basking in its sweetness as everything around me crashes like waves upon the seashore.

⁹There I find rest in His love—comfort in His presence—my heart will not cry out—for it is renewed in Him.

¹⁰Inwardly all is quiet—all is at peace whenever He resides in my vessel—my confidence is restored when I rest next to the Master.

¹¹Push onward, my soul, push onward—until you have conquered the last barrier—the final frontier of darkness—then you will be swathed in the light of His glory.

¹²The natural eye beholds uncertainty—while the eye of the Spirit clearly sees that the governing of God's abode has jurisdiction over all.

¹³Who could possibly be busier than my God?—not even the highest-level executive in the most famous Fortune 500 company has a schedule like His.

¹⁴In spite of Your bustling schedule You still make time for me—You have never failed to show up for an appointment—nor have You ever been late for any meetings.

¹⁵All who have made time for You are met with joy—the light of Your Word is made real in their hearts.

¹⁶The lamp of God shines through the lives of His saints—He uses the godly to show righteousness in the dark places—He disperses His light throughout the nations.

¹⁷Those who are pleasing to God will complete their earthly walks—not as shackled prisoners—but as favored sons—because He has taken delight in them.

¹⁸He is pleased to bring them into their desired destination because they have made it the portals of heaven—His good cheer has guided them into His safe harbor.

¹⁹With each new morning I will rise to greet the day with victory in my bones and a new hope coursing through my veins.

²⁰The joy of the Lord infuses me with strength—His Spirit gives life—His thoughts are the oxygen that flow through the passageways of my existence.

²¹I have kept Your Word, O God—it has been the encouragement of my soul—intently I have leaned upon Your strength—Your eyes have seen my forming tears.

²²Your great love has forgiven my fickle emotions—Your mercy is attempting to replace them with the foundations of truth.

²³The voice of the righteous is lifted in contrite and humble living before the Father—together their lives form a deliberate memorial of worship before all mankind.

²⁴The God of all heaven will abundantly bless those who trust in Him—for they have given their praise to the Giver and not the gift.

²⁵The song of the heavens has covered the earth—it has entered the hearts of the godly—it will cause their souls to praise the Creator.

²⁶With joy they will sing "How great is Your holiness, O God"—their hearts are made light through their worship.

Psalm 148

Follow Me Into Life Everlasting

¹The longings of my soul were expressed unto You, my God—long before I knew You—now Your glory has opened my eyes to Your ever-abiding presence.

²I open my hands to receive Your good gifts—but I will not cling to them—I rest and am made complete in You—all I ever need is Your presence.

³Who has never had a fearful moment come upon him—who has not known dread and terror in dark hours?

⁴The wise man does not share it with his wavering friend—nor would he expose it to his enemy—he would only whisper it into the ear of his Lord.

⁵No single moment in time is able

to manifest complete spiritual maturity—nor does lasting triumph come by it—these things happen only through a lifetime of moments.

6The judgment of God is laid to rest on those who refuse to take heed of His Word—for they have set their minds against it and will not budge.

7The eyes of the Lord are upon each man—to see all that might be contained within his heart.

8He looks to see whether the motives that surface are pure—to see if righteousness is reigning in victory or whether the intents are bound up in worldly desires.

9My hunger for You, O God, drives me to Your outstretched hand—let my appetite for righteousness become ravenous until it cries out for more than a crust of bread.

10Satisfy me—but not with contentment—until Your revealed Word becomes my meat—I need Your river of life to quench this thirsting of my soul.

11I will feast on the bread of heaven—my soul has tasted from the unending tree of life—my spirit craves the delicacies from Your Word—You fill me with good things.

12In faithfulness He watches over me all through the night—all through the day—His eyes are upon me.

13He guards my ways in case I walk into a trap—His eyes never tire nor does slumber come upon Him like a drowsy night watchman.

14His faithfulness unto me has not been due to any outstanding debt He has owed—or any unfulfilled obligation I could bring against Him.

15He does not grow weary in watchfulness—His eyes do not quit watching like a burned-out light bulb that ceases to give light.

16His strength is never taxed—fatigue never lays a hand on Him—lethargy does not lay stripes upon Him—He will not succumb to exhaustion.

17How could my heart be despondent in view of all His mercies—are they not greater than any of my vexations?

18My soul will cling to Him more than saran wrap to a China plate—it will fasten tightly unto Him and not be drawn away.

19O Lord—You have held my life in Your hands—You have salvaged it from the wrecking yard of the enemy—You have preserved it for a better day.

20You have redeemed it and paid the full ransom demanded for it—Your payment has increased its worth many times over.

21In the pressures of tribulation is the making of our souls into bread and wine—to be edification for the perishing—a commemoration of our Lord's sacrifice.

22Who has not felt the grinding of the stones used to crush the wheat in making bread or the feet used to mash the grapes for wine?

23Remove any bewilderment or doubt—my understanding has not made sense of Your wisdom—yet my spirit will trust in You.

24In the heat of the day He has lovingly showered me with raindrops from heaven—clouds of shade roll in to cover me with mercy.

25When I am down in the dumps—He lifts my spirits—soon I am walking in new light—I will sing a new song to Him—for His generosity has made my steps light.

26He has sprinkled my path with joy—He covers me with strength when the strain of my journey becomes too great—His understanding causes me to rejoice.

27I will offer my sacrifice of praise today—for my assurances are not held in tomorrow—I will praise You, my God, for Your wonders never cease.

28His words came like a gentle breeze upon my face, "walk with Me down pathways of peace—enjoy My presence on your daily walks while I shower you with gentleness.

29There is multiplied blessing behind each dark cloud—do not pray that it be removed—for your eyes are unable to see on the other side.

30Your mind is the fertile soil into which I plant My Word—let it grow unhindered and I will give the great harvest—it will be food in time of famine.

31I have called you to a quiet place so that you might find holy rest—it is there I will meet with you and give you the desires of your heart.

32Because of My faithfulness—I will let your naïveté follow Me all the way home—My Word will enable you to stay on the path of truth."

Psalm 149

You Honor The Prayers Of A Sincere Heart

¹You will not turn down the prayer of an earnest heart, O Lord—though it only contains a single word.

²Longwinded prayers do not impress You—yet a simple prayer will move Your heart because of its simplicity.

³The great King will hear even the most timid knock—it is not lost to His ear—it is more than a bowing of the knee—it is a bowing of one's heart in worship.

⁴Your heart, O God—is stirred by the cries of those who seek You—their prayers are made known throughout Your house—they resound across the heavens.

⁵You value them not for their wordiness or charm—but their candor, openness, and sincerity have kindled Your passion.

⁶I have experienced when the cry of my heart has touched Yours—before I had the chance to utter a single word.

⁷My spirit had crumbled—like dry bread, ready to sop up the milk of Your Word.

⁸You began reviving my soul when I waited on Your voice—it came not at my bidding but in Your time—the nearness of Your presence has filled my heart.

⁹Teach me to pray, my God—to understand Your will—to know Your heart and come into alignment with it.

¹⁰What would You have me say?—I have no words of eloquence to offer—for they have left me high and dry—I am not fluent in powerful prayers.

¹¹What would I ask of You, my God—which petitions shall I bring before You—which request could I render that would be pleasing to You?

¹²Let me set aside my solicitations and appeals in lieu of my worship to You—I will lift my servant heart in exaltations.

¹³Your words, O God—bring peace to the seeker and make Your solace available to him—his heart is freed to speak without pretense.

¹⁴You will not make a truce with sin—but with a wholesome heart You find pleasure—its prayer will not go unheard—nor will it be in vain.

Psalm 150

Walking The Highways Of God

¹Those who live as if on the edge of a precipice must walk carefully—they must be guided by the great hand of our God.

²His children have learned not to stare down over the edge of the embankment or search for glories far below—otherwise fear may seize them and render them useless.

³A sideways glance can cause them to become disoriented and lead to their downfall.

⁴While they walk cautiously—their hope is in the unseen hand that guides them daily—He alone is their safeguard upon this precarious journey they travel.

⁵It is not their desire to test the edge—to find where its strength lies—for in so doing that edge may crumble—and they would fall from a great height.

⁶The way of the godly can be no other when their trust is in the eye of the Almighty—they surrender their hands unto Him without fear—they are confident in His guidance.

⁷They will not tempt fate by clinging to the edge—by living for the thrill—when their security is threatened—it is then that their trust is tested.

⁸They are at peace with their guide—He knows the path well—He is not alarmed at the dangers that surround them—for they are nothing to Him.

⁹The righteous walk with deliberation—for they have measured their steps and are most vigilant in their walk—they will not stray from the center of the path.

¹⁰They have guarded their course and choose not to run with abandon at this time—they will walk in responsibility and steadiness.

¹¹The enemy of their souls would seek to avert them from the straight path so that their feet might slip and they would somehow be hurtled down to everlasting ruin.

¹²Although their trek has encountered much steep terrain—their eyes have not looked away from the prize—their gait is steady and their belief is sure.

¹³And when chasms and steep slopes have surrounded them on every side—their walk will not waver—for the Lord Almighty has been their navigator all along.

¹⁴He will usher them into avenues of glory reserved for the faithful—as their escort He will lead them forth into the halls of His Kingdom with majesty.

Psalm 151

The Nearness Of His Presence

¹The words of the Lord God Almighty belong to Him alone—sometimes He chooses to share them with His creatures.

²He is gracious and kind and loves to commune with all who earnestly seek Him—those who are serious about Him.

³When I was silent before the Lord He heard the cry of my heart—in the stillness I knew that He alone was God.

⁴Obedient—as a servant—I waited upon His bidding—without desperation—I waited patiently for His voice—His leading.

⁵All I could hear was the beating of my heart—He could hear much more than that—He could hear the longings of my soul as they marched in cadence to His rhythm.

⁶My heart was hoping to hear His audible voice—are there any alive who have not had that same desire—will He hold that against us?

⁷Know this—He will not satisfy these desires because they are of an earthly origin—but to the godly He will speak truth with directness and conviction.

⁸The pure in heart have heard His voice and seen His manifestations—He comes before them with light and beauty.

⁹He has made His voice known throughout the lands and in the midst of many people—but their ears have failed to hear it because they were not listening.

¹⁰Resistance melted and futility fled as I waited for Him in stillness—He poured His blessings over me and peace attended my waiting.

¹¹Then His embrace came to me and spoke louder than many words—and I knew He had drawn me close to His bosom.

¹²His words were revealing—"My presence is as close as the heat of the sunshine you feel warming your body right now.

¹³It's as close as the gentleness of the sun's rays as they lay upon your skin—even though the source for those rays is millions of miles away.

¹⁴My sun will soon be descending below the horizon and you will no longer feel its heat—but My presence will still be with you—for I will never turn my back on You.

¹⁵I will kiss you with the nearness of My presence and bathe you in the sweetness of My oil—My Spirit will bear you up with tenderness and affection.

¹⁶Those who are so inclined to draw close to Me will not fail to find Me—for they will be satisfied with nothing less—I will grant them the pursuits of their hearts."

Psalm 152

The Voice Of God Made Plain – Can You Hear It?

¹Who has not heard the voice of God as it thunders forth in power leading the storm—or heard the crack of lightning as its splendor decorates the sky?

²I have been an eyewitness to a measure of the majesty and power of the Lord Almighty—His rushing waters and mighty ocean waves are sights to behold.

³Through the crashing of His mighty waters I have observed His power at work—their force and intensity have directed my thoughts upward in praise for my Creator.

⁴Their mighty strength is displayed day and night—at His bidding He causes them to be stilled—they are given rest by His command.

⁵I marvel and am amazed at the home His waters provide for His abundant sea life—He cradles them in the depths of the oceans and blankets His creatures with love.

⁶Does He care less for the sea anemone than for the great white

shark—does not His love cover all His creation?

⁷I look for You, my God—then I see Your mighty waves rolling in without ceasing—I listen and hear their voice speak with authority.

⁸He shows forth His power to all who have opened their eyes to look at His wonders.

⁹Your power, O Lord—can be seen even without the flexing of Your muscles—it is evident from long range.

¹⁰The voice of God is made plain to those who seek to hear it—it resounds in majesty and distinction.

¹¹Do not dismiss His voice when it becomes calm—it is no less important.

¹²The thundering of His mighty ocean waves can strike sheer terror in the hearts of those who are not wrapped in the cloak of God's peace and covered with His tranquility.

¹³In the midst of the tumult He captures my soul and decorates it with comfort.

¹⁴Who has witnessed the power of His oceans and not paused to catch their breath—to consider His majesty and to tremble before His greatness?

¹⁵His power and majesty have caused the foundations of the earth to reverberate with praise—to sing forth His worth.

¹⁶He has brought my soul a great delight so that I might enjoy a small portion of His majesty—it has overturned my greatest expectations and replaced them with a new awe.

¹⁷If His display of power had not suspended—I would have surely perished.

¹⁸The paths of righteousness and truth go deeper than the deepest ocean—they lead to the fathomless depths of God's love.

¹⁹He has purposed to lead the godly to them—His will has set them on the right path—although it is not a heavily traveled way—He will guide their every footstep.

Psalm 153

The Lord's Presence Fills My Home

¹The Lord has entered my residence and filled me with His presence.

²I have raised a banner and welcomed Him with open arms—now He feels at ease and accepted.

³He has applied for a permanent residency and been accepted.

⁴I will keep my house in order so that He might be pleased with my living arrangements—it is not His desire to abide in an unclean house.

⁵My heart is filled with His goodness—how I love to meditate on Him—He shares His treasures and I am perfectly content with what He gives me.

⁶He has placed a wreath on my door and groceries on my table—He has filled my closets with His belongings—I will give Him thanks with a heart of indebtedness.

⁷Friends have come to join us because they are welcome here—we will all bid Him to sit in the honored seat as we gather around.

⁸We will be uplifted by His words—His songs will be music to our souls—He has filled our spirits with His presence.

⁹He will never cease to bless the house in which He abides because those in it have made Him welcome in word and deed.

¹⁰Let us humbly bow before Him so that we might return to Him the best part of all He has given us—a yielded and settled heart He will not turn down.

¹¹Let those who have breath praise and give Him thanks—for He loves to hear the words of a thankful heart.

Psalm 154

His Glory Lights The Way

¹The light of the glory of the Lord has shown across the face of the deep—it has blanketed the earth and all of His creations with truth and light.

²He has not forsaken mankind—nor has He failed to show His love to those who would seek Him in earnestness—He has seen man's sincerity and will duly reward it.

³His glory has shown forth throughout all of time and eternity—but the darkness of night has failed to recognize it—the ugliness of sin has been blinded to it.

⁴Even though a bright light shines in a room—those who are blind will never see it—even those who shut their eyes to it will never see its radiance.

⁵He has kept the light of His glory for His faithful ones—for those who will choose to draw close to Him—it will light their way.

⁶He will use those who have seen His glorious light to guide those living in darkness—those who are willing, the righteous will lead to safety.

⁷Those who refuse will be left to grope around in the darkness—content to taste the joy of sin for a while without viewing the light that exposes their wickedness.

⁸Seek Him, so your blinded eyes may be opened—then you will see a glorious light.

⁹Search for Him while you still have opportunity—before His glory departs like a scroll that has been rolled up—seek high and low that you might unearth His glory.

¹⁰Call out to Him and see if He will not hear you—He will not fail to answer the sincere—He will come quickly to those who have lifted their voices in desperation.

¹¹Exalt Him with a humble heart—there is no way that He will turn down this praise.

¹²Pour out your soul before His majesty—let Him fill it with goodness and joy.

¹³Bathe yourself in His presence—let it cover you like a soft and gentle shower.

¹⁴Worship Him by the light of His Word—stretch forth your hands in praise—let the light of His glory fill the room where you reside.

¹⁵His presence will cover you and His glory will be shown all about—darkness will flee in the light of His glory and grace.

Psalm 155

Unseen Victories Are Yet To Come

¹The Lord—my God—has covered me with a robe of righteousness—or I would be unclean in His sight.

²My garments were grimy and full of soot—in my own eyes they begged for cleansing—all this I saw as I looked for the One my soul loves.

³His love transformed my life and gave rise to my spirit—on the wings of the wind I will soar unto Him—high above all the distractions of this life.

⁴When my spirit longed to behold Your dazzling beauty—You covered my eyes so that I might walk in faith—Your presence surrounds me and does not disappoint.

⁵My God shines a strong light on the path all around me—because of the darkness, He makes it shine exceedingly bright so my foot will not stumble.

⁶The light of His glory leaves a celebrated trail in my wake—so that scores of others might see His light and follow along.

⁷He has paid attention to my needs and does not look down upon me in scorn because of my destitution.

⁸Only He knows the outcome of all my trials—these I do not need to know—let the people of faith follow Him without hesitation.

⁹His faithful ones will not fret the day of reckoning—for they shall see victories for the battles they had deemed as lost.

¹⁰They will rejoice with many banners waving in the city of our conquering King—the battle truly belonged to the Lord and they never knew it.

¹¹On that day their Hallelujahs will roll as the waves of the ocean—in ceaseless tributes of praise to their great God.

¹²He will not fail them in their earthly times—He will supply them with all they need prior to the coming battle—His strength will be their armor.

¹³He has shown me victories in the present—but even greater triumph is yet to come—I will trust in Him and not be afraid—for He is as certain as the morning light.

¹⁴In the darkness He comforts me—He is my attendant when weariness weighs me down—His presence is my first aid kit—let me praise Him in my weakness.

¹⁵Does He not hear the wind howling outside my hut—threatening to tear it apart?

¹⁶Yes—He is right here beside me—so I will pay no attention to the wind.

¹⁷Even before the daybreak He saw my distress—my cry did not fail to touch His heart—His Word will be my crutch and I will lean heavily upon it.

¹⁸Just to know He stands with me in all my trials has blessed my soul—He will hear its song of praise and be exalted by it.

¹⁹He will grant everlasting life to those who trust in Him—He will be their reward and they will clearly see that He has never abandoned them.

Psalm 156

Praise Him With Your Measure Of Life

¹The Lord God Almighty who reigns over all—abides in the heavens above—He makes His home far above all the earths below Him.

²Although He created mankind as an underling—His purpose was to make a searching heart—one with a yearning for communion and friendship.

³Each life He fashioned with a measured aim and existence—few of His mortals have exceeded His limits.

⁴To some He has measured a cupful—some have enjoyed the measure of a pint or possibly even a quart—others have held the measure of a teaspoon or a tablespoon.

⁵Who are we to bristle against His Majesty concerning His measure-

ments and purposes—or whether He has measured out a full quart —or perhaps only a dash?

⁶Some recipes call for only a pinch of this or a teaspoon of that—so our lifespan is of little consequence— it is what we have added to the recipe that really counts.

⁷A life born of shortness is but a ray of sunshine in a dark valley or the few grains of salt thrown in to bring needed flavoring—who can argue against the pinch of spices needed to bring out the proper zest?

⁸Let those who have been granted a heaping measure praise Him with a full heart as well as those granted a lesser amount.

⁹The Holy Spirit of God has called those aside who will listen—those who would take time to be holy He has humbled their hearts and minds.

¹⁰His riches have been laid bare before the soul of those who would seek to please Him—they have been set apart in accordance with His will.

¹¹He directs their thoughts and plans against the grain—His Spirit is gentle and will not coerce.

¹²His ways have often caused their thoughts to wonder—and even question His course of action.

¹³He has settled their hearts by His Word of truth and they are good to go.

¹⁴He will shield the minds of His saints from the cares and concerns of this life—or they might lose sight of the finish line.

¹⁵They have made the Almighty their refuge and look to Him for strength—they have made up their minds and will not be deterred.

¹⁶He has made the lives of His saints to be like steam from a tea kettle —dispersed with purpose into the surrounding atmosphere.

¹⁷Now He has allowed love and faithfulness to be my companions— they have bolstered my spirits in lonely times and been my attendants when I sat in darkness.

¹⁸My spirit has linked hands with them in praise—praise to my Redeemer.

¹⁹He will cause the righteous to shine through their state of unworthiness—the oil of His Spirit will prevent the rust of ineffectiveness from disabling their light.

²⁰They have learned not to doubt His love—they have not taken offense in the simplicity of their mission—theirs is the security of endurance to the end.

²¹He has swallowed up the emptiness of my soul and filled it with His divine presence—with eternal wonder.

²²I will praise You, O Lord, beyond my final breath—past this veil of tears and this body of mortality—my soul will rejoice forevermore in Your presence.

Psalm 157

We Are His Light To The Nations

¹I have seen the perfect light from above—glowing through the lives of His saints—their mission has been one of shining light and sharing encouragement.

²Their happiness was not found in the things of this life—but in the hope of glory—they took satisfaction only in the Lord their God.

³With hearts shining brightly they have cheerfully reflected the light of His purity in the settings in which He placed them—they have done this unto God—their Creator.

⁴He has scattered them abroad so they might light up His entire universe—in wonderment the nations have seen the lights of the righteous and been blessed.

⁵In the shining forth of their lights He has brought much glory unto His matchless name—their offspring has been a further extension of that light.

⁶His saints, some clustered, while others are spread about—have brought Him praise through their obedience—they have shined with gladness throughout their lifetimes.

⁷They have provided guidance for the lost and for those seeking to find their way—the Father has used their lives to plot a course—to map out a plan to draw them to Him.

⁸The steadiness of their lights has caused many to see His glory—at times the flickering of the lights of His chosen ones has brought attention unto their God.

⁹They have been faithful in their service during the time He has allotted them.

¹⁰The Lord blows gently across the lives of His saints—and like the candles on a birthday cake—their lights are extinguished.

¹¹They have burned brightly for their appointed time—serving their appointed purpose—it is necessary to cease from their earthly works so they might enter His eternal rest.

¹²They have now come into His eternal Kingdom where their lights are no longer necessary in that city where the Lamb is the light.

¹³If you listen closely you will also hear the praise song that emanated from the hearts of His devoted saints—their song that has brought glory into their world.

Psalm 158

A psalm for Dot & Jerry

¹Though the mighty waters rage against the doorsteps of the righteous—their confidence remains steady because their hope is in the Almighty One.

²They have seen the power of His handiwork rushing past their dwelling places and yet their hope is secure in Him.

³He will keep them safe and hold their lives as a ransom against the evil one—by His Word of truth He commands the winds and the waves and they obey.

⁴Even while their eyes beheld the onslaught of the storm—they have also searched for Your rainbow, O God—the covenant of Your faithfulness.

⁵You heard their downcast cry and became the peace in the center of their storm.

⁶To those who trust in Him—His mercies are never dependent on whether the river is running high or whether it has dried up altogether—their trust will prop up their spirits.

⁷His eye was upon them when the banks of the river overflowed—dismay was quick to rise within their hearts—He sent His precious ones to hearten their spirits.

⁸With a song in their hearts and praise on their lips His faithful ones were quick to come to their aid—they sent forth a shield of praise throughout the house.

⁹You, O God, latched on to their cries and sent the waters fleeing—yes how we will not fail to praise Your name—in our troubles we will lift unto You our exaltations.

¹⁰We will bless Your name and make this home a sanctuary of Your presence—You will not fail to abide in the midst of praises unto Your name.

¹¹O praise the Lord aloud—for He has caused His faithfulness to appear—His mercies have given us reason to rejoice again.

¹²My soul will find gladness in the praises for my King—it will overflow in heartfelt worship—for He is my delight forevermore.

Psalm 159

Call Upon Him And Receive His Favor

¹"I, the Lord, am speaking even now—to those who will listen to My voice—what were you expecting—drum rolls and blaring trumpets—pomp and ceremony?

²Today I will come into the heart that simply says come in—do not wait for special seasons to invite Me in—I am an anytime God!

³Call upon Me with authenticity—see if I will not meet you at the place where you currently are—let your heart be guided by truthful uprightness and candor.

⁴I will bring My favor to rest upon those whose hearts are committed to Me—My Presence will chaperone their steps and My Spirit will govern all their thoughts.

⁵I will apply the anointing oil of My forgiveness to those who are bruised and hurting—in their weakness they shall find strength.

⁶By My Word you will receive power to vanquish your rivals—through My strength your failures have been swallowed up by forgiveness.

⁷Do not let the exhaustion of your spirit put you to shame—for your strength is unable to cope with My assignment for you—there is much weariness even in well doing.

⁸Your battle is Mine—but only if you allow it to be—it is a struggle that crosses the grain of the world in which you live.

⁹I have seen the heaviness of your heart—and I have noticed your despair—do not allow cold feet to turn aside your passion for Me.

¹⁰You should not serve Me with trepidation by always looking at the way things were—I have placed a new day before you and a fresh path awaits you—go forward in faith.

¹¹Your heart will yet again praise Me—and I will send My joy your way—to accompany you along your walk and to lift your drooping spirits."

Psalm 160

Usher Me Into Your Holy Presence

¹At the laying down of our anxiousness there is rest—as there is for a traveler who happens upon an oasis and is renewed—it is there he is fortified with new strength.

²He has bid me to walk the longer route so I will not lose sight of His Presence.

³Then He will lead me down the paths of truth until I come upon the Highway of Holiness—I will follow that until I reach my Father's house.

⁴I am but a short distance from His house—I can see Him standing at the gates of glory with outstretched arms.

⁵The Spirit of God has instilled words for my soul and I have learned to be still and listen—a wise heart makes Him so glad.

⁶Let the glory of the Lord be seen not only in the heavens but on the earth below—may it be manifest by the prayers of Your saints and directed by Your Spirit—O God.

⁷Use the prayers of the faithful to command the forces of righteousness—Your saints have given their petitions to You—intensify their energies to bring about godliness.

⁸He has introduced the prayers of the godly within the heavens—He has translated their sounds into a heavenly language—He has honored their sincerity.

⁹He has made it known that their prayers will precede them—they will cause great joy among the heavens—a mighty sound will be heard as a result.

¹⁰And I heard the heavenly choir singing around the throne and giving glory to the Lamb—and we were singing;

¹¹We've been chosen by Your grace—chosen by Your grace—we praise the Lamb who has taken our place;

¹²It wasn't works that we had done—grace came through God's Holy One—now we've been chosen—saved by Your grace.

¹³Your temple and Your throne I have longed to look upon, O Lord—to gaze upon their magnificence so that my eyes may see their loveliness.

¹⁴I will enter into your temple with thankfulness—for You have shown me the way inside—my ears have already heard the joyful sounds coming from within.

¹⁵Lead me O God, past the outer gates so that I will not loiter around them—take me beyond the outer courts—show me the inner courts of Your sanctuary.

¹⁶Then I will see the beauties of Your house—my eyes will look upon Your majesties with astonishment.

¹⁷He has taken me deep within His chambers and shown me untold mysteries—He has filled the deepest longings of my soul in His Presence—and there I find unspeakable joy.

¹⁸All the intricate ornateness of His house does not compare with the light of His glory—its indescribable beauty is a marvel to behold.

¹⁹His Presence has ushered me into the throne room of the Most High God—it is there I am swept off my feet and content never to be apart from Him for eternity.

²⁰My eyes look to Your Word—You have answered my heart's prayer and opened my ears—there are glories my understanding heart knows about, of which I cannot write.

Psalm 161

Your Faithfulness Is Witness Of Your Perfection

¹He has gathered up the energy of my soul and bound it for eternity—now through His energy this poor weary pilgrim has been given everlasting life.

²I will allow Your Spirit, my God, to lead my heart down the path to the place that pleases Your heart.

³My heart will abandon itself unto Your will—it is there I will find my peace—Your security will be made mine because I trust in You.

⁴So great is the Lord—He has carried all my struggles upon His shoulders—for He makes my load light.

⁵He has painstakingly addressed my predicaments with great care and administered mercy and grace unto them all.

⁶His faithfulness is more certain than the tolling of the evening bell—more than the shining of the North Star.

⁷No one is able to fathom Your faithfulness—though they would try for an eternity—it cannot be quantified with the measurements of mankind.

⁸His faithfulness has supplied all I need to walk with holiness through this present hour.

⁹The voice of the Almighty has spoken unto my soul from the depths of eternity—His place was secure before time began.

¹⁰He has displayed His love unto me through the unfolding of His Word—ratifying it by the written commands of His prophets.

¹¹Those who would become intimately acquainted with the presence of the Almighty have not neglected the subtleties of His declarations.

¹²They have heard His voice through the close proximity of His Word—its power and authority has drawn them close.

¹³The truth of God has preceded the earliest traces of mankind—it had no beginning because it was forever with Him.

¹⁴His voice has spoken unto all creation and it has known Him as He is—the great Almighty—the great I AM.

15He says, "to those who would seek Me wholeheartedly I will block out the noises of the earth; their spirits will hear My Spirit and I will speak to them with clarity of speech.

16They will be strengthened in righteousness while being renewed—they will set aside their weaknesses and I will clothe them with power not of their own.

17I have allowed a seed of repentance to germinate in the hearts of the godly—their prayers are not useless—I have entertained their desires for revival."

18Holy Spirit—stir within me the fire of my God that has settled down low.

19Let the breath of God blow across the kindling of my desire in order to revive the fire in my soul.

20Allow this fire to spread and ignite the dryness in the souls all around me so that they too, might have a fire that burns with fierceness.

21He has opened up the way before me and now I can step forth in confidence.

22Pause and give glory to the Lord all throughout your day—never miss a chance to proclaim His greatness.

23Do not hesitate to share His Majesty with those passing by—His greatness with any who inquire.

24Who has not witnessed the inanimate objects of His creation praising His wonders?—even the trees of the woodlands wave their arms in praise to their Creator.

25Stop and contemplate His perfection in the middle of your day—remind yourself of His loving kindness—be an example of His mercies to others.

26Blurt out His virtues to all who will listen.

27Let all your words speak forth kindness and goodwill overflow from a tender heart.

28Vocalize the vastness of God to your neighbor—do not hold back airing His excellence to all people.

29Remember His goodness all day long and dwell upon it with a thankful heart—I will let the wonders of my God saturate me continually.

Psalm 162

A psalm for Mary M

¹I have seen the way to nearness with my God—it is found on the path of the next praise-filled breath.

²His joy is made to overflow by those who bring Him a sacrifice of praise and a thankful heart.

³It is the godly who have desired each breath to go forth in praise—they have set the labor of their hearts heavenward.

⁴He will give health and strength to His faithful ones that they might complete His good work until the last sentence of their stories.

⁵Their stories have been published with significant and profound care by the Lord—the author and creator of their souls.

⁶His banner of love has been their protection because they have refused to seek riches and fame—their aim has been the Kingdom of their God.

⁷Because their lives have been bound up in the will of their Father—He will bless them with sublime peace like that of a gentle flowing river.

⁸The ways of the Lord have been precious unto them and His will has blessed them—because they have put Him first He has heaped His favor upon them.

⁹They have looked for His glory and found strength—His Word has made their bones strong—He has spoken life unto them—everlasting life to His saints.

¹⁰See how His truthful ones marvel at His greatness—He has welcomed their praise for all His creation—His joy has infused the marrow of their bones with wellness.

¹¹He has granted them the desires of their hearts because of His purity and truth—His eyes have seen the depths of their souls and heard their cries.

¹²Their longings have brought His good pleasure to many around them—and His righteousness has become their garment.

¹³In power, they initiate their lives to proclaim His Majesty in boldness—their voices sing forth His praises again and again and yet again.

¹⁴Let them be strengthened and lifted up—their service has made His heart glad—His anointing has touched the lives of many others through them.

¹⁵He has smiled sweetly upon them —and they have seen it—because their eyes were looking unto Him.

¹⁶Their lights will continue to burn brightly all the days of their lives —and others will be blessed to see the light of their Redeemer.

Psalm 163

I'm Giving You My All

I'm Giving You My All [a poem]

O precious God of wondrous love who charms the raging sea
His power enthroned in heav'n above yet reaches you and me

He speaks to howling winds below they hasten to obey
He gives us grace for every hour new mercies for each day

He touches lives not randomly His purpose to fulfill
He's waiting for that yielded heart to work His perfect will

O precious God of wondrous love I'm yielded to Your call
No matter what the price may be I'm giving You my all

Psalm 164

I Praise You For Who You Are

¹I will let the love for my God be manifest through my daily living —it will speak with the force of ten thousand words.

²God has set over me glory, power, and honor—He looks out over the handrail of His balcony in the heavens and smiles on those who please Him.

³He has planted His kiss of redemption upon my cheek—O how I will praise Him for His faithful-

ness unto me.

⁴And yet I am amazed that He, a King, would so much as cast a glance upon me—a lowly servant—and then I ask the question—who am I?

⁵He watches over me—He will not sleep in comfort while I toss and turn in restlessness—He is ever attentive to my groaning.

⁶Light up, O heavens, and spill forth your decisions—make all your proclamations known to us.

⁷The Lord has examined the ways of the righteous and finds them pleasing.

⁸Keep me close to Your side, O Lord, as a piece of elastic keeps the cloth gathered closely to a person's body.

⁹While I am in Your presence—teach me not to be hasty but to linger there and soak it in—as we might absorb the sun's rays on a cool day.

¹⁰Instruct me in Your ways, my God—and I will walk graciously before You all of my days—I will not test the limits of Your control.

¹¹His peace will always be your portion when you learn to walk in the secret places of His presence—let them be your great reward.

¹²Holy Spirit—lead me straight to the desires of my heart—let them be comprised of pure holiness and not just gold plating.

¹³May the desires of my heart be marbled with Your will, O God, so that they would be made strong by the lamination of our spirits.

¹⁴The royal road of praise leads me near to my God—I will exalt Him for who He is.

¹⁵He delights when His children fill the spare moments of their lives with praise.

¹⁶He kept me from tragedy and great loss when the foolishness of my youth wanted to consume me—His mercy did not allow the error of my ways to come to fruition.

¹⁷His mercy was the guardian of my estate when wrong choices threatened to leave me homeless—His amazing grace became my virtue—it was kind and longsuffering.

¹⁸The presence of my God has entered my soul through the doorway of my inadequacies—His approach is one of gentleness.

¹⁹He has extended the scepter of hope unto me by exchanging my weakness for His strength—it has become my lifeline from heaven.

Psalm 164 - I Praise You For Who You Are

²⁰You, O Lord, are the furthest reach of my imagination—the most distant of my dreams—the nearest of my thoughts—the breath that issues forth from my being.

²¹Be both my conscious and my subconscious—let them be aligned with Your will.

²²The godly have become His living—walking—billboards and are not shy when advertising His goodness.

²³He has plastered His truth across their countenance and they will proclaim it to all who come across their path.

²⁴Who is that wise man who has learned to trust Him through the calm days as well as the days of adversity?—it is he who is storing up his treasure to enjoy at a later date.

²⁵So great is His love that He has offered His mercy unto me—it touches the soles of my feet—it has traveled through the fingertips of my upraised hands.

²⁶His mercy has caused my sins to go into hiding—now He has buried them.

²⁷How His love has gone to great lengths to draw me to His side—He has wasted no efforts to show me its depth.

²⁸See how it beckons to you—to me—it will not sneak up behind and force you to His side—it only beckons and waits.

²⁹I will run into my Father's arms—there He will soothe my spirit—there He will caress my soul and sing lullabies unto it—there in His arms I am comforted.

³⁰Nighttime will not faze me—for He is there also—I will not shiver because His warmth surrounds me like a fleece blanket.

³¹His voice calms and reassures my anxieties—it pacifies uncertainties.

³²It is there in the stillness that my soul has found what it has sought hard after—His gentle peace afforded unto me.

³³I will praise You, my God, because of Your wonderful greatness—how can I contain that which overflows from my spirit?

³⁴Your Majesty is abundant—its range has stricken me with admiration and worship of Your marvels—O how I must praise Your name forever and ever.

Psalm 165

You Even Change The Thoughts Of The Heart

¹The thoughts of a man define his heart—his actions reflect his meditations—his conduct shapes who he will become.

²He is plainly able to portray his life story from the things that originate inside him.

³His mouth cannot help spilling forth those things he deems important—the causes that lie deep inside.

⁴Even his actions will give evidence of the passions that lay claim to his longings—the obsessions that wrap their tentacles around the fibers of his soul.

⁵Righteous living will emanate from his being—his presence in the lives of others will show a marked sign of God's glory.

⁶His very words will be pleasing to His God as well as those around him—he will speak with authority and wisdom.

⁷Those who have a tendency toward evil will spew out things of a like nature—their message will surely show others the inclinations of their hearts.

⁸They will thrust forward their intents like a dagger—to slay any who might cross their path.

⁹They will not be able to keep concealed the kind of people residing within—they will eventually break loose as strong men who snap the ropes that bind them.

¹⁰Prepare your heart and come before your Maker with honesty and humility—for only He is able to change a heart.

¹¹He will never refuse those who come to Him with a whole heart—He will draw them very close.

¹²I will praise You with my whole heart—with each breath I give You praise—I will bow my heart in worship—and I'll serve You all my days.

¹³Take this praise that I offer—use it as my gift of love—let it rise with sweet aroma—'til it fills the heavens above.

¹⁴I will praise Your name, O God, and You will draw near—I will call to You and You will hear—praise the Lord—O my soul—praise His name.

Psalm 166

My Soul Is Complete Under Your Rest

¹The distant stars and the heavenly planets all point directly to Your attention to detail—they speak to mankind in waves of truth and beauty.

²Throughout the realms of glory there is none like You, O God—where could I search and find someone that was Your equal?

³Who can flex his muscles like my God—who can put on a show of strength like He can?

⁴And who can challenge His Majesty to a duel?—no one—for there is none like Him.

⁵Can anyone else tip his watering can with precision and water the earth evenly?

⁶Which god or man is able to distribute his snowflakes—in a similar manner to salt being shaken from its shaker?

⁷Show me who else can pucker his lips and exhale the winds of the Almighty so that they blow across all His creation.

⁸The strength and might of His little finger is greater than all of man's stamina—if He were to display the power of His right hand, it would crush mankind to a fine powder.

⁹So who am I that You would give heed to even one of my petitions?

¹⁰You are my God—for I have made You Lord over all my possessions—nothing will I withhold from You.

¹¹He will cause the plants of my garden to flourish like the garden of Eden because of His great love for me.

¹²Today His message came to me in a familiar voice—He said, "those who have heard My call have expressed it through the many ways of ordinary life.

¹³Their devotion to Me is plainly seen by their service to others—they are allowing My Father to release His good pleasure through the revelation of His own Son in them.

¹⁴Never allow the perception of misspoken words—of stammering lips and faltering voice—to block your path to My blessing and anointing on those who would obey Me.

¹⁵I desire obedience more than eloquence—I will do the needed work through your surrender to My Spirit—only then can My will be accomplished.

¹⁶I will never require you to understand My requests—it is truly not your place to comprehend My workings—nor should you even be concerned with them.

¹⁷Do not try to figure out who My message is for or the purpose behind it!

¹⁸Just continue to walk in faith and trust My leadings—that is all I ask.

¹⁹Never squelch those blessings I have prepared for both the giver and the receiver by failing to act upon the promptings of My Spirit.

²⁰I will pour out My richest blessings unto their searching hearts—they will receive the sweetness of My treasure with tenderness.

²¹Then I will reveal the delights of My heart to them and they will rejoice with gladness at the truth of My Word.

²²I will let My love cover you like the night stars blanket the heavens—your soul will snuggle under My protection and will not shiver.

²³My love has been a buoy for your soul—you will not fear the depths because you are supported by My strength—your mind will be at ease in My presence.

²⁴I have hewn you out a place in the mountain of tribulation where you can run into until the storm has passed by.

²⁵I will hide you in the cave of My glory and protect you with the shield of My righteousness—it is there you can come into My rest and be complete."

Psalm 167

Each Life Has A Story To Tell

¹Your Spirit, O God—has become an active ingredient in the formula of my soul.

²Let my thoughts continually be near to You—may they cause me to hang on to You tighter than a body suit on a skin diver.

³O that Your love would consume me as inebriation consumes a drunken man.

⁴How blessed are those who refuse to take shortcuts—especially so close to the finish line—they will not be sidetracked or unwittingly delayed.

⁵When I bow before Him and count my blessings—none is so great as He.

⁶He has written the pages of my book—His will has become my story—His nearness has become my glory.

⁷I will serve my Lord on purpose because His love for me was no accident—it is the purpose of my heart to follow Him all of my days.

⁸The godly bump up against the love of God daily and are blessed—they are not afraid to rub shoulders with those around them—in this way they spread God's love.

⁹The moving of God's Spirit never ceases—sometimes it whispers gently without ever moving the wind chimes—at other times they swing wildly and ring melodiously.

¹⁰Yet on both occasions He moves—regardless if seen or felt.

¹¹His currents from one direction may begin a stirring—causing those nearby to hear a sweet sound of revival.

¹²But this same current from the north may produce no movement at all—so the perception is one of little or no value.

¹³Never reject His moving based on what you see, feel, or hear—He will judge that at the proper time.

¹⁴Continue in faithfulness that which He has called you to do—His reward will be greater than your imagination and you will stand amazed.

¹⁵God holds His knowledge in abeyance for those who wholeheartedly seek Him—He sets aside special venues of instruction for them.

¹⁶He hides His ways from the worldly ones but He shows His paths to the seeking heart—they see the light of His Word and are glad.

¹⁷Daily He gives me basketfuls of blessings woven together with strands of His mercy and adorned with ribbons of His grace.

¹⁸The fullness of God Almighty contains the length, width, and depth of His knowledge and wisdom—His love is the frame holding it all together.

¹⁹Who among us is blessed and has not received our portion from His hand—who is wise from his own supply of knowledge?

²⁰He renders His blessings upon those He created so that they might reciprocate kindness unto others.

²¹Who has found the locale of God's insight—the establishment where it abides—the area of its lodging—the place where He divvies it out with knowledge?

²²It resides in the domain of the heavens—in the secret places of the Almighty—the whereabouts that are not within reach of mortal man.

²³Teach me Your ways, my God—my soul sits in rapt attention as Your pupil—willing to soak up all of Your injunctions—eager to follow the dictates of Your heart.

²⁴My ears are attentive for Your voice—I will let Your truth enter my spirit—then I will be led in the ways of my God.

²⁵I am but your servant, O God—give me a willingness to follow all Your ways—then I will choose the right path.

²⁶Saints of all ages have chronicled their lives in countless ways as a record of God's mercy and love unto the ends of the earth.

²⁷Each thread of their garments has a story to tell—when that strand of fiber was upon the spool it was of little consequence—now He has made it to be of value for the body.

²⁸The lives of the godly are like the threads of a well-worn jacket—some have become frayed and tattered but still produce a measure of comfort to those around them.

²⁹Even though the hue and sheen of their colors have faded—they have an interesting story to tell because of what the Lord has done.

³⁰He has found and mended the broken threads so they will continue to be useful.

³¹They do not despair in their weakness but give praise to God through their story.

³²The Lord will summon those He loves unto His holy mountain—there they will bring Him their finest sacrifice of praise and find His favor.

³³They have heard His call and carried out His righteousness—they have made the Eternal One their refuge.

³⁴The Lord Almighty will be their glorious reward because they have looked to Him as their Rock and fortified place.

Psalm 168

He Surrounds Me With High Walls So I Am Safe

¹To those who have learned to pour out praises upon their God—He in turn lavishes on them His kindness.

²The Lord is quick to eat up your praise anytime you favor Him with the gift of your worship—He does not let any of it go to waste.

³Let each day begin with a grateful heart—let your soul be silent before Him—there you will find His presence and it will draw you unto Him.

⁴The faithfulness of my God keeps His promises close to my heart—His Word is my contract—for in it I find all my provisions.

⁵Long before the first glimpse of daylight I searched for strength as with a fine-toothed comb—but it was nowhere to be found.

⁶That is when the Lord directed my eyes unto Him and He became my strength.

⁷I most assuredly would have looked for it in vain if He had not taken heed of my frantic seeking.

⁸My paltry quota of strength He set aside and empowered me with the wealth of His.

⁹He surrounds my soul with high walls so that nothing can penetrate and reach it.

¹⁰Howling winds may shake the house where I live—but my soul stands secure—You fill it with grace and my heart with wonder—O how Your greatness overwhelms me.

¹¹I will rest in Your presence daily—for it is there that You bring joy to my heart—in fact I am speechless with delight.

¹²Lord—I have come before You just as You asked me to—I've laid all my concerns before You—spreading them across the floor.

¹³He has shushed some of my most incessant concerns and covered them with His mercies—my cares He has made His own.

¹⁴Not a single one of my uncertainties has He made to seem trivial—His composure is soothing and quick to obscure my uneasiness.

¹⁵The strain of my apprehensions has not caused Him a bit of sorrow—He never neglects my qualms.

¹⁶He will let His light shine upon those whose hearts have been darkened by heaviness—if they will listen—He will sing a melody unto their souls.

¹⁷His great love has cast out my sadness and dismissed my heaviness of heart.

¹⁸I will lift my hands unto You, my God—when my heart has been dealt sorrow—I will rejoice with the voice of thanksgiving.

¹⁹Let your feet go free and dance before Him—praise Him with a light step and a joyful heart—find gratification in dancing upon your doldrums with contempt.

²⁰I will quickly praise Him—for He has come to my aid once again—He is able to thwart those who would come against me.

²¹His love reached out and drew me close—suddenly I could no longer see my cares—His presence has come between them and me.

²²He has given me a resolute heart that will not flinch in the face of unpleasantness.

²³He has appointed me to pronounce blessings in His name forever—I will maintain His truthfulness and holiness without end.

²⁴Let your heart now come before Him in worship and adoration in the way He has uniquely prescribed for you—and with that He will be pleased.

²⁵Be sure to accept from His hand all the instructions He has laid upon your heart—let Him lead you down a straight path.

²⁶How is He able to speak words unto you if you do not become silent before Him—if you do not yield your soul and spirit unto His voice?

²⁷His revelations will be lost to the rambling of your voice and the muttering of your words.

²⁸Praise Him with few words and praise Him with silence—He is accepting of all your worship.

²⁹Release unto Him a sincere heart—let it be honest and above board—He is interested only in a bona fide and genuine heart.

³⁰The contented heart is at peace with God and finds grace in each moment.

Psalm 169

His Abiding Presence Covers All

¹The strength of my heart has overtaken the feebleness of my mind—it will put to shame the failures of this carnal mind.

²In those places where my passions have fallen short—His purposes have captivated my convictions.

³When my thoughts betray me—when they take a side road along my journey—my Lord comes beside me with reassurance.

⁴I will dismiss my feelings—those that clamor for my attention like a classroom full of rowdy children—so that my walk of faith will be enhanced.

⁵So great is the love of the Lord that He brings me to the sea of His mercy and invites me to jump in daily.

⁶It is not in His best interest to make snap judgments concerning a man—His mercies and compassion do not allow this.

⁷He rules with justice and His verdicts are true—honesty is His measuring stick.

⁸His grace has become my hope—it is the lifeline by which I am anchored directly to the throne of His forgiveness.

⁹O God—I long to remain in your presence—in its nearness I find comfort—there I am guided by Your Spirit and move about in freedom.

¹⁰The saints of the Lord Most High are His inheritance—the tithes of all people—they contain His portion from the whole of mankind.

¹¹They are the sons and daughters of His family—the children that bring Him great pleasure—in turn He has blessed them with wisdom and a discerning spirit.

¹²The glory of the Lord fills the whole earth with completeness—it stretches throughout the cosmos and purifies the heavens.

¹³His presence abides beyond the extremes of knowledge and imagination—is it possible to travel anywhere that He does not exist?

¹⁴The vast reaches of space cannot provide enough room for Him to fill—the very essence of His being encapsulates all of time and space

15My heart will praise You, O God, because You inhabit its inner chambers.

16Let praises soar from the soul of saints—let them purify the heavens with His glory.

Psalm 170

Your Light Brings Beauty To My Soul

1It takes the light to bring out the beauty of the wood's grain—to showcase the intricacies of the carving.

2The light of Your Spirit, O God, brings beauty to my soul—showing forth the loveliness of the works of Your hands.

3Honor the Lord with all that you have—not just ten percent—in so doing His presence will illuminate you.

4Stay in tune with the Master in all that you do—and it will be sweeter than any melody ever heard by mortal ears—moving mightily in the spiritual realm.

5O Lord—You have filled my life with many blessings—may not a single one of them ever become greater to me than You are.

6Your will resides within the godly—it manifests itself daily through a clear conscience and an innocent mind as they praise You with all their hearts.

7Your Word renews their lives daily—it has become the strength of their spirits.

8They have found thankfulness to be the hot air balloon that whisks them above their circumstances—their grateful hearts allow them to view things from a higher perspective.

9I leaned upon my God for mercy and He answered me in kindness—I searched steadily for another answer but He was insistent with me.

10He revealed His sovereignty when He opened my eyes unto His sufficiency of grace.

11Then my soul was quieted—humbled within His presence—my spirit was released to pursue Him along other avenues.

Psalm 170 - Your Light Brings Beauty To My Soul

¹²The understanding of my mind was left unsatisfied while peace became its replacement—the anxiety of the moment was displaced by eternal assurance.

¹³Whoever would be pure in heart has learned to sacrifice the stubbornness of his heart upon the altar of God's forgiveness.

¹⁴I will fill my home with praise for my God—for I know He delights in that and dwells there daily.

¹⁵Praise for Him begins from the foundation and flows up past the rafters—its gratitude touches every article within the house.

¹⁶I will bless His name with each breath that proceeds from my mouth—for He has purchased my life to be a sacrifice unto His glory.

¹⁷His Word clothes me in fine linen—I will go about arrayed in the splendor of His holiness—His Word comes forth in liberty and power to accomplish His purposes.

¹⁸He satisfies my heart with the bread of heaven—I am made complete by His manna.

¹⁹Marvel at His glory—declare it passionately unto all the nations.

²⁰Do not forsake your neighbor—for to some he is all the nations—he stands as the farthest ends of the earth.

²¹"I—the Lord your God—have opened your eyes and shown you the way—you do not need to go abroad to reach the lost—for they are at your doorstep.

²²Those who love Me with their all—will be ecstatic at everything I am preparing to fill their hearts with—I have desires they have not fathomed yet.

²³I will make their lives finely tuned instruments of praise unto Me—both now and forevermore.

²⁴I have often withheld My sovereignty from your minds—I will allow it to become the resistance training of your faith building.

²⁵Trust in Me—do not struggle with your own understanding—lest you grow bitter and disillusioned.

²⁶You only need to trust Me and lay every disappointment at My feet to acquire a perfect and total surrender—and I will do amazing things through you."

Psalm 171

Your Love Shows Us The Pathway Of Peace

[1] Like fresh tracks across the new fallen snow—His Word leaves indelible impressions upon my heart.

[2] May all who know me see His wonders written across the landscape of my life—the direction of His path is leading upward.

[3] Like a beneficial medicine—the Lord has prescribed for me all the paths I am to take—He knows which direction I should be headed.

[4] He has shown me the pathway of peace and invites me to walk in it —where He goes I will follow.

[5] What flows like a mighty river from the throne room of my God except His abiding peace and everlasting love?

[6] His saints partake of it daily and it enriches their lives immeasurably.

[7] Gather a fresh supply of His mercies daily—for yesterdays have evaporated—and He will not loan to you from tomorrows.

[8] While His grace is totally amazing —you must apply it daily—enjoy it like the warmth of the sunshine and never take it for granted.

[9] The Lord has blessed His saints— His chosen ones—those who have yielded to His call, with everlasting life.

[10] They have begun to live it while here on this earth—they have not made their formative years a high priority.

[11] Their hope is not in manmade things—the Lord Himself has been their sustaining life flow.

[12] Even if the earth should crumble like a dried and stale cookie— even if it should shrink and wither like a dried prune—their strength is in the Lord.

[13] If all they had going was the hope of this life below—they would just throw up their hands in defeat right now.

[14] But they walk a steady pace while looking forward to stepping over the threshold and through the doorway of glory.

[15] They have not been swayed by the here and now philosophy—they have made the ever after their hope and joy.

¹⁶Love the Lord—not with your words—set them aside and show Him your true heart.

¹⁷Draw near to Him while you can—come into His presence through your reflective thoughts—meditate upon His greatness.

¹⁸Let your pen capture His thoughts—transcribe His desires to the whole world so others can praise Him after you pass on from this life.

¹⁹Never jealously guard His revelations unto you—freely share them with your fellow man—then they can reap a portion of your blessing.

²⁰I will bless His name forever—so I might as well get a head start on it now—my soul rejoices in God alone—for there is no other name like His.

Psalm 172

Wherever I Am, You Are There

¹Healing for the body—rest for the soul—do they not both belong to the Creator of all—are they not at His disposal and for His great pleasure?

²Does He dispense them only to the deserving and the guilt free—or does He offer them without merit?

³His mercy has reached out to the wayward and the disobedient because He has heard their cries of desperation.

⁴The healing compassions of the Lord have often been known to touch the lives of sinners on behalf of the prayers of His righteous saints.

⁵Do not fail to bring your petitions before Him—whether for yourself or for your brother in need—then your fellow bondservant will be blessed by your prayers.

⁶There is only one chance to pass this way before these flimsy bodies rest in sleep.

⁷I will cling tightly to His hand and not go my own way—He guides my steps daily.

⁸And if He should withdraw His hand so I can walk by faith—then I will trust Him all the more because I know He is nearby.

⁹I will not be alone when His voice is there to guide me—it directs my walk if I will pay attention to it.

¹⁰The darkness of night will not deter me because He is with me—His Word will not leave me forsaken because it resides within my heart.

¹¹He is with me when I walk in the sunshine at midday—when its brilliance would blind my eyes and I am unable to see my footpath—yet He is there to direct me.

¹²When dark clouds gather overhead and the rain is beating down upon me—when I am unable to make out what lies ahead—then He makes known the way I should go.

¹³If I should find myself in a strange land and uncertainty seizes hold of me—even then He will not leave me on my own.

¹⁴At those times when I walk in familiar places and along well-beaten paths—His presence goes with me—it surrounds me with the light of His glory.

¹⁵He is with me walking on the valley floor or on the heights among His clouds.

¹⁶He is my song and the praise of my heart—because of His strength He has allowed me to go the distance—I have run the race with courage and dignity.

Psalm 173

You Are Fully Attentive To Our Worship

¹The Lord God Almighty reigns with all power—all of us can attest to this if we would allow honesty to answer truthfully.

²He has made us His people and we are His crowning glory—at the same time we will inhabit the earth and fill it with His delight.

³Let your praises be full of exaltation unto Him—He has set your life aside for His purpose and His praise.

⁴Is it too much for Him to ask for your worship—is He not worthy of all praise and all glory?

⁵Why then be hesitant to pay Him His due—why shortchange Him of your worship—why take what

Psalm 173 - You Are Fully Attentive To Our Worship

belongs to Him and give it elsewhere?

⁶Do not hold back—pay Him your tribute from a grateful heart—ignore the clamoring of outside influences and settle your heart before Him.

⁷He will only exchange His glory in lieu of your praises—He will be fully attentive to your worship.

⁸Let tears well up in your eyes—let them run down your face as you lift your heart unto Him without hesitation.

⁹I will not withhold from Him any portion of my strength—I will devote all my praise to His cause—praise be unto my Redeemer for this life that I live.

¹⁰You are my Rock, O God, lead me to Your hiding place—You are the strength that I am in desperate need of.

¹¹He has called His saints—not to do great and mighty works of righteousness—but to walk daily in faithfulness.

¹²The very words of my God have encouraged my soul—I will exalt and praise His name forever.

¹³Lord, I worship You and You alone—for You are the God of all the heavens—You have made all that is seen and all that is unseen.

¹⁴I lift my hands and my soul unto You in acceptance and submission.

¹⁵I am desperate for You—somehow I need You more than my consciousness permits me to be aware of.

¹⁶You have created us to praise You, and if that is all we ever do we have accomplished Your will.

¹⁷You, O Lord, have given each man the ability to praise You—it is contained within each breath he takes.

¹⁸Let him breathe out praises to God instead of threats and grumblings against his neighbor—then he will be pleasing to his King.

¹⁹Why does man waste his opportunities of praise with all kinds of cursing and condemnations?—when those prospects are gone he will have no more.

²⁰Is not life found within each breath—and does that not come from God above?

²¹As for me—I will praise Him as long as I live—and with each breath He gives me—my soul will shout Hallelujah!

²²Do not forget to crown the King of Kings with your praises—let them be a garland of glory unto His Majesty.

²³No one is deserving of life—yet He gives unto each man an equal chance to praise Him—therefore no one can stand before His Presence with a shred of an excuse.

²⁴Let all who have breath and all His creation praise Him—for who is as worthy as He—who can expect praise more than our Creator?

²⁵Open your heart and mind to Him and He will fill them with many occasions to praise Him—times to lift high and exalt His name.

²⁶Be exhausted by your worship and wear yourself out with praise—then He will come quickly to you with strength.

²⁷I will bless His name every chance I get—both now and forevermore—my voice will sing to Him new songs of praise—sing aloud O my soul.

Psalm 174

As For Me – I Will Praise Him

¹When the effects of aging have come against this body and my soul sings unto You fewer times than it ought—I will lift my soul unto You, O Lord, with gratefulness.

²I will not let the condemnation of my heart stand against me—for You, my God, are the giver of songs and the One in whom I trust.

³You will not forsake me even during my latter years because of Your great promise.

⁴Though my enemy would put shackles on my hands and legs and gouge out my eyes—even then will the eyes of my heart look to You.

⁵I will come against him in Your great power—for I have no power of my own—such as I have comes from You alone.

⁶You keep my hands steady so that they might refrain from beating against the rock—instead You give me a strong voice so that I can speak to it in power.

⁷And when the strength of my hands has slipped away and I have none with which to stand—you encourage my steps like a toddler being taught how to walk.

⁸You brighten my outlook and give me hope for the day—my heart will refuse to be downtrodden because You are with me.

⁹You have measured my knowledge and the length of my days—they are not hidden from Your view.

¹⁰Although my love for You may not surface as often as I desire—You, my God—know its depths and are pleased.

¹¹No matter how I long to walk the paths of days gone by—today You are showing me fresh ways and giving me new desires so I will walk in them.

¹²I will not rest in contentedness and let my past lull me into complacency.

¹³You use flickers of the past to remind Your children where they have journeyed—blessed are they who are not willing to linger there.

¹⁴I will trust in You, my Lord, while allowing my frailties to lead me further than I have gone before.

¹⁵My soul looks up to You and sings a new song at this time—for I shall never pass this way again.

¹⁶Praise the Lord exclusively with your soul and worship Him only—for He has sustained you for that very reason—let the thoughts of your heart make Him proud.

¹⁷Never forget where He has brought you from and His marvelous salvation—let those thoughts bolster your heart and lead you forward in the confidence of the Lord.

¹⁸I will reverence Him in holiness and know that He alone is God—would He refuse the honor I bring Him?

¹⁹Do not let despondency on account of your short memory overpower you—for He knows how we are made—and the desires of our hearts are not foreign to Him.

²⁰He will rule and reign in the hearts of those who allow Him to—He will not force Himself upon the unwilling.

²¹Praise the Lord, all you people—through the readiness of your heart—do not hold back what He deserves.

²²As for me—I will praise Him with all that is in me—I will let each breath be a courier of praise—it will honor Him and lead forth with a thankful heart.

²³Into His glory I will come with praise—for He does not just dwell behind a dark cloud—He is present in the midst of thanksgiving and praise!

²⁴He has not left me penniless—he has showered me with the riches of heaven.

²⁵His grace has given me thanksgiving in abundance—how marvelous—how marvelous—He has shown me the light of His glory.

Psalm 175

His Wisdom Comes To Those Who Seek Her

¹Let us be people of destiny as well as children of glory—until we come into the Kingdom designed and ordered by the will of our God.

²The glorious light of His throne shines from above and surpasses the brightness of the sun—the God of all civilization has founded it on truth and discretion.

³Wisdom has called out to me and I have answered—I have inquired of her—to know her beauties—to feast on her truths.

⁴What I seek is not the wisdom of man but that of her creator—to rejoice with her in God's presence—to delight in the wonders of His ways.

⁵Wisdom is no respecter of persons—she has come to the simple as well as the learned—to the young and to the aged.

⁶She will not become elusive to any who truly seek her—for her heart is fashioned after her Creator and she spills forth His desires and knowledge only to fervent seekers.

⁷Let wisdom bombard you—let her come at you from every direction.

⁸Wisdom has displayed knowledge as a banner in the window—let your eyes take her in—and she will be good to you and guard your heart.

⁹She will place a crown of righteousness on those who keep her close—she will bestow honor upon the heads of those who follow her ways—for her name is wisdom.

¹⁰Your mouth—O God—has no need to proclaim Your mightiness—Your works have already shouted forth Your greatness.

¹¹At other times they have witnessed Your splendor in silence without spectacle—they stand starkly against the backdrop of eternity in stateliness and affluence.

¹²Who can count the number of Your wonders—are they not more than the sands of the seashore—are they fewer than the stars of the heavens?

¹³Open me up like a clamshell and pour into me Your holiness and I will praise You with uplifted hands and a pure heart.

¹⁴Your praise is on my lips from the get-go of each day until it has run its full course.

15My praise for You, O Mighty One, is close to my heart—but I release it unto You with total abandon—let it strike the strings of Your heavenly harp with sweetness.

16Let the worship of a blameless heart spew out excitement—its joy cannot be contained any more than water from a fire hose with a broken shutoff valve.

17Make sure your heart sings forth its melodies of praise in clear tones—not muffled or unclear—but with distinct tones that magnify the Lord—that is what stirs Him up.

18Do you dare hand over your heart's desires to Him—can you release them to Him?—if so, then He will meld them along with His and do an amazing thing.

19O God—You are the throb of my heart—You are the beating within my chest—You are my passion that stands at attention and salutes its commanding officer.

Psalm 176

The Breath Of God Sustains Me

1Look to God for all your needs—seek Him daily and He will supply them from His abundant storehouse.

2O how the Master of the universe, who has established time only for the benefit of mankind, loves to fashion a brand new day for each of His children.

3He does it with the utmost care and precision and never fails to take into account all of your needs.

4Do not neglect to thank Him for each day—because you may not have another one like it to enjoy.

5Fill it with the praise of your lips and the good deeds of righteousness He created you to do.

6Do not look upon a single day with disdain or dread—it is a thing of beauty—not meant to be taken lightly.

7Take my words to heart and enjoy each day to the fullest—do not waste the smallest part of even one of them—then your Creator will rejoice right along with you.

8Make His heart glad and thank Him for His creation—because He tailor made it for you—He longs for it to be no other way.

⁹Praise Him now with your whole heart—and His peace will come alongside and be your comforter.

¹⁰I will call upon Your name, O Lord—I will breathe out Your praises continually.

¹¹The breath of God is all I need to sustain me—it keeps me going through the tough times and helps me breeze through the easy times.

¹²Each time I inhale—I draw in His goodness—He fills my soul with delight.

¹³Each time I exhale—it is filled with praises and exaltations—it is impossible to exalt Him too much—let righteousness emanate from my being.

¹⁴I will worship Him with my whole heart—I don't have far to look for Him because my soul has made Him my close companion.

¹⁵Surrounding me is the order of His creation—He is perfect in all He does—who can deny his perfection?

¹⁶Thankfully He is steady and unchanging—He is not moved a bit by the whims of man—nor is His nature affected by our fickleness.

¹⁷On close examination He is found to be unflappable—uncertainty does not bring Him grief—for that is not the place where He dwells.

¹⁸Faithfulness is the ground upon which He stands and the place from which He cannot be moved.

¹⁹I would have stumbled and fallen in the darkness had His hand not been there to guide me—He sees my faltering steps and brings steadiness to my gait.

Psalm 177

Build Our Cities On Your Salvation

¹The army would have been overwhelmed coming against the entire city at once—so the fighting men isolated one stronghold at a time for destruction.

²Lord—we look to You for our help because we see that our strength is puny and insignificant in our own eyes.

³Even before we suit up for battle—

Psalm 177 - Build Our Cities On Your Salvation

before we step one foot on enemy soil—we come against our own sins and those of our fathers.

⁴We examine ourselves and find that not one of us is without sin—we come against the sins of slothfulness and self-righteousness.

⁵Purify our garments so that we can stand confident in Your grace and forgiveness.

⁶Clothe us with the armor of Your might, O God—and prepare us for the battle.

⁷May the prayer of humility grace our lips as we ready ourselves for combat—and let that supplication be a weapon of might through the Spirit.

⁸We have built the foundation of our city upon education and knowledge, teaching and learning—but where is the wisdom that comes from above?

⁹We ask that You would instill righteousness in the hearts of the teachers and leaders of this community—for how can godliness abound when righteousness is not present?

¹⁰You have given us Your precepts and commandments—now help us practice them daily and not look for ways to abolish them.

¹¹We are Your people and we have made You our God—therefore You are the God of our city and we lay claim to it in victory.

¹²Let those people who are proud to be called by Your name rise up all across this land with fervency and desperation.

¹³Cause Your Spirit to breathe new life into our bodies as revival floods our land.

¹⁴Sin loves to occupy the areas of darkness—because sin rejoices beneath its cover.

¹⁵Let the light of heaven shine upon us—so that those You have called will be drawn to it—and darkness will be forced to take flight in the light of its glory.

¹⁶Grant permission, O Lord, for the pathways of salvation to come into our city from many directions—as the saints of the Most High live and walk among the people.

¹⁷We will submit and humble ourselves under Your mighty hand as we allow Your sovereignty to lead us to Your light.

¹⁸Let the burning of Your heart cause our cold and listless hearts to burst into a fire of renewal—one that might reach the most distant parts of our city.

¹⁹And if the blaze should start among the faithful few—it will spread like a sweeping wildfire—devouring all within its borders.

²⁰Give us this city for the sake of Your name and the glory of Your Kingdom—let it be a catalyst unto other towns and governments.

²¹Appoint the bodies of Your believers scattered throughout to be locked in unity and purpose—seeking Your truth and the will of Your Kingdom.

²²At the command of Your Word we lay bare our hearts and seek You for the welfare of this city—we look to Your hand for divine deliverance.

²³Lead us to willing hearts—those hungry for You and the salvation of Your Word—turn over each stone and expose the readiness of those to whom You send us.

²⁴We search after You, O God, with diligence and desperation—fill our hunger and grant our desires of passion and longing.

²⁵As we release our prayer unto You we look forward in anticipation of Your life-changing miracles.

²⁶Our hearts pour out the exaltation of Your name and give praise unto You alone—worship His holiness with me and applaud His unending greatness.

Psalm 178

Catch Sight Of His Form And Be Blessed

¹The sounds of heaven sweep me through its outer gates and lead me down the thoroughfare of its streets—I am drawn there with a longing not of earthly origin.

²Will the Lamb hide His face from me—will I search in vain for His presence—will my failings and inadequacies keep Him away?

³Not at all—for He has borne all my grief and sadness—He summons me to come close to His side—and I will gladly come.

⁴He marks my path through the pages of His Word—it is there I find light for my way and endurance for my journey.

⁵Lord—You are my strength in the morning and what remains at day's end.

⁶Strengthen the inner man, O Lord, when this outer man grows weak—let my seeking heart be set on You all the days of my life—then evil will not come near my tent.

⁷How blessed are those who are God-filled—they have left the footprints of their Lord across the hearts of all they come in contact with.

⁸They refuse to waste a single opportunity to invest each moment of every day for the Kingdom of their God.

⁹My heart stands safe and secure because the faithfulness and truth of my God stand guard to its entrance—my trust and thankfulness have joined them in celebration.

¹⁰Are you the one the Lord has blessed because you refuse to hold hands with anxiety—have you allowed your trust in the Almighty to steer you clear of trouble?

¹¹He has given me a heart that tends toward love—one with a leaning toward truth—all because of the light of His mercy and grace.

¹²His Spirit has instilled truth within its inner chambers—and I have tilted it toward my God—I will bless His name forever and heap upon Him thankfulness.

¹³The dread of night will not come against me as long as the Lord is by my side—what could possibly alarm me when He is there?

¹⁴By the light of His truth He has made the blackest nighttime—like the parting of the Red Sea—for His children.

¹⁵Sin and evil have abode in the womb of darkness until their birth—when their time came to full term they ventured forth.

¹⁶Who can define the light of my God?—in its purity it is indescribable and in its brightness it is immeasurable—its beauty is inexpressible.

¹⁷He demonstrated His awesomeness the moment He said "Let there be light"—He revealed His character to those He would create—His magnificence is eternal.

¹⁸Humanity could now catch sight of His form and be blessed through the revelation of this dimension—this facet of exposure has brought us into relationship with Him.

¹⁹His light was now the opening of His truth—the seed that He longs to plant in the hearts of all who are seeking.

²⁰O Great and Most Holy God—we are most deserving of Your judgment—meanwhile You are more than deserving of our praise.

²¹We will praise You with clean hearts—You have publicized Your worthiness and made it known to us—we have seen it with our eyes and our hearts welcome it.

²²O Lord—what do we have that does not belong to You—which of our possessions have not come from Your hand—is it not all Yours anyway?

²³"Yes indeed it is all Mine, and it is to your credit when you are able to focus and reflect upon that.

²⁴To what can you boast that you have acquired on your own—or what can you hold within your grasp and know is yours because of your strength?

²⁵Who is that man who can engineer one glorious sunrise or cause the planets and heavenly bodies to make one revolution?

²⁶Which mortal can speak a word and have that which is not come to be?

²⁷And where are your philosophers who can unearth wisdom that has not already come from My Word —or knowledge that has not previously been spoken?

²⁸Who by banishing their strength is able to create wealth or by throwing away intelligence can hope for wisdom?

²⁹Can you—by your own futile attempts—order and produce your next breath—is breath not life and does that not come by My command—at My Word?

³⁰Are you able to combine any of the elements I have produced and make a living soul—or is that not within your power?

³¹Make sure and give thanks for My blessings and do not get puffed up by your achievements for I, the Lord God, am the author of life and I hold the keys to it.

³²Go ahead and take a risk for the sake of righteousness—lay your all on the line for the sake of My Gospel.

³³Leave a trail that is longer than your earthly years by sharing My Word —let My message live for all eternity."

Psalm 179

Your Love Covers All Mankind

¹I have reserved blessings and gifts for those who have elected to walk by faith with Me—they will not be disappointed with My selection.

²They have looked unto Me with steady faith—esteeming the loss of the temporary in exchange for the assurance of the eternal.

³My Spirit has made sure that they lack for nothing because the unwavering focus of their minds has been upon Me.

⁴What were you looking for when you sought Me with your whole heart—an apparition perhaps?

⁵Were you striving to see Me with earthly eyes instead of looking for Me in the dimension and beauty of My holiness—in that realm unseen by the physical?

⁶Let your soul search after Me in the depths of your desire—let it reach out and grasp for Me like a mountain climber who has lost his footing and grabs for the safety line.

⁷I long for you to know the joy of My being—in things other than material blessings.

⁸You have spent your entire life seeking purpose and meaning when I have been right here all along.

⁹Allow Me to be the reason for your existence—make Me the centerpiece of your praise and I will fill your soul.

¹⁰You have shown me a better path, O Lord,—not one of my own choosing—a narrow way lined with the cotton-like softness of peace.

¹¹You revived my spirit—it perked up the minute I realized that I am homeward bound—O what glory awaits me.

¹²My soul has heard Your voice, my Lord—truly no other sounds so sweet.

¹³I am a man hungry for You, O God—who has scarfed down Your Word like someone who has not eaten for a month.

¹⁴You have exalted and lifted me up into heavenly places—it is there I am at home in the light of Your glory—free to discover the multitudes of joy set before me.

15 Yet while here on earth I will let each breath I take praise You—this is the one thing I have desired and to which You have purposed for me.

16 Let us sing together the song of the Lamb and tell the story of the redeemed to the nations—we will glorify Him with the praises of our hearts.

17 He has ordered my ways today—how can I allow myself to be stressed about anything?—I will cling to His hand and tell of His greatness.

18 Though my words fall far short of describing His Majesty—He translates my thoughts and words into heavenly languages.

19 He will never tire of my heartfelt exaltations because they come from His Spirit bearing witness with mine, to lay aside my weakness and established strength.

20 I have set out the welcome mat at the doorway of my heart for Him.

21 He has captured my soul and set it free—how can I help but praise Him with elation?

22 He has delighted in the persistence of my heart rather than its perfection—or else He might have despaired at my shortcomings.

23 He has shown light unto my pathway and His Word has been my truth and goodness—His divine power gives me strength to walk uprightly before Him.

24 He has washed my heart with clean water and rinsed it with fresh forgiveness—He has dried the tears of my soul with a spotless towel.

25 What does it take to know the greatness of the Lord—isn't His glory evident every time you look around?

26 He has not kept it hidden from us—we only need to open our eyes and acknowledge His creations as coming from Him.

27 Can the man who closes his eyes see anything—are those who sleep too much able to discern His Majesty?

28 Listen intently for His voice so you can discern His whispers among the distractions of the day—strain to hear His message as His voice falls upon the willing ear.

29 Do not set it aside but purpose in your heart to seek out and know its wisdom.

30 Do not keep your desire to wholly know Him wrapped up as a present would be in order to hide the contents from its receiver.

³¹Instead—offer your longing to know Him as your gift without wrappings—and do not keep it concealed—then He can look upon it with pleasure and pure delight.

³²What can you bring before Him that is too insignificant if it is brought with a heart of thanksgiving and a measure of praise?

³³I will bless His name with all that is inside me—my soul will not cease to reveal His name wherever I go—both now and forevermore.

³⁴Let us lift our voices unto Him and join all those of this present age as we pay tribute to and adore our Eternal King—praise Him with surrendered worship.

³⁵The assurance of His presence daily has caused me to flourish—how blessed and sweet is this promise.

³⁶His strength rises within me—otherwise I would be unable to move—because of this I can look forward to the coming day without foreboding.

³⁷If it were up to my mind to recall all of Your blessings I would be a miserable letdown—but with gratitude my heart will list each one of them without fail.

³⁸Our God has spread His great love across all mankind—much like mayonnaise upon the bread of a sandwich—we have all been touched by it in our lifetimes.

³⁹Take me deeper, O Lord, take me higher—just take me anywhere You go—then my soul will celebrate and be uplifted.

Psalm 180

Unending Praise For His Majesty

¹Let all Your works praise You, O Lord; the sun, the moon, the stars, and all the heavens—even they cannot refrain from exalting Your greatness.

²How much more should we—with the breath of life—emit the praises of God?

³You have given my soul access to worship since its creation—it will not refrain from singing anthems of praise unto You and no other.

⁴I lift my hands to You—and not

Psalm 180 - Unending Praise For His Majesty

timidly—for they are but extensions of the praise of my heart—they are pointers of the way to Your throne.

⁵When I consider the privilege I have to praise Your name—I am brought low in humbleness—my soul will lay prostrate before You in reverence.

⁶See how the praise of my heart overflows the confines of my lips—it rises past the atmosphere with no hindrances—straight to Your throne.

⁷It will be stationed at the outposts of my soul—it has forged new frontiers and will not be fainthearted—it will be mighty until strongholds lie in ruins.

⁸I will honor my Creator with all of my worship—the devotion of my adoration and desire will then be pleasing to Him.

⁹Marvel with me at His unspeakable measure—no one can estimate the extent of His renown—His reach stretches far beyond our scope.

¹⁰See how great His fame is—from everlasting to everlasting is not able to contain it.

¹¹To what can His reputation be compared—is there another that comes close to His caliber—is His competence in question—who can discredit His rationality?

¹²The breadth of His character is unsurpassed—it has become the nucleus of our being—the backbone of our worth—and speaks meaning to our makeup.

¹³The sum of our praises cannot begin to equate Your magnitude.

¹⁴When You deal the barrier of time a final blow, then our praise will be unending.

¹⁵The desires of the Lord draw praise out of willing vessels so praise Him from an eager heart—do not wait for Him to wring it out of you—instead bless His name forever.

Psalm 181

Trust In The Lord Brings Peace

¹Trust in God defies all natural logic—it declines to consider human reasoning as part of the equation.

²It puts a bear hug of blessed assurance around faith and refuses to let go.

³Belief will not make friends with sanity nor confide in doubt—it does not lean heavily upon rationality—for that would be against its grain.

⁴Trust has slain the evil giant of skepticism with a single stone—it rises before the crack of dawn without regard for sleep.

⁵Spurning apprehension—trust has no misgivings about the omnipotence of God—anxiety is terminated in exchange for confidence.

⁶Trust has become the strong Morse code signal unto the soul of the believer—even through the darkest night.

⁷Faith does not do business with uncertainty in any case because that becomes a black mark against God's provision and thus presumes His insufficiency.

⁸Let trust cry loudly and let it call out to those who are being swallowed up by fear—it will be a pledge for them—let it urge them to forsake disbelief.

⁹Trust does not look through rose-colored glasses but prefers to keep any qualms under suspicion—to view all fears with a dose of contempt.

¹⁰It will not stumble with foreboding or be tripped up by uneasiness—it does not peer through the prison bars of hesitancy.

¹¹Do not lean your trust up against worldly riches as a ladder against a wall—for the ground may shift and the ladder will tumble.

¹²Trust is not a commodity that can be purchased—nor can it be acquired by superficial means—it only comes from a sincere heart with pure motives.

¹³Let trust lead you down the quiet path—His strength will guide those who lean upon Him in dependence.

¹⁴The trust of His saints is manifest throughout their daily walks—

they take action with no thought of failure—the Lord holds their lives in esteem because of their faith.

[15]They will let it rule in all they do and will not consider any other point of view—they have made it their way of life.

[16]He makes His grand and glorious way visible to trusting souls—for by this they have acknowledged the Lord their Savior.

[17]Trust will lead your heart in righteous ways when your desires are dedicated to His purpose—let your behavior be secure in reliance on Him.

[18]The light of His glory has brought wisdom to the eyes opened to His truth—let it fill you with understanding.

[19]When understanding has moved behind a cloud and is not visible to the discerning spirit, and you cannot get a grip of any kind on perception—let faith and trust rescue you.

[20]Transfer your confidence unto Him for safekeeping and you will find inner peace.

[21]Toss foresight to the wind and give deliberation the heave-ho—then He will be swift to validate your trust in Him.

[22]All who have a strong reliance upon His abilities will not be ashamed—He will bring about more than presumption—instead poise will be theirs in the midst of battle.

Psalm 182

Let His Love Set You Free

[1]Let your love for the Savior draw you closer to His side—let it flow from you freely—it will keep you from drifting off the pathway.

[2]When we hear nothing except God's voice of silence—we should take note quickly—for He always has our best interests in mind—His will is more vital than our happiness.

[3]Never permit your earthly desires to be scrambled with the purity of His—do not let them intervene into areas of spiritual holiness.

[4]Impound and drag them to the pit

where they belong—banish them from your mind—shoo them away like pesky flies.

⁵Encourage His love to reign in your thoughts—You, O Lord, need to reel in my thoughts like a determined angler pulling in a prize catch.

⁶Praise leads temptations captive and directs our vision heavenward—it gives us favor with the Father as we walk in His light.

⁷The godly have allowed the plans of the Lord to unfold in their lives like a dinner napkin at a costly banquet affair.

⁸How marvelous is the love of our God—which those in this world have seen—His servants have clearly shown it to them like a sign on the shoulder of life's highway.

⁹The child of the King is a torchbearer of His great light—he holds it in his hands and it shines on those nearby.

¹⁰His mercies each day are better than freshly picked berries from the vine—their freshness enhances their sweetness.

¹¹The God of heaven will speak His mind unto those who truly seek after Him in truth and humbleness—He will make His message clear unto their spirits.

¹²The Lord prompts the footsteps of the ungodly—but the evilness of their hearts will refuse to follow—yet at times their yielded hearts will find salvation.

¹³He will set free with joy those who allow Him to guide their daily walks—their steps will be straight and their hearts unburdened.

¹⁴Let all who hear the voice of the Lord heed and obey it quickly—when the handwriting on the wall comes—it is too late for action.

¹⁵He strips us of those we love sometimes in order that we might lean harder upon His mercy and taste more richly the blessings of His grace.

¹⁶O Lord, my God, the desire of my soul is to walk blamelessly before You all the days of my life so that all I say and do will praise You in spirit and in truth.

¹⁷You lead and guide me in the way of all truth—You establish my feet securely upon the pathway of righteousness.

Psalm 183

Physical Strength Is For A Season – His Power Is Forever

¹The saints of God have not lost their focus on heaven because hope has become the lure that draws them closer each day they live.

²Hope to the godly is like the scent of prey to a hound or like the smell of bacon frying—it invites hunger to all within its reach.

³The Spirit of God will speedily draw any yielded heart closer because that is what pleases Him the most.

⁴Those who are led by God have allowed His Spirit to rescue them from the grips of materialism—they will sacrifice the desires of their hearts unto Him.

⁵Do not cling to those things He has given you—those things that have come from His hand—for He may take them back if you don't have due respect for your Creator.

⁶He has filled my cup with His goodness—I have found much gratefulness of heart with which to lavish upon Him.

⁷I will rejoice when He places my cup so that the overflow of its blessings spill onto those less fortunate.

⁸He leads my soul around scattered objects—giving me the righteousness I need to navigate around them—watching over my heart the entire way.

⁹I will praise You, O God, with all my resources—I will let my way of life speak volumes more than my expressions.

¹⁰Measure your words carefully as you would when adding salt to a recipe—too many words will only bring regrets.

¹¹Sow your utterances in a straight row—not haphazardly—so that at harvest time you will be blessed with a fine crop.

¹²The godly do now allow their feelings to goad them into speaking rashly—they are quick to ask His Spirit for wisdom and guidance before vocalizing their thoughts.

¹³He has cleansed the God-fearing man from the feeling of unworthiness for receiving His blessings—his grateful heart has set him free from the chains of self-condemnation.

¹⁴You, my God, have introduced my weariness to Your strength—You have shaken hands with my fragility and the two have found close friendship.

¹⁵Even when I awake refreshed with new strength—I will lean upon You, O Lord, because Your strength is so much greater.

¹⁶And when the strength of my youth has disappeared—and feebleness has wrestled it to the ground—I must depend upon Your strong right arm.

¹⁷Physical strength is only for a season—the power of Your Spirit is forever.

¹⁸When a man is subdued and has exhausted his last ounce of strength—You, O Lord, remove his breath of life and he is laid to rest from his days of toil.

¹⁹You provide the night hours to restore the vitality lost in the undertakings of the day—You re-create new vigor and re-establish soundness of mind.

²⁰You have given me sharpness of thoughts as I concentrate on Your presence—Your Word brings clarity to my spirit.

²¹I am stunned by Your greatness—I've been taken aback by the marvel of all Your creation—how can I help but praise You?

²²Do I have any works to offer that would qualify me for Your marvelous grace—do I have any redeeming qualities that would acquire even one particle of Your mercy?

²³My finest offerings would not be enough to scrape together a speck of significance for me to pay my dues and merit Your salvation.

²⁴I will let the works of a grateful heart offer unto You thanksgiving forever and always—You have satisfied my heart like no other.

²⁵Sorrow has multiplied repentance and turned it into joy—with that, O God—You are exceedingly pleased.

²⁶Come let us fall before Him in reverence—let our voices cry out and praise Him for His majesty—we will exalt Him in our praise—for He alone is worthy!

Psalm 184

He Will Set Your Heart Free

¹If you will only quiet your heart and mind before His presence He will draw you to His side with hushed whispers—do not neglect your time with Him.

²Let Him and Him alone entice your heart—let His Spirit guard your thoughts and keep your prayer centered on wholeness of the mind.

³I love You, Lord, and my heart declares its love for You daily.

⁴May the hallowed thoughts of my soul follow after Your good pleasure—let them seek out Your wisdom—and petition Your mercy again and again.

⁵The imparting of truth and the revelation of His Spirit will come in spite of those who stand opposed to it.

⁶He sweeps them aside and removes them like a river discarding riff raff downstream—the doomed are moved along like mighty waters surging at flood stage.

⁷The light of His glory will cleanse every willing heart so it can purify and govern freely without recourse.

⁸Do not be frightened by the advances of His Spirit or be intimidated by His calling—instead embrace His arrival with open hearts and see where He leads.

⁹Seek with determination and pray earnestly that He will open the eyes of your spirit—He will not fail to lead in righteousness those who sincerely search for Him.

¹⁰As this life is metamorphosing into glory—You surround me with Your presence and I am never alone—no alarm can overrun me as I walk this road to eternity.

¹¹You, O Lord, enable us to move into your physical presence as simply as walking through the doorway and into the next room—how we praise Your name for this light.

¹²The life dedicated unto God has drawn support from the smile of His pleasure.

¹³My feet carry me from place to place—but Your Spirit, O God, sweeps me into Your presence.

¹⁴He has put time on my side—and given me just enough to accomplish His will and purpose for my life—that is only if I do not fritter it away frivolously.

¹⁵The rejoicing of my soul has made my enemies scatter—O how it sings forth in praise as I view all the works of Your hands, my God.

¹⁶My soul has become enamored by Your greatness and needs no further indication of Your majesty.

¹⁷I cannot help but marvel at all the vastness You have set before me—and how insignificant I am in the middle of it all.

¹⁸And yet man is unable to see many portions of Your greatness—because You have kept it hidden for a later time.

¹⁹I will let Your greatness flood my mind—for out of it shall come extreme praise—my heart and soul will sing a duet unto You.

²⁰Even out of the randomness of my thoughts—You, O Lord, are able to bring order—You have settled the determinations of my heart and found them gratifying.

²¹As I praise You with my whole heart—You fill me with wonder and I am smitten with silence—You have made my soul speechless and I am unable to articulate any more.

Psalm 185

He Has Bid Me Come Closer – How Can I Do Less?

¹Those who search diligently for God come to Him with open hearts—longing for new visions and dreams.

²How blessed is that man who has opened up his heart before the Lord—he will walk clear minded and with a steady focus each step of his day.

³The Spirit of God will steer him in the right direction whenever he lifts his thoughts higher than the ground upon which he walks.

⁴When I asked God to open my eyes so I could see His glory—He showed me His starlit sky—and I bowed before Him in awe.

⁵I asked Him for answers to my questions—and He bid me to simply trust Him.

⁶He showed me even greater glories when I opened the eyes of my heart and saw that God dwells within man—He has invaded my soul and filled it with the light of His glory.

Psalm 185 - He Has Bid Me Come Closer – How Can I Do Less?

⁷I will let my heart dwell on all of His wonders—then I will be filled with delight—His hand will escort me in joyfulness.

⁸Praise Him now with all the breath He has placed inside you—let it come forth with exuberant worship while you delight in the heart of your Father.

⁹Every breath I take belongs to You, O Lord; I reserve each one unto the praise of Your glory.

¹⁰Let your heart devote each breath unto His holiness—allow it to dictate the purpose for each mouthful of air unto your Creator.

¹¹Make known your purpose unto Him with a heartfelt prayer—and He will encourage your soul at all times.

¹²Pray unto the Lord that your soul will prosper and be well—seek His healing of your mind so it will dwell upon Him continually.

¹³I love to be swallowed up by the presence of my God and to view my intimate relationship with Him all around me.

¹⁴He has bid me to come closer—so how can I do any less?

¹⁵Who do we have but You, O Lord?—You have set your hand against the righteous as well as the unrighteous—the faithful count it as nought because their trust is in You.

¹⁶Do not shrink from the drawing of His Spirit—He is willing to set His Word into action at your request.

¹⁷He feeds the hunger of those who look to Him for righteousness—to all who thirst for truth He will satisfy by the light of His Word.

¹⁸The sincere heart will seek to know God's eternal pleasure instead of its own—He has shown my condemnation the exit door and His forgiveness has ushered in true peace.

¹⁹Before I arise each morning I make a mental note of my need for You, my God, I find it always registers in the desperate range.

²⁰My mind is quick to fill with gratitude for Your allowance of a new day—the nearness of Your presence refreshes me.

²¹He has caused me to stand in the house of God and to walk through the gateway of praise—with a heart of thanksgiving I will enter heaven's domain with joy.

Psalm 186

You Are So Worthy Of My Praise

[1] Those the Lord has called He has redeemed in glorious fashion—they will walk in His light and reflect His glory every place they step foot.

[2] They will walk with quiet assurance and their trust will not waver in the least—they will bear up resiliently under dark clouds.

[3] The marvels of their God will be made clear unto them because they have exalted Him as holy.

[4] He has exchanged all of our sin for endless worship so that His glory might be made manifest unto all—speak forth His praise on earth as it is in heaven.

[5] O Lord—You are near to those who walk through the desolate places—when loneliness overshadows them like a sheet covering a bed—even then You are present.

[6] For those who choose to serve You—Your love is not measured by a lifetime but for an eternity.

[7] Our unwillingness to look inwardly is the roadblock to all that God has purposed for us—He seeks a heart inclined toward Him.

[8] The Spirit of my God gives my heart discernment—He tells me which path to follow.

[9] Let me absorb Your Word, O God, into the pores of my soul—then I will be strong against the enemy.

[10] He has shown me new paths where the righteous have walked—He beckons me to follow closely without turning aside.

[11] The joy of the Lord becomes the highlight of my day when He is my focal point.

[12] He gives me permission to fill His courts with praise—O how He rejoices when I abide by His desires—He then showers me with affection.

[13] God has allowed my sorrows to accumulate with those of saints gone by—all the while knowing He will address them at the proper time.

[14] His mercy quickly runs forward to meet all who call on His name with sincerity.

[15] Sin lurks in the heart of the ungodly but joy abounds in the heart committed to the Lord—He gives His rewards to the devoted.

[16] The joy of the Lord has stood up and catapulted over my grief and woe—even they are not enough to suppress His delight.

[17] My soul will kneel in ecstasy and bliss before Your throne, O God—it will not fail to prostrate itself in Your presence.

[18] After periods of testing and walks along dry and dusty pathways—He has brought me full circle to familiar places—His Spirit has guided my steps with care.

[19] He has made my way to prosper when I was not even aware of it—His Word has become my daily rations and the meditations of my heart.

[20] My soul looks for You more regularly than the great lion that prowls the jungle in his hunger.

[21] Because You are worthy, O Lord, I will give You praise—there is no higher calling or greater destiny.

Psalm 187

Entertain The Glory Of The Lord Daily

[1] God spreads His love over the people He calls by His name like the snow that covers a barren land—He clothes His people with fresh mercies.

[2] He opens the eyes of those who long for Him to nuggets of truth—He will not fail to bless them with abundant provisions.

[3] In their barrenness He causes a spring to come forth unto their souls—then they will rejoice with many words of praise unto His name.

[4] He has burned the song of the redeemed down deep within the souls of His chosen ones because they yield their hearts unreservedly unto Him.

[5] O how they love to praise His glory—that is all they live for—they know the glory they achieve from their own efforts will fade like a cloth bleached out by the sun.

[6] He reveals Himself unto them because they have learned to seek Him in the secret place—it is there that their hearts will not be denied.

[7] They will not stumble in darkness because His Word has become their flashlight.

⁸See how quick the Lord is to jot down even the smallest deed that pleases Him—He will not fail to write it in His book.

⁹The Lord is kind and generous with His benefits—He allows sleep to those who offer Him a clear conscience.

¹⁰He will not look away in revulsion at my inadequacies—no—He is stirred beyond belief by my weakness and offers me His strength.

¹¹The Lord has dealt love unto me from His hand of mercy—and grace from His hand of justice—I will praise Him for His compassion.

¹²Sit at the feet of Him who knows you best and be comforted in His presence—sit still and listen—He will speak all you need to hear.

¹³He brings the hungry heart close so He can fill it with good things—does He leave the inquiring mind unfulfilled or let those who sincerely seek Him go away empty?

¹⁴He makes the Spirit-filled mind a tabernacle of purity—an abode of righteousness where He can reside.

¹⁵A yielded heart brings the diverted mind back into focus.

¹⁶Integrity shakes hands with honor and invites a man to a life of wholeness—it offers to lead him down the paths of truthfulness—past the gates of iniquity.

¹⁷Grace and mercy are currencies of the Father—just think of how lavishly He spends it on us—His children.

¹⁸God's faithfulness has inundated those who have received His peace—His mercy has smothered them with a hush in their souls.

¹⁹The Lord is never chintzy with His love—He is always liberal and bighearted—I will not forget to think on His goodness or fail to give Him a thankful heart.

²⁰He is not the least bit stingy to those who seek Him wholeheartedly—they have heeded the promptings of His Spirit.

²¹He honors them with life so they might praise Him with offerings of thanksgiving—it is His good pleasure to bless them beyond measure.

²²When faithful people let their hearts pray to God in place of many words—even their feeble groans are more effective than a top-notch speech at a motivational seminar.

²³The godly are anxious to crown Him with praise because He is worthy and they have seen His greatness.

²⁴He awakens His chosen ones with songs of praise—with promptings He points them toward the completion of His call.

²⁵Their hearts are content to dwell on all His greatness and He delights in the desires of their hearts—they aim to please Him.

²⁶The devout heart is not sporadic in its search for truth but is set on a path of purpose.

²⁷Daily I will entertain the glory of the Lord—His presence I will make welcome—let His servants never cease to delight in calling on His name.

²⁸God moves His children along the path of righteousness in order that He might pick them up and place their feet upon the highway to glory.

²⁹This is a glorious road that leads to the gates of His Kingdom—He allows His adopted children to travel it with joy and dignity—the Lamb is the light of their lamps.

³⁰After those close to His heart have lived lives of truth and righteousness He honors their faithfulness by dismissing them to their lives of eternal reward.

Psalm 188

You Are The Keeper Of My Heart

¹You, my God, are the keeper of my heart—when my mind disappoints me—You look inside my being and are satisfied.

²Your eye keeps a close watch over this heart of mine—You send Your Spirit to keep it in check or else it might stray from Your path.

³When the stress of my walk causes my feet to ache and my limbs to grow tired—when my vision is blurry and my knees grow weak—then I call out to Jesus.

⁴He reveals my mortality through the lens of eternity—I have seen my calling and purpose and accept it from His hand.

⁵Because of this my confidence is not inward but upward, yes, He is always my strength.

⁶Let your life blaze a trail of peace for others—straight to the Savior—walk this path in confidence and you will find rest for your weariness along the way.

⁷My waking thoughts belong to You, O God; they fasten upon Your goodness and prepare me to walk in Your ways.

⁸I bring You my gaping hole of inadequacies and You fill it with Your presence—Your strength bolsters my neediness.

⁹Which foe or alarm can come near me with Your hand guiding me? —O Lord be the source of my delight.

¹⁰You have shown your people the path of righteousness—now we are glad to walk in it because its end leads to glory.

¹¹Holy Spirit—You are the fullness of my worship unto God—led by truth through my yielded heart.

¹²Worship in the mystery of God—not in the understanding of your mind—reverence and bow in awe of Him and not His creation.

¹³Do not search for explanations of His greatness—instead praise Him for His greatness—then your spirit will touch His with humility and true worship.

¹⁴Let His voice speak to your heart—hear the stillness of it in its majesty—hear it in its simplicity—let it guide and direct your every step.

¹⁵Kneel before Him and adore Him—let your heart lift up your praise—there in humbleness exalt Him—He is worthy of all praise.

¹⁶He leads by the might of His counsel—by the strength of His arm we find guidance—His knowledge marshals us onto paths of truth.

¹⁷Truth is the genuine fabric of His being—the molecules of His character.

¹⁸Bring truth to every part of me—line the walls of my heart with it—let me be as steeped in it as a teabag is in a pot of boiling water.

Psalm 189

I Will Follow Your Voice Down The Narrow Path

¹The ways of the Lord are made clear by His Word—and truth is revealed unto the searching heart by its light.

²With each new day that comes my way I will renew my choice to praise my God and serve Him with all my heart—the choice is mine to revive or to make brand new.

³Listen for His voice and let Him guide you down the simple path—an unadorned trail that leads to righteousness.

⁴If you follow this solitary lane it will bring you into a clearing of truth.

⁵There are other voices calling out to you that would have you follow the wide path—it is adorned with many comforts but will lead to unfaithfulness.

⁶The voice of the Savior is gentle and directs our steps along a narrow passage—it arrives at calming pastures of freedom—His voice will not lead to confusion.

⁷Because there is breath within me I can still give praise—because I have another day I'll give Him all my praise.

⁸Now I'll take this time—while I have the chance—to give my God the praise—to take His hand and dance.

⁹Any time of day or night He delights to hear your praises—He never tunes you out—for such a time as this I will give Him praise.

¹⁰The persistence of my praise achieves a great victory in the same way that water wears a channel through the hardest stone.

¹¹My carnal mind cannot possibly comprehend the greatness of God—its limited capabilities cannot even begin to fathom His eternal perfection.

¹²Only You, O Lord, can broaden my vision and enhance my sight so that I can take in Your wonders.

¹³Your love, O God, is deeper than the ocean—mightier than its power—more vast than the farthest reach of all its shores.

¹⁴When I listen to the sound of its crashing might I am held in awe—then I praise You for my hearing and Your witness to me—its deafening roar is greater than a lion's.

¹⁵My soul is stirred as a vessel tossed about by its mighty waves—I exalt You, my God, in Your strength and in Your greatness.

¹⁶I am humbled by Your power and moved by Your mightiness—I have both seen and heard them in the amphitheater of my soul.

¹⁷The song of my soul has been borne upon the waves of Your ocean—its melody has carried me unto the shores of heaven.

¹⁸The earth is filled with continuous praise as Your glory, O God, covers its surface.

¹⁹What is there in all creation that does not owe allegiance to You, O Lord; indeed have not all things in heaven and below it received their existence by Your hand?

²⁰The galaxies are alive with the sounds of worship—not even pausing for breath.

²¹Are not the winds and the waves subject to Your command—do they not move at Your bidding—how can I do any less?

²²My heart belongs to You, my God—and I will direct it to esteem Your faithfulness as its highest offering of praise—You have filled it with the wonder of Your greatness.

²³Come humbly into His presence—and bow before His majesty in meekness and reverence—He is the fountain of all life—the healer of nations.

²⁴Let His name, Jehovah, be spoken breathlessly and with awe—surely heaven's moment will be worth far more than earth's lifetime.

Psalm 190

You Do Your Will Through Thankful Hearts

¹The works and wonders of God plainly reveal that there is none like Him—they ratify the truthfulness of His Word.

²I will praise You, O Lord, in this place among the heavens—I will give glory to Your great name while here on earth, which is too small to even be Your footstool.

³Since the breath of God gives me

Psalm 190 - You Do Your Will Through Thankful Hearts

clear license to praise Him I will not neglect my right to worship.

4What gift can a man present unto His maker that he has not already received—what gift can he offer that would be pleasing unto Him?

5The Lord has never refused the gift of a thankful heart.

6My heart will lead me to the altar of thanksgiving where I will bow before Him with my gift of worship.

7He has parted the heavens and filled me with waves of glory—my soul belongs to Him and I will not give it to another.

8Let Him call forth nobility from among the simple things of your life—if you give Him His rightful place in all you do, blessings will be abundant.

9I held my hand out to Him and He filled it with His—He said I will lead and direct your path since you are willing to let Me do so.

10Your love, O God, has surpassed the most noble of our deeds and the vilest.

11Your grace has outmaneuvered our best efforts and instigates hope to flourish within our hearts.

12Let the gifts of the prudent be passed on to others so they will magnify His greatness and bring glory to Him.

13The wheels of faith move undetectably in the lives of those who follow God's Word.

14Open my eyes that I may see none of this world but God's glory—You, O Lord, are great and glorious—grand and majestic and full of power.

15Help us accept Your bounty of blessings with thankful hearts—may we also view adversity as a measure of the workings of Your hand.

16This day belongs to You, O Lord, I readily submit my portion of it unto Your majesty—enhance my submission so that my life consistently pleases You.

17Those who focus on the Savior find the cares of life drop away like the shackles off a prisoner set free.

18Never discount the workings of those He chooses to bless you through—for His hand of providence sends many agents.

19Your kindness, O Lord, has kept my feet on solid ground—you have directed my path around the miry clay that was before me.

20Fill the hearts of the godly with light so the darkness on the outside will not distract them—they will only see the light that surrounds them.

²¹You have set Your light, O God, upon the lamp stand of my heart so that nothing will detract from it.

²²I will seek nothing outside Your will, my Father, let it be done in me and my soul will sing praises unto Your name.

²³Your strength has been my glory all the days of my life—if it had not been I would have passed on before now.

Psalm 191

Fresh Praises Prevail Against A Faded Mind

¹When my mind has faded sharply and no longer brings me constant daily remembrances of You, my God, I cry to You in desperation.

²When advancing years have kidnapped my intellect and the evening of life has snatched its freedom—I will still be fearless because You are with me.

³And when my brain no longer recalls the longings of my heart with precision—I will rest my anchor securely in Your faithfulness and love to me.

⁴When my mind's eye is blurred and cloudy—when its sharp edge has been dulled like a mower blade hitting a rock—even then I will give You untarnished praise.

⁵I will press into You when the bleakness of my mind comes against me, and my soul will sing unto Your name and prevail.

⁶Yes my soul will rejoice with fresh praises throughout the darkness— O how I will praise You—You have flooded the windows of my soul with light.

⁷Your Spirit comes to my aid, plucks the strings of my heart, and makes sweet music—the glory of which You will accept as I yield unto You a sincere heart.

⁸When I was glum and doleful You showed me the warrant You signed for my soul—thereby assuring its salvation.

⁹Because You have built my whole heart upon the truth of Your Word I will not falter when my mind fails me—You are the rock upon which I stand.

¹⁰Let me feast on Your truth and be nourished by Your Word—I have tasted the springs of heaven—their cooling waters have touched my lips.

¹¹I will glory in Your steadfastness and strength—I will lean heavily upon Your mercy—Your grace will guide me until I come into the light of my new home.

¹²The promises of my God stand forever—because of them You will never forsake me—my hope remains tightly linked with Your Word.

¹³As I close my eyes to the world around me, I will lift my hands in praise to You.

¹⁴I will let my soul speak of Your immortality—I will exalt Your wonders unceasingly—for all eternity.

Psalm 192

A Faithful Walk Brings His Rewards

¹Who is the friend to the publican and the sinner—is that not what I was while here on earth with you?

²They are My beloved ones who share My Word in truth and deed with everyone they encounter—I will not judge them as unrighteous and neither should you.

³Do not look down on those who go against your grain or do not conform to your expectations—I, the Lord—will only hold you liable for the straightness of your walk.

⁴I will relieve you of any responsibility to judge your neighbor, foe, or friend; trust in Me as the Supreme Judge and leave all such matters in My capable hands.

⁵Honor Me with your strength and integrity—use My Word as your plumb line and level—remain founded on My principles.

⁶It is My place to inspect and scrutinize the lives of those around you—I have not given you that concern—nor have I made that your livelihood.

⁷I see the heart—whether evil or good—and I will make My judgments based on that—do not fret yourself with My job.

⁸You will receive My reward in future days only if you let your life shine with the light I have placed inside you.

Psalm 192 - A Faithful Walk Brings His Rewards

9 The soul that walks close to the Master is peace and light to a watching world—it is blessed by leisured trust.

10 When the Lord of heaven takes a righteous man from this earth and receives him into glory—He will leave many roots from that man's stump for succeeding generations.

11 Many will taste the fruits of his labor and find abundant life because of his witness.

12 His family will also find great peace in the midst of earthly sorrow while realizing heaven's gain—He who has promised this is more than faithful to the ends of the earth.

13 The Lord has chosen to inhabit the simple-hearted—their hearts are adorned with the fabric of praise and the tapestry of worship.

14 Seasons come and seasons go but the faithfulness of my God stands forever—undaunted in the face of change—unflinching throughout many revelations.

15 Do not take lightly the presence of His glory that surrounds your daily life—and never fail to give thanks for His fellowship—it will surely light your path.

16 Worship the Almighty in your earliest morning hours—it will set the course for your entire day—then you can walk with ceaseless praise and be joyful.

17 Let your praise rise higher than the words you speak—then it will be seen through the deeds of your life.

18 The soul of the mighty, O Lord, will praise You even in silence.

19 I will let the beauty of Your holiness come to me in the rapture of the stillness.

20 I listened closely and then I heard His voice—at first it sounded like the crashing of many thunders or waves beating against the rocks.

21 Then I listened closer still—it was as light as the wings of a butterfly next to my ear—as soft as a gentle breeze upon the leaves of a tree.

22 He spoke directly into my thoughts and I was amazed—speechless by His greatness.

23 The farthest horizons stretch out before man's view and disappear into oblivion—they are only entrances to His unseen worlds.

24 Even a speck of power in the little finger of the Almighty far surpasses the greatest power of man—one cannot even begin to compare the two.

²⁵A simple flex of His muscles causes all mankind to tremble—the mere clearing of His throat makes the nations quake with fear.

²⁶He smiles and covers the earth with the warmth of His sunshine—His tears water the terrain from above.

²⁷The wave of His hand makes cooling breezes—the heat of the land is stifled for the moment.

²⁸I have gathered my thoughts to present them in the company of my God.

²⁹O how I delight to think on His greatness—to rejoice in His power—He gives my soul gladness of song before His majesty.

³⁰I take delight in Your goodness, O Lord—may I find equal delight in pleasing You each and every day of my life.

Psalm 193

I Will Praise You While Looking Mortality In The Eye

¹He has set His joy before me and bids me to reach out and take hold of it—now it fills me to overflowing.

²When I waited silently for the Lord to come—then I knew He was God.

³Lead on, Holy Spirit, teach me the assignment of my God for this day—stay close and be my mentor so that I will find success and please Him.

⁴Does youth last forever—do the hands of time stand still for any man—does vitality stay with us all of our days?

⁵Does God promise us that our strength will outlast our limitations—that our potency will outlive our purpose?

⁶Can physical effort overcome our loss of stamina—or do we just throw in the towel?

⁷When the best of our strength has been crushed by weakness—when fatigue has traded places with health and exhaustion has caused vitality to yield to its dominance;

⁸When brawniness is not able to pounce upon the enemy of mortality or look feebleness in the eye—when it has been stretched

further than an overused rubber band;

⁹And when the vigor of youth has dried up like a spent flower off of which most of the petals have fallen;

¹⁰And there is no sign of it found in this decrepit body where health was once its stronghold—where its weather-beaten flesh totters with the daily breeze;

¹¹Then my spirit will rise up in praise to You, my God, I will rejoice again from the depths of my soul —for Your greatness has become my strength.

¹²My hope in You will overpower my faulty faith—then I will stand in power and prosperity while reveling in Your truth.

Psalm 194

Your Majesty Is Inescapable

¹I will not fall down and worship the star, it only points to who You are; I bow and worship Christ, my King, and bring to Him my offering.

²Never stop praising His name as long as there is breath within your body—can you somehow claim that as your own?

³Our days have increased and here we are enjoying another one because of Your blessing, O God; and we have food to go along with it.

⁴Let us never refuse to acknowledge Your divine hand by our sincere gratefulness.

⁵Do not fail to encourage your brother when you have opportunity—it may be the very word that enables him to go on.

⁶He will be blessed because of your counsel and uplifting—and you will have rescued him from falling.

⁷I will praise Your name, O Lord, because of Your goodness—my heart will sing of it all the day long.

⁸O how I love to begin each new morning with the taste of praise on my tongue—I am filled by the nectar of worship unto my God.

⁹Let your heart reach out for that genuine encounter with the

Almighty God—let the burning of your soul demand it—lest you worship only an idol.

¹⁰Watch for that bush around you to start burning—then your heart will stand before Him without shoes—then you will know you are on holy ground.

¹¹Allow the fire of His presence to jump the fire line around your heart—you will burn with zeal and holy righteousness without being consumed.

¹²Then your soul will be led to that divine encounter it so desperately longs for.

¹³O Lord—You continue to bless those who are alive with added days and new ways to praise Your holy name.

¹⁴I will give Him praise in the house for His goodness—I will carry it with me all the day and disperse it unto Him continually.

¹⁵The Lord—the Faithful One— has allowed those who seek Him wholeheartedly to find nuggets of truth within the field of His Word.

¹⁶He has shown them caves of wisdom wherein they can mine His truth and store it up for their future prosperity.

¹⁷They will not be content to be rich but will share this treasure with many others.

¹⁸Feelings of inadequacy do not belong in the hearts of the godly— they will let the hope that dwells within mount up and slay those emotions with a spirit of humility.

¹⁹The truly satisfied heart desires nothing more and nothing less than God Himself—it can want for nothing to be added.

²⁰He has caused me to walk with a limp so that I might not hurry along the path ahead of Him.

²¹He has shown me the correct way to go and I must choose to follow it—even though it is not the path I would have chosen.

²²O how blessed are they who move along with a steady pace and do not run ahead of His commands —they will not be disappointed or cast down.

²³I will not look in the distance for my God—I have found Him to be closer than the air I inhale—His Word resides within me.

²⁴I will let every breath I take be like a trumpet blast of praise—an overture of worship unto my God and King:

²⁵I will present each breath as a grand and glorious exaltation of His Majesty so it will continue in accordance with the desires of my heart.

²⁶He will open wide the doors of heaven and come in splendor unto that soul who has come before Him in sincerity and fervor—His presence will brighten that person's day.

²⁷He is greater than the scope of His heavens and the span of His universe—He is inescapable like a pinching of your skin—the utterance of His name brings intimacy.

²⁸O Lord—You are the champion of my heart—You have defeated him who would come against my soul to bring it down.

²⁹Join with me and magnify the Lord—His name is glorious and praiseworthy—it is supreme and to be hallowed above all others—O praise the Lord, O my soul!

Psalm 195

I Will Bring Forth Your Beauty In Due Season

¹The Lord covers the earth with His love and moves the earth through the midst of His glory—at His Word it stays on course.

²He patrols my neighborhood in faithfulness—He keeps a close eye on all my ways—He sees even the smallest disturbance.

³I never need to sound an alarm because He has sent a company of His angels to care for me—I am secure in His watchfulness.

⁴Because of His great mercy His hand has kept me from tragedy—He has caused my great enemy to turn back in utter confusion.

⁵Speak the praises of His name out loud in the rooms of your house —in the secret places of your dwelling let your exaltation of Him be heard;

⁶Bring your finest offerings of praise before Him—make your song of worship known to Him with a heart overflowing with thankfulness;

⁷Then all of heaven and all nations will hear and receive Your song—You will reveal Your voice upon the mountaintops.

⁸Never fail to speak His praises in the darkness—for out of this your

testimony will come—your heart's desire will be made known to all—it will not be held back.

⁹He has put you on this earth to be a flower of His glory—so bring forth His beauty in your season and you will be pleasing unto Him.

¹⁰Do not cry unto the Lord for a place other than the one He has granted you—refuse to go after other pleasant lands—for He has not given those to you.

¹¹His voice comes unto the yielded soul with a strong and steady tone—it does not stutter—nor does it falter in its message—neither does it come with vagueness.

¹²Let your ear be open to hear Him—He who speaks with truth longs for you to gladly follow His commands.

¹³Those who take His Word to heart will not be stymied—He has made their path clear—they will walk in unhindered devotion to their God.

¹⁴Let your pain show the depth of your commitment so that He might know what is in your heart.

¹⁵I will praise You, my God, with my whole heart—both in the reality of life and in times of uncertainty—when skepticism would try to overrule me.

¹⁶During those times when my heart may hesitate or my mind may discredit my beliefs—I will cling to Your faithfulness and not let go.

¹⁷My heart will need no prompting in order to praise my Redeemer—it has decreed to worship Him forever.

¹⁸Those who have walked the road of faith will stand before Him with gifts to bring.

¹⁹O how I will praise Him—for a new day has dawned and my soul has been set free.

²⁰The best part of waking up is worshipping my God and praising my great King.

²¹Where can you find that willing heart—a heart moved beyond its natural desire—if not in those who have surrendered to the Spirit of the Almighty?

²²He has led them to walk in heavenly places—in realms of glory—because their hearts have opened up and revealed the Spirit that God has placed in them.

²³While they have crossed paths with the wayward souls—their desires have led them past—for they know the end of the wicked is an earthly one.

²⁴The righteous have devoured His Word and He fills them with understanding.

²⁵They will let their praises ring true and He will lift them high above the shadows.

²⁶He has loaned His faithfulness unto me for but a season and given me clear vision for my path.

²⁷He has come down among the common people so they might be rescued—His light will show them truth so they will find salvation.

²⁸To those He has called to be holy He has given the extra mile to run —and He will be their sustaining strength in their final hours.

²⁹They will not stagger but will bear up under His mighty hand—they will pass the finish line with their torches held high and burning brightly.

Psalm 196

Cradled In His Holy Hush

¹Let the influence of God drape you in His love and power—it will clothe you with glory, honor, and strength.

²To those who would believe—He has made the sun to break through the dark clouds so they have a bright hope to cling to.

³Make the desire for God that thing you dwell upon and it will only be a short time until you have yielded to it—it will be a consuming fire upon your forests.

⁴The heart after God only needs to draw inward—there He is just waiting to commune with you, Friend to friend.

⁵He has let His goodness go before me like a locomotive in front of a long line of railroad cars—it prepares my path for the coming day.

⁶Like a snowplow after a blizzard it clears the way so I can travel in safety.

⁷To those who walk with Him daily —He shows Himself real through all they say and do—the light of His glory and presence has become their confidence.

⁸He allows the faithful to walk in victory—their spirits of earnestness will guide them all the way—they have not made it their place to wonder at His calling.

⁹He will safeguard them and not allow the slayer of souls to come against them—they will rejoice once again—for He has seen their hunger and filled it with abundance.

¹⁰The richness of His Word has displaced their leanness and given them fleshiness upon their bones.

¹¹To those who would ask of Him the Lord grants a wise and discerning heart—then they will gladly choose gratitude over complaints.

¹²I will look daily upon Your glories—the manifestations of Your love—then my heart will be glad and burst forth with song.

¹³Let us call upon the name of the Lord Almighty in full faith—He will answer and show us His truth.

¹⁴Like the parting of the Jordan—He has parted the chaos and strife of my world and led me to a retreat in the midst of it.

¹⁵There He covers me with His blessed quietness and I am healed—this is where I can find true peace.

¹⁶He calls me to His side and summons me to listen—He reveals to me that there is no better clamor than the stillness of His presence.

¹⁷It is not His intent to compete with the riotous sounds of singing—nor will He intrude upon the tumult of disorderly worship.

¹⁸His voice is heard much more clearly in the quietude of my worship than in the bedlam and clamor of commotion.

¹⁹I will marvel in His reserved glory—for He cradles me within His holy hush.

Psalm 197

Behold, I Come Quickly...

¹The Lord populates the earth for His good pleasure and takes great delight in those who choose to worship Him.

²He began by planting it with the good seed so that He might reap a bounteous harvest of righteousness—but alas—the enemy has sown weeds of sin in His garden.

³"Who are the mighty ones I have called by My name—are they not those I have placed My righteous

seed within—those who do not look to their own strength?

⁴I can use them because they have positioned Me above all gods and will not consider any other.

⁵By the fertility of My Word they have sown many seeds with no thought of a harvest—they are content in planting My Kingdom.

⁶Their lot was not in the harvest but in the planting and watering—I have kept the reaping hidden from them but I will reveal it when I have purposed it.

⁷I planned a great harvest—one of many souls for My Kingdom—it is not the rich and powerful who will be taken but the small and weak.

⁸I will gather the humble in heart because of their hunger for righteousness.

⁹How long will I resist the prayers of the godly and ignore their urgings for My return to come quickly?

¹⁰For I have indeed been moved by their pleas—they have caused Me to reconsider My timetable more closely.

¹¹Although it has always been My heart that not even one should perish—I have always known that many will not accept the free gift I have to offer.

¹²Soon I will sweep the earth and gather My harvest—those who are watching and waiting will not be surprised.

¹³I will not neglect My chosen ones much longer because they have been faithful to My call—they have laid aside earthly pleasures in exchange for a crown of glory."

Psalm 198

What Is Too Great A Sacrifice?

¹My heart longs to know You, my God, until nothing else matters.

²What is that hard thing He would ask of you in order to know the sincerity of your heart—so that He might know your devotedness?

³Do not lay it aside and hope it will go away—do not pray for relief from the heaviness of its burden.

⁴Do not decide to give Him another sacrifice or present a different offering than the one He wants you

to give—the one He has already asked of you.

⁵When you pray to Him do not seek release from that hard thing or He may ask an even harder thing—then what will you do?

⁶Settle in your mind that you will please Him in no other way than doing what He has purposed for you to do—then He will multiply His blessings unto you.

⁷Set aside the pride of your heart and humble yourself before His majesty—never let the enemy of your mind sidetrack you from the promised blessing.

⁸I have immersed myself within You, O God, until I am no more—You are all of me and I am all of You.

⁹What could He ask of me that I might consider too great a sacrifice—has He not already led the way in the line of sacrifices?

¹⁰How can I do less than to accept from His hand those things He has given me—whether I perceive them to be good or bad?

¹¹He brings deliverance unto those who have turned their hearts over to Him.

¹²My soul revels in Your greatness, O God—it can only gasp at Your marvelous wonders.

¹³I look forward to that day when my spirit will know only Your Spirit and the things of this life will be swept away.

Psalm 199

See Him For Who He Is

¹Trust and thankfulness will swing the door to the heart of God wide open.

²Who among us has knocked upon His door in faith believing, and He has not answered?

³Are you prepared for His answer even if it is not what you want to hear—or even if you must wait a little longer to get it?

⁴Place your trust in His wisdom and He will reward your patience—let Him secure your soul and He will wrap it in a cocoon of His love.

⁵Whoever walks close to the Master abides daily in His presence—he

will not view it as an obligation but as joyful service.

⁶O that everyone would praise my God for His greatness—that all would see Him as big as He really is.

⁷Let us not confine Him to our mind's eye but observe Him in the grandeur of His holiness through the eyes of our hearts.

⁸Those who have looked through the telescopic eyepiece of God's Word have seen Him in larger-than-life form.

⁹This does not make Him any bigger—but those who view Him through His holy scriptures are able to see Him in a way the natural man does not.

¹⁰Blessed is that purposeful man who has determined to walk closely to his Lord while taking no thoughts for his own plans—instead he relinquishes everything to Him.

¹¹The Lord looks down upon the land and watches for those who rise up and seek Him wholeheartedly —for those who bow before His throne in humility.

¹²As for me I will let every breath I take praise the Father—because He is so worthy.

¹³The beauty of His holiness is not in the abundance of things but in His abiding presence and peace.

¹⁴Join with me now and see His glory and majesty—let it wash you clean through the water of His Word.

¹⁵If He is not Lord of all your life—if He does not own you—then surely He walks far away from where you stand.

¹⁶Call to Him and sever your worldly ties—He will draw near to your heart—do it now because if you hesitate it may be too late.

¹⁷He will lead you down paths of righteousness if you will put your hand in His—go wherever He takes you—He always knows the right path to follow.

¹⁸I will not fall because of Your hand, O Lord, which holds me securely.

¹⁹Do not be distracted by worries— they are a sin against God's holiness—they are a rebellion of your will against His great faithfulness.

²⁰Let us not forget the majesty of God and treat Him as common—worship Him for who He is and not for the sake of His works.

²¹I will let my spirit look upon Him with awe and my soul will delight in His greatness again.

²²Come before Him with reverence—do not let your mind take control—listen to the dictates of your heart and fall prostrate before Him.

²³Seek Him with total sincerity and the candidness of your heart will shine out.

²⁴Let Him reveal the simple things of His Word before you ask for the deep things of His Kingdom—He will reveal the basic truths before He shows you His grand designs.

²⁵Quiet your voice and stop your speech—revel in His holy quietness—then you can be still and know that He alone is God.

²⁶In that particular moment do not look for Him to be God—and do not listen for Him to be God—simply let the depths of your soul be still and know that He is God.

Psalm 200

He Is My Story

¹I will praise the name of my God forever, because of His great love for me.

²When He woke me early this morning my heart could only bless Him—He has given me a clean fresh page on which to write my story.

³I must write with care upon this page since no man knows whether he has many chapters left to write—or whether this is his final page.

⁴He is the theme of my story—so let me tell all who would read about His greatness—without Him I have nothing to write.

⁵If it had not been for His grace—my story would have been thrown on the garbage heap—so I will praise Him all the more.

⁶He steadies my hand as I carefully write so that no blots will come upon this page—for I have dedicated it to His glory.

⁷I will walk with grace and dignity because His hand leads me on.

⁸He has put good thoughts into my mind so I might express His greatness to all—so the multitudes might praise His incomparable name, as well.

⁹Listen closely and you will hear only words of truth—He is the glow of my lamp and the motif of my song.

¹⁰O that only His praises would come from my lips—may they run rampant all through my story.

¹¹He is the freshness of my song and the originality of all things created—I will let Him infuse me with new boldness.

¹²I will glory in Him for He is my story—He is my tale of joy.

¹³Sing to the Lord of hosts—the hope of heaven and earth—the breath of all mankind—acknowledge His majesty with all of your being.

Psalm 201

He Takes The Barren To New Heights

¹Rise up today and seize hope by the horns—shake off the feeling of doubt and cast aside unbelief.

²Let the faithfulness of the Almighty take you to new regions of His delight—then you will experience the newfound might of His hand.

³He will show favor to those who seek Him with their whole hearts—not because of their great works—but because He has seen their resolve to follow His ways.

⁴O Lord—You have honored the intentions of their souls and not regarded the weaknesses of their flesh—Your mercy has removed their stains and stigmas.

⁵He has chosen some to walk the solitary road—the lonely path—to travel upon the barren heights as their birthright.

⁶They must not let the altitude of that place deter them, however, because He has called them to a higher calling.

⁷The Lord their God has let them roam the loftiness of those peaks and survey heaven's glories from that vantage point.

⁸They will have little communion with those of the earth—He has purposed to show them His splendor—and that is its price.

⁹He has called them aside to a walk of faith and to pursue delight in Him only.

¹⁰The ugliness of sin will not be their viewpoint any longer—He has made them to emerge far above it.

¹¹They will not squint to see because He has shown them His wonders in panorama.

¹²The survey of His grandeur will be their reward—His fellowship will be their peace.

¹³His purpose is eternal and they will tread upon His paths in contentment.

¹⁴Then He will show Himself real to the desires of their hearts because they have come close to Him—their souls have searched for the better thing.

Psalm 202

The Earnest And Sincere Heart Will See God

¹O Lord—I long to hear Your voice—not only in the stillness but also through the ruckus of chaos.

²He has settled the offerings of the righteous in their souls—they will bestow their gifts with gladness in their hearts.

³Because of the willingness of their hearts He has blessed the works of their hands—He will make their toil go much further than its initial efforts.

⁴They will not become weary in their labors but will have strength for the day—He will multiply it unto them many times.

⁵His strength has overpowered my weakness—now I will declare Him to be my joy.

⁶I will verify how He has come near to me and become my security—He has replaced my lacking with vitality.

⁷Offer the Lord fresh praises and discard those that are stale and weak—dump those that are well worn and give Him something crisp and new.

⁸Hit and miss prayer will not take you to the deep desire and longing of your soul—only consistent and earnest prayer will lead you to that place.

⁹Let your soul run to Him—then it will be happy and at ease.

¹⁰My heart will not give You forced praise or insincere worship—I will let it come as the irresistible offering of my soul.

¹¹Open your heart to Him—lay it bare before Him and He will give you the richest of His plentiful treasures to sustain you.

¹²Do not be afraid to go forward in the strength that you have —through it He will perform mighty works—then your deeds will bring glory unto His great name.

¹³The graciousness of the Lord has permitted us another day so that we would choose to give it back to Him filled with praise and thankfulness.

¹⁴He awaits our eager expressions of gratitude—He is honored by a life of praise.

¹⁵Adore Him with all that is in you and bow low before His majesty.

Psalm 203

His Grace Can Heal Any Disease

¹When sickness comes against the house of Your children—when it infiltrates the ranks of Your righteous ones;

²When the enemy of their souls is pleased to wreak havoc against their bodies—to put an end to their godly witness and to snuff out their light;

³Then You will allow the cries of their hearts to lay Your stripes upon them as a blanket of healing— their praises will erect a standard around them.

⁴Praise will cause a spirit of power and strength to be unleashed throughout the house as they proclaim the everlasting glory of their Creator.

⁵Disease and affliction will be ushered out the front door of their dwellings because they have trusted in the Most High.

⁶He will turn their suffering into rejoicing and come against their plight with mercy.

⁷With their prayers they solicit His healing—by their praises He advances wellness into their bodies.

⁸He will let healing flow because of their praises—they have aroused the heart of their God and He has moved on their behalf.

[9]When the scourge of the enemy seeks to silence their testimony they are able to say—blessed be the name of the Lord.

[10]For the name of the Lord is their strong defense—even in their weaknesses He is the praise of their hearts—the joy of their hope.

[11]His grace has become their ransom—He is their shield and portion—they have let His mercy reign enthroned upon their praises.

[12]They will declare His worthiness—for He has blessed their souls—His grace is enough for every hour.

Psalm 204

Bow Before Him Today Like There Is No Tomorrow

[1]Let the praise of the whole earth be directed unto You, O Lord—may it go forward and touch every distant star—let every high and low place be filled with Your glory.

[2]Your name, my God, is one of goodness and high merit—in it there is no blemish.

[3]Come before Him with the sacrifice of a clean heart—worship Him because of who He is—call on His name with trembling.

[4]Shiver in His presence and be still before Him—shudder under His mighty power.

[5]Focus upon Him only and do not be distracted in His presence.

[6]I will shut my mouth and listen only for His voice—then I will be glad when He speaks unto me those things I need to hear.

[7]His presence has removed my unworthiness and replaced it with the peace of His holiness—I will acknowledge Him with humble silence.

[8]In this moment He has caused stillness to be born within my soul—I will give pause with anxious hush.

[9]I will not recoil or shrink from His authority—He has heard my soul's cry—neither will I squirm while I am in His embrace—it is there that He comforts me.

[10]He has made me to flourish in His presence like a well-nourished plant.

¹¹His strength has given steadiness to my hands and my spirit will not draw back—I will praise Him in all my ways and throughout all seasons.

¹²The child of God weighs carefully what he would ask of the Father—to make certain it is in keeping with His will.

¹³As he grows he becomes more deliberate and practical in his requests—he leaves sentiment for another time and place.

¹⁴Seek for your heart to be in perfect alignment with His—for you know that gives Him immense pleasure.

¹⁵He longs and loves to bless His children—His blessings never run short because abundance is at the core of His heart.

¹⁶Lift your hands to Him and bless His great name—praise Him all the day.

¹⁷Let your mind be pleased and let your heart be dignified to worship His Majesty in innocence—with purity—free from challenging the loftiness of God.

¹⁸Knowing that God's plans are lifted above our conceptions and that we are not permitted any say in His proposals let us stand back and give Him our submissiveness.

¹⁹Instead—shouldn't we bow before His great wisdom and acknowledge that He alone has the first and the last words in all matters?

²⁰O that the whole earth would praise Your name—You are deserving of the praise of all Your creation.

²¹If only my praises could intercede for all mankind—that they might take the place of the praises others refuse to give you, my God.

²²Even though darkness comes upon these earthly eyes and the light of day no longer shines for me—even then Your Word will be the light of my heart.

²³Let us not become bashful in coming before our Father's throne—He has motioned and called for us to come close.

²⁴Let every day be a great day in the Lord—this is way better than a heart attack!

²⁵Serve Him today like there will be no tomorrow—then we will have no regrets.

²⁶Let us carry the blessings of the Lord everywhere we go—like taking a first aid kit with us when we go camping in the woods.

²⁷Since He distributes His blessings to us freely—should we not pass them along to others?

²⁸He has resurrected my soul unto His good works—therefore I will not be stingy with the gifts I bring unto Him.

²⁹Never allow the blessings of the Lord to become an idol of your heart—the thing that takes away your focus from the giver.

³⁰Even if He gave me a multitude of lifetimes to make this discovery—I would never be able to find another that compares with my God.

³¹Every breath I take exalts Him because that is my utmost desire.

Psalm 205

He Reveals Himself To The Passionate Soul

¹I have seen a great hope for me—the Lord does not regard the outward man with special fondness but looks deep within the heart—what joy I find in that.

²Rejoice with me in this mighty revelation—if the Lord Himself does not look upon the outward appearance of a man then neither should we.

³Are we, the sons of man, able to look deep into one another's heart?—then we should not judge anyone because that belongs to the Lord alone.

⁴I will marvel in the Word of the Lord and give Him thanks for His great light.

⁵Yes, how I will praise His majesty because the God of all eternity looked down upon me and sanctioned my beginning.

⁶I will praise the One who formed my life from nothing and gave it purpose.

⁷Who would dare to label His existence—is it not pure and holy—without beginning or end, timeless and forever?

⁸He has fashioned my start and given me no ending so that I might reign supreme with Him throughout all eternity.

⁹Do not withhold your praise from such a God as this—worship Him and bring Him the glory due Him.

¹⁰Never let your lack of comprehension lead you to the place of frustration and despair—He does not

require your understanding in this or any other matter.

¹¹My soul will sing unto Him the praises of my heart—I will encourage the depths of it to rise and declare His greatness unto all who will listen.

¹²I have looked for Him in the mornings but see only a small portion—my rational mind holds me in restraints—it holds me captive and will not set me free.

¹³How I long for the day when I will be able to see You, my God—in all Your glory—to know those things my mind is unable to grasp.

¹⁴All mankind is held subservient to Your greatness—we are held hostage by our denseness.

¹⁵Let us search to know that small fraction of what He has allotted unto those who seek after Him wholeheartedly—that part and parcel He shows unto the passionate soul.

¹⁶I will not pursue Him with my rational mind—it has no insight with which to fathom His mightiness—my spirit must guide me into His truth.

¹⁷Like gloves for the hands and stockings for the feet—the Lord's compassions cover all my insecurities—His mercies wrap each of my fears with His great love.

Easter day 2013

¹⁸The victory of the Risen One has come my way and lives mightily within me.

¹⁹It has given me power to rise with wings at His call—my soul stands dressed and waiting to hear the thunder of His voice.

Psalm 206

The Word Of Our God Stands Forever

¹The Word of God has been uttered through the lives of many—it has been spoken with power and authority in many dialects and tongues.

²His Word can go where no man can go—it is able to touch the hardest heart and make it pliable like putty.

³It is suitable for emperors and no-

bility as well as the child of a slave and the common man—it works powerfully on the front lines or undetectably behind the scenes.

⁴You, O God, have sent Your Word into the forsaken places of this world—whether by printed page or spoken words—it has moved in power and with precision.

⁵Those who send forth Your Word are sowers of righteousness—they are unfazed when tracking across enemy territory.

⁶Your Word can guide the hearts of the blind if they have a willing spirit—it uplifts the weak and gives power to the needy.

⁷You have sent it into the most unlikely places to lead the searching to salvation.

⁸It has been trampled underfoot and burned at the stake—it has been drowned and cast into prison—it has been pierced by bullets—yet it grows stronger.

⁹The Word of the Lord has been ridiculed and despised but its love will not falter—it has cheered the downhearted and given faith to the hopeless.

¹⁰It has cost men their lives but given freedom to many—it has been from the beginning and will last throughout eternity.

¹¹His Word contains His plan and gives man the promise of salvation —His Spirit will guide the truly searching heart.

¹²The power of His Word causes the demise of empires and upholds justice—it can trigger truth to spread faster than a deadly cancer.

¹³At times it moves boldly across regions and sometimes cautiously—its power cannot be contained by a penitentiary or placed in solitary confinement.

¹⁴It has been passed down from generation to generation without regard for the cost—the Word of God will not fail to accomplish its purpose because it is truth.

Psalm 207

Peace In The Midst Of Despair

¹The Lord and His great majesty have given me stillness—the quiet of the hour is my disconnect—it melts the distractions away so I can hear His voice more clearly.

²He shows me the way to closer communion with Him each time I enter His rest.

³What is like the beauty of silence when it is met by His tender voice?

⁴Flush away those earthly interferences of the mind as you might flush the commode—let His peace refresh and quicken your spirit.

⁵Where are those who are willing to devote their whole hearts unto Him?

⁶They need to come out with the boldness of His Spirit and He will cause them to shine forth with the brilliance of a lightning bolt so that His glory will not be hidden.

⁷He will make the wisdom of His Word clear to the seeking and the open heart—then His laws will not be concealed from them.

⁸Where can I go that His mercies do not go before me?

⁹His kindness overshadows my life—I have witnessed the results of His angels protecting me from my own clumsiness.

¹⁰I will marvel and praise His great name—He protects all my ways—should I fall He will safeguard me from even greater harm.

¹¹Does He not watch over all my steps and harbor me safely under the shadow of His Almighty shelter?

¹²Yes, I will give Him all my praise; His love is my stronghold and His mindfulness is my retreat.

¹³Let us make a pledge to commit all the remaining days of our lives unto Him—let us submit each and every future breath irrevocably unto His glory.

¹⁴When He has become your song of praise you will have tasted the benevolence of His good pleasure—then the joy of the Lord can be your strength.

¹⁵O God, Your confidence has entered the hearts of those who have lifted their eyes unto You—because their trust is obviously in You.

16 They have dismissed their doubts and forbidden them to rise up—they will not look behind but only forward into the light of victory.

17 Seek Him now and He will make your welfare of utmost importance—how often has His care for you been overwhelming?

18 He has caused me to rest content in His good message—His Words have ministered peace unto my soul.

19 In all my searching He has shown me the doorway to quiet peace—my spirit will prosper because of my trust in Him.

20 I will not fear the uncertainty of the ages because He is with me.

21 When the enemy would tout the direness of the days—it is then I throw up my hands in joyful praise unto my God—for He is greater still.

22 Even in the hub of troubles and predicaments He is there to bring me hope—He speaks assurance to my anxiety and all is well.

23 I will not allow the dread of the coming days to fill my mind—but I will again focus upon His greatness—then my soul will be revived with inner strength.

24 No hour holds terror for the child of the King—he knows his Father holds all power in His hands and victory is His to give.

Psalm 208

You Are The Desire Of My Heart

1 My soul has stirred me awake with a twitching of the body and a fluttering of the eyelids—long before the light of daybreak.

2 It has overcome the desire to sleep because of its passion for You, my God—it has not regarded the luxury of rest as top priority.

3 When it rises from my bed and leads me by the hand we come into Your presence, O Lord, with a refreshment of spirit and a reviving of my senses.

4 Then I am satisfied as the praises of my soul are lifted unto You and the fondness of my heart is revealed in worship.

5 I have set the affections of my soul

to bow before Your majesty—then I will regard nothing else but You.

⁶Your friendship has aroused my soul to sing once again—Hallelujah is its refrain—my soul will sing its joyful melody unto You.

⁷O how I hate the ways of this world I have been born into—the rapture of my soul awaits Your coming Kingdom.

⁸The cravings of my soul have driven me to seek Your will—yes how the ache of my heart will not allow me to go my own way.

⁹To dwell in Your eternal presence is the song of my soul—the desire of my heart.

¹⁰It will leave no stone unturned in the thirst to find my God—my devotion will be fastened upon hearing His call and seeing His glory.

¹¹The rapture of my heart will never cease to be inclined toward Him—then my life will be driven with purpose toward His Kingdom.

¹²My soul will never fail to gravitate unto His calling as I retreat from worldly pleasures—His love has influenced my heart and draws it upward.

¹³Give the Lord a loyal heart and He will not forsake you in any way—acknowledge Him without hesitation and let your truthfulness bless His name.

¹⁴They who are able to step aside and follow His leading in all matters—regardless of how small or great—will see the works of heaven accomplished right here on earth.

¹⁵Who is blessed like those who have allowed the Holy Spirit to take them beyond themselves—at times into dimensions of spiritual exploits?

¹⁶What He orders—do not rearrange—what He desires—do not seek to change.

¹⁷Let us allow our daily lives to be punctuated by praise and thanksgiving—like a well-structured and grammatically correct sentence.

¹⁸I will praise You, O Lord, in the moment—when all else around me has forsaken and fled away—You are there.

¹⁹You never fail to receive my praise—it falls upon Your heart with gladness.

²⁰It flows endlessly from a grateful heart—it will not waver—it is the sacrifice of a clean heart and a willing attitude.

²¹He has given a crown of splendor to those who would walk the daily walk with Him—they will wear righteousness as their veil and truthfulness will be their boast.

²²Who is he that is confident in his own strength—yet fails to consider where that strength comes from?

²³In due time it will be stripped away as the bark is peeled from the log in a lumber mill—as a hillside is eroded by the constant rains—as daylight passes into darkness.

²⁴Will his self-sufficiency allow him to rise up as a body builder lifting a large weight?

²⁵Look to the Lord—though your strength may be small—and He will lift you up.

²⁶Give Him thanks for His greatness as you acknowledge your weakness—exalt His holy name and you will receive power from on high.

Psalm 209

The Yielded Spirit Stands Triumphant Before God

¹The spirit of a man can sustain him in life—it is able to befriend him while he is in the valley of death.

²It is able to build a mighty tower to reach the heavens—it has also grappled to touch the distant planets that man can see.

³Some have even wielded their spirits with a strong disposition of defiance all the while mocking their Creator.

⁴Has not the Lord given a spirit unto each man for his benefit—has He attached it with limits or restricted its use?

⁵God has allowed free will to govern man's spirit—this has exhilarated him oftentimes with reckless power.

⁶Although God has granted man a freedom of his will—His deepest desire is that man will use that liberty to honor Him.

⁷Man's spirit can lead him to the pit of pride or to the peak of humility—it is controlled by the mandates of his heart.

⁸From its depths can arise ultimatums that will either lead him

righteously or condemn him for life.

⁹The surrendered spirit has relinquished all claims of authority back to its Maker—it is at peace with God.

¹⁰A yielded spirit has won a great victory—it will stand triumphant in submission and concede all rights unto Him.

¹¹Who is able to control his own spirit by single-minded tenacity—are we able through sheer resolve to conquer its force?

¹²Consider the meekness of our Lord when His final words were uttered—Father into Your hands I commit My spirit—shall we do less than this?

¹³O that my spirit would be surrendered with total abandon to You, my God—and that my will would be swallowed up by Yours.

Psalm 210

Every Day Is A New Day With Him

¹O Lord—as I lie awake in bed—before I even rise to greet the day You have made—I put all my shortcomings squarely on Your shoulders.

²I should not feel hesitant to do this because that is what You invite me to do—Your Word instructs me to toss all my pathetic deficiencies upon Your broad shoulders.

³With an offer like that—why should I be hesitant to hold anything back?

⁴Look for Him in the least likely places and seek Him among the ruins—you just might be surprised where you find Him lingering.

⁵Let Him bring you face to face with your inadequacies and you will discover how great your need for Him really is.

⁶Let us allow our faith to be worthy of the trust our God has placed in us.

⁷When I look behind at earlier days I notice there was never a time I needed Him more than today.

⁸Open your heart to Him so He may come in—just as you would open

your garage door and drive your car inside.

⁹Check your commitment level to Him in a similar manner as you might check the oil level in your engine.

¹⁰He has made my life into a funnel for pouring His goodness into the lives of others.

¹¹He has narrowed the days of my life here on earth—much like the bottom of that funnel—so His glories may be poured out with pinpoint accuracy.

¹²The trust of the righteous is their stronghold—peace is theirs as they wait silently for God to reveal His glory—a lack of the visible rewards will not thwart them.

¹³As they bide their time for the unearthing of heaven's proclamation they are filled with the joy of hope.

¹⁴The Lord is loving and merciful both in the day of disaster and the day of peace—let us learn to thank Him for whichever has come our way.

¹⁵I will delight in the Lord while in this present life—so on the day I see His face my joy will be made perfect.

¹⁶I will praise Him in the sanctuary of my worship where there are no walls to contain my praise.

¹⁷The peace of God brings calmness to the troubled soul and steadies the uneasy heart.

¹⁸Even though the strength of my youth has slipped away His love will never abandon me—what else do I need to trust in except Him?

¹⁹Let the intimacy of His Spirit stimulate the inclinations of your heart —then it will awaken a new urgency in your spirit.

²⁰Show your inward godliness through acts of good will—then others will see the generosity of your God and praise His name.

²¹Many spread their time, money, and service unto numerous lands and invite God's glory and intervention—these gifts have journeyed to places the giver could never go.

²²I will let my praise for God be like a city without gates, a country with no walls, a prison with no bars, a river with no dam;

²³Like an electric wire with little resistance, my praise will have few barriers to slow its travel to the throne.

²⁴Every day is a new day in my God —therefore I will set before Him a fresh variety of added praises— I will discard those that are out of date—tattered and unresponsive.

25 Offer unto Him your unpracticed worship—let Him give you a clear mind and an unstained heart—then you can worship Him in true holiness.

26 Let your awe and reverence of Him be wide-eyed wonder—He alone belongs on the pedestal of your worship.

Psalm 211

For Lonnie & Linda

1 How great and how far reaching is God's love?—it has circled the earth upon which you reside.

2 It has even touched your own heart—you who read these words have been touched by it—even though you may deny it.

3 Is there anywhere you can go that His love cannot reach—why do you fight it then—does it make you feel powerful to turn Him down again?

4 It is not His intention to force your acceptance of His love—although He could.

5 He has all the time in the world—but you do not—so why risk the final tick of the clock?

6 Nothing in your past is too great for His forgiveness—nothing—nada—zero—zilch—zip—I think you get the drift.

7 His love stands waiting—so why don't you come to Him while you still have breath?—nothing would excite Him more than to have you around for all eternity.

8 He has made salvation as simple as can be—Lord, forgive my sins—take me—I'm Yours.

9 Do not turn Him away again—it may be your final call.

Psalm 212

Sacrifices Of Praise Draw Us Closer To Him

¹All those who are known as the sons and daughters of God Almighty are only too happy to be led by Him daily.

²You have taught me to delight in You, O Lord, even in my sickness; is that not better than to be laid in death with no breath left with which to praise You?

³God's faithfulness never goes on vacation or takes a holiday—do not let yours lapse or take a break.

⁴Honor the Lord with dependability—be rational and levelheaded in all that you do—show your loyalty to Him throughout the day.

⁵The lips of the godly have been parted with praise and their tongue is only too happy to tell of God's goodness.

⁶Unto those who have a teachable spirit the Lord will do mighty and surprising things—this is His way of changing them into His likeness.

⁷Let teachability clothe you like an outer garment—allow your spirit to be a training ground for all of your days.

⁸The godly are reliable in all that they do and please Him by their truthfulness—they rise up in faith so they can walk the road He has positioned in front of them.

⁹He has seen a better way for me to go so I will not dare to depend on my own leading, besides, my own guidance would never lead me to that most excellent place.

¹⁰Marvel that the God of all creation would choose for His presence to reside in such lowly and plain temples as these bodies we are clothed in.

¹¹That He did not demand to reside in something more palatial is no small wonder—even the Taj Mahal would not be lavish enough for His dignity.

¹²What would it be like for you to allow Him to take you down a different path than the one you are used to walking?

¹³Forgo the plans you were making right now and try His handling of your day—see if His ways are not better than yours.

¹⁴Let His Spirit take you places you might never have thought of—be prepared to see things you may never have noticed before.

¹⁵Could you possibly dare to trust Him to direct you down an unfamiliar path—down a God-forsaken lane?

¹⁶Let the joy of the Lord increase with each passing day that He delays His coming—because you can be certain it is that much nearer.

¹⁷To those who have a heart after God—He will allow His grace to lift them higher than their weaknesses—then they can praise Him for His added strength.

¹⁸I looked and saw that He was greater than all that was around me—then I fastened my gaze upon Him and was able to see His faithfulness.

¹⁹Let His Word shed the light of understanding upon your eyes and His Spirit anoint you with the truth of counsel—then He can direct you with perfect advice.

²⁰I will not let my heart be overcome with grumbling because of my physical ailments—nor will I let criticism come from my lips against my God.

²¹How can I possibly protest the trials He sends my way when I see my fellow-man bear even greater hardships than the ones I do?

²²Perhaps I should consider the adversities others must endure that I cannot see—those afflictions they carry that are hidden from view.

²³I can only praise my God from the depths of my soul—He has intervened on my behalf—in His mercy He has made my suffering light.

²⁴Be overwhelmed with rejoicing—let praise move you past your pain.

²⁵I will praise Him—He has undoubtedly been my support—He has taken an interest in all my troubles and has sent His Spirit of peace to my aid.

²⁶I am thankful He renews me inwardly in spite of the decline of this fleshly body.

²⁷When your strength for the journey ahead is too little—when even the upcoming day looms larger than a nearby mountain—you can call on His name.

²⁸He hears you and will certainly be there before the words are out of your mouth.

²⁹Today begin to look upon challenging times as opportunities of praise—allow your difficulties to draw you closer to the Master.

³⁰I will offer Him a sacrifice of worship at all times—that is what pleases Him most.

Psalm 213

There Awaits Your Heart's Desire

¹Walk an unimpeachable walk—let the Holy Spirit authenticate all your ways—then no other man will be able to lay a label of counterfeit upon you.

²Live so all you come in contact with will see the genuine Gospel—show love that is the real deal and up-front grace.

³Darkness cannot be snuffed out like a candle or extinguished like a match—but it can be caused to flee by the smallest infiltration of light.

⁴I offered Him my battered and bruised soul—He took it, lovingly bound it up, and put the ointment of His love on it.

⁵O how I will praise Him for His tenderness—He has restored my soul unto me.

⁶His Spirit has taken my submission—the yielding of my heart—unto the throne of His grace and offered it as a pleasing sacrifice.

⁷He has kept the hand of the destroyer steady and far from my dwelling because I trust in Him.

⁸How mighty and powerful is the faithfulness of our God—what can stand up against it—what can put a stop to it?

⁹He has shown me it is greater than all time and eternity—if you can number His days you will know its origin.

¹⁰Is it more outstanding today than it was yesterday—will it be more impressive tomorrow than today—can He improve on any aspect of it?

¹¹It never fluctuates or wavers in the least—if it did, it would not be something we could ever count on because it would be imperfect.

¹²Trust only in the Lord and the power of His strength—stand strong in the certainty of His faithfulness and you will never be without hope.

¹³He rules with righteousness and extreme order—His plans are precise and systematic—He has regulated all He does with accuracy.

¹⁴All His creations show His attention to detail—His exactness is something to be marveled.

15Praise Him for His faultless nature—worship Him only—He is perfect in all He does.

16Give glory unto Him because He has given us insight into His conscientious nature.

17Let the diligence of your heart and soul be drawn unto Him—search untiringly for His presence—when you find it—there awaits your heart's desire.

18Lord, rule and reign within the confines of my heart and I shall want for nothing else, I surrender its domain unto You.

19The Lord Almighty has set aside a large harvest for the godly because their hearts are turned unto Him.

20They have not seen the season of reaping with their natural eyes—but by faith—they have caught a fleeting look at His heavenly Kingdom.

21It was not up to them to search for the fruits of their labors nor to observe the yield of their toils.

22They did not strain to see the produce of their crops—neither the springing up of their plantings.

23Sowing and planting were their main concerns—they happily watered in season.

24The Lord of the harvest has given them credit for reaping outside their natural loins.

25They have disregarded race and creed because they desire salvation to be known to all who would receive it.

26God has also given them honor because of their adopted offspring—righteousness will be their compensation.

27The Kingdom of heaven has advanced because of the faithfulness of their prayers.

28The salvation of a multitude of souls has been set aside as their reward and crown because they have not failed to pray for their children.

29They have had many additions to their descendants—those they do not even know about—their lineage has been a godly dynasty and their ancestry is one of a royal birth.

30Because they have looked unto Him in their season they will in no way forfeit their prize—it will be given to them as a sanction of honor.

Psalm 214

Let His Wisdom Forge New Paths

¹The ways of the Lord are often baffling even to those who are personally close to Him because His paths are too lofty and unattainable for mankind.

²His behavior is holy and beyond our limited knowledge—His nature stands in unapproachable truth and light.

³The being of the Almighty cannot be traced with human reasoning—nor can it be discerned with philosophy or sound judgment.

⁴Give Him honor in all your thoughts about Him and respect His mysteriousness at all times.

⁵Never second-guess His ways—that will only lead to doubt—exalt Him in all His decisions and worship Him in spite of your confusion and uncertainty.

⁶Acknowledge the excellence of His ways—let His wisdom overwhelm you with admiration for His greatness.

⁷I will command my mouth to be silent and my lips to stay shut so that I might worship Him with my heart only—then I will glorify Him simply in spirit and truth.

⁸My words will melt away like an ice cream cone on a hot summer day—I will let the fullness of my soul lift its praise unto Him alone—with that He will be pleased.

⁹I will let my soul praise my God—for He has given it permission to pour out its ultimate cravings in His presence.

¹⁰He has shown it all His starry hosts so that it might worship Him—not them.

¹¹Last night He covered my pillow with whispers from heaven—their sweetness was my delight—His words were so gentle.

¹²He said, "do not long to revisit your past—you may botch it even more than you did the first time around—give thanks for My grace and its covering.

¹³That which I have cleansed cannot be made any whiter—trust in My completed work in your life and move on.

¹⁴Do not desire to return to your former days—whether good or bad—because I have unseasoned agendas for you to follow—new proposals for you to seek after.

¹⁵Open your mind to My leading—I will never steer you down the wrong path.

¹⁶Give Me your persistent and yielded heart and I will do things such as you have never seen.

¹⁷Worship Me unceasingly and you will not fail to see My glory.

¹⁸I will open your eyes to My truth and My delight if you will seek Me only."

Psalm 215

He Dwells In The Secret Place

¹The secret place of the Most High God is made known to those who seek Him from the canyon of their souls.

²The doors to the inner chamber of my heart are open—He is already there awaiting my arrival.

³I will go there, meet with Him, and sit at His feet; there in the secret place He speaks words of promise.

⁴I am overwhelmed that He, the Almighty One, would come into my house; that He, the Holy One, would choose to inhabit my dwelling.

⁵He has shown me mercy and not reproach—because of that I will call this place Hallowed Terra-Firma.

⁶My heart will come barefoot before His majesty—my soul has refused to wear shoes in His presence.

⁷I have reserved myself unto His calling and I set myself apart for His glory.

⁸Come before Him with no other motive or intention except to rendezvous with the King of all Kings and worship His majesty.

⁹Allow your sincerity of heart and your singleness of mind to escort you into His presence—then His pleasure will generously fall upon you like a drenching rain shower.

¹⁰He leads me—and where He goes I will not fear because He is well acquainted with the paths we are walking.

¹¹I will spread His great Word to many people because I love His Word—I will be a conveyor of His glad tidings all of my days.

¹²He has not anointed me to go to the nations—on the contrary—He has directed them to come to me.

¹³The land in which I reside is a melting pot of many nationalities—the Lord God has caused the races of all mankind to make their homes in my nation.

¹⁴I am surrounded by diverse and ethnic peoples who have come a great distance at His command.

¹⁵My praise for His greatness will be heard in their midst—as a result it will carry His great name to many nations without stepping foot off my homeland soil.

¹⁶The prayers of my heart have gone up for many nations even though my feet have never walked their lands.

¹⁷The Lord God has allowed the prayers of the righteous to produce a mighty harvest even to the ends of the earth.

¹⁸By His Spirit He has moved upon the hearts of those they have never seen or met—as a consequence their prayers have drawn them close as a family.

¹⁹The prayers of the godly have advanced His heavenly Kingdom on all sides of the earth—reaching the most insignificant people in the nooks and crannies of our planet.

²⁰He has given me a lifetime appointment to dispense His Good News to a multitude of societies around me.

²¹By His sovereignty His will is accomplished across the lands He created—He loves using hearts yielded unto Him—at times He has used resistant hearts.

²²What if each person you come in contact with had been sent specifically by God?

²³Let this thought guide your heart and transform your walk into light from heaven.

²⁴O that the stones of your altar would be assembled in accordance with His will—as prescribed by His directives—then your offering will bring a pleasing aroma unto Him.

²⁵His pleasure comes from a pure and meditative offering—do not let it consist of whatever you have laying around—He does not look with favor on willy-nilly offerings.

²⁶Do not hold back your best gifts from Him—what on earth are you saving them for?

²⁷His delight is in your highest praise, your most desirable worship, your finest offerings belong to Him alone; He finds great satisfaction in your Sunday best.

²⁸He is honored mostly by a yielded heart and a pure attitude—these He will not turn down.

Psalm 216

Intimacy Brings Almighty Blessing

¹The wisdom of the Almighty is written in the language of man so he might give glory unto Him—the Lord makes plain the complex and simplifies the unimaginable.

²You, O God, have verbalized a tiny portion of Your wisdom into a vocabulary that we might be able to grasp—and yet we still struggle.

³You do not speak with an accent or eloquent speech—so we have no excuse for misunderstanding Your Word.

⁴Humble your heart before Him and let Him come in—He will not hide from those who are sincerely seeking.

⁵Lord—when Your grace stymies me—when it overwhelms me like the waves of the ocean—then I will praise Your name.

⁶Never refuse His gift of mercy just because your feeble mind cannot comprehend it.

⁷Let your heart pull it close and quickly embrace it with gratefulness before your understanding gives it the thumbs-down sign.

⁸The Lord has promised healing for the mind and rest for the soul of those who seek hard after Him.

⁹My God—I want to seek You with a boundless passion—all I am praises You.

¹⁰When this passion wraps around me I will be more than just charmed by You—I will fall deeply in love with You, Lord.

¹¹Who, besides the lowly in heart has heard the voice of the Savior; have the meek not felt the gentle touch of His hand upon them?

¹²It is not those who are high and exalted—those puffed up by their misguided imaginations and their unbridled loftiness—who have been moved by His gentleness.

¹³He will hasten to the side of the poor in spirit—His timeliness will be their comfort.

¹⁴Who am I that You, O Lord, would love me—who am I that You would dole out so much grace upon me—to rescue me from my past?

¹⁵Even if the earth should crumble and fall apart—and all things around me are perishing—my hope is securely in You.

¹⁶I will praise You, Lord, because that is my soul's desire—that is the urging of my heart—then I will seek the intimacy of Your nearness.

¹⁷My praises will approach Your throne even during the bad times—is this not a simple matter when times are good?

¹⁸Let your heart salute His Majesty in reverence—for He is so worthy!

¹⁹Which path could I take that He would not know about—which passage could I follow that would escape His attention?

²⁰My God has become the fullness of my heart—it overflows and runs down the sides of my vessel—when He fills me there is room for no other.

²¹The Lord delights in those who choose to spend time in His presence—He gathers their praises and keeps them close to His heart.

²²The power of darkness has been decimated through the light of Your Word—daily You bring light to the nations through the fellowship of Your saints.

²³Their offerings shine throughout the lands You have placed them in—their lives have been torches to a dark world—one that closes its eyes to the light of Your Word.

²⁴When their intercessory prayers have risen upward like smoke from a burnt offering—all heaven is moved at Your command, O God.

²⁵You unleash Your will and might at their bidding any time it is aligned with Your desires and purpose.

²⁶At times they do not see Your hand moving on their behalf—but their faith keeps them anchored securely to You—the Rock of all hope.

²⁷All heaven is moved by the sounds of their prayers and a great and mighty army is led forth in triumph—it will not shrink in battle.

²⁸You, O Lord, have given purpose to their lives like a multi-pronged fork—the enemy is unable to come against the power of their prayers.

²⁹You have blessed mightily through the simplicity of their prayers—the humility of their hearts has made You rejoice.

³⁰I will praise and exalt my God because He has heard my prayers—those of a yielded heart and a willing spirit.

Psalm 217

Rejoice In The Mile Markers He Places Along The Way

¹The Lord is my protector—He safeguards me from every one of my fears—He is my guardian and defender of all that would come against me.

²He oversees the walks of all who trust in Him—He will usher their every step.

³Deliverance belongs to the mighty—to those who have made Him their stronghold.

⁴The glories of the Lord are revealed unto any who seriously seek Him—to those who do not grow weary probing for His presence.

⁵He has shown me those things I might not have known just because I chose to draw closer to Him.

⁶When I said good morning, Lord—let me hear Your voice when You become my choice—then I could not help but rejoice with gladness.

⁷Make it your aim that every breath—not every four out of five or even two out of three—yes, each and every breath be given unto Him for the glory of His name.

⁸What could be more pleasing to Him than you realizing your purpose in life?

⁹Do you see that place of weakness within you—is it a barrier to your daily walk?

¹⁰Would you be willing to let His Spirit invade that area?—if so, He will bring victory while giving you power to walk in righteousness.

¹¹The Lord has seen the desires of my heart and made good on those that are righteous and upright—any others He has caused to break and fall off.

¹²He has brought those godly desires to pass even in spite of myself—I will not permit the failing of my mind to make me a hostage to pangs of guilt.

¹³When I finally grasped that the King of the universe looked forward to meeting with me—my heart was broken that I had not realized this fact sooner.

¹⁴Now my heart will bow low and I will worship Him with reverence—my soul has seen His beauty and rejoices.

¹⁵I will not fill my remaining days with remorse—I will use every occasion to honor Him with all that is within me.

¹⁶Let the surrender of your heart and strength be lifted unto Him —knowing that He is the lover of your soul.

¹⁷Each time your desires harmonize with His they will be more exquisite than the most beautiful harmonies of a passionate love song.

¹⁸I will trust Him in the questionable moments of life—they may take me by surprise but they never shock Him.

¹⁹The children of God have been scattered throughout the earth in much the same way one randomly places lights on a Christmas tree in order to cover the whole thing.

²⁰It would be illogical to put all the lights on the bottom portion or senseless to put them only on the top half.

²¹Practicality dictates their consistent placement in order to light up the entire tree.

²²Has not God in His wisdom chosen to distribute us across His whole earth so we might show the light of His glory all about?

²³Each of His children should shine His light with the intensity the Holy Spirit gives—so there will be light in all areas of His Kingdom.

²⁴The prayers of His saints have mingled with those of His Spirit and they have become a mighty force to contend with.

²⁵What power of darkness can resist this mighty effort or is able to grapple with the strength of the house of faith?

²⁶His people have armed themselves for battle and with power from on high so that they will withstand every front of the enemy.

²⁷Their prayers of intercession have intruded upon the realms of darkness with increasing fury—causing the powers of heaven to escalate.

²⁸Which dominions are able to withstand the prayers of the righteous when they come in unity?

²⁹The Almighty will be moved on His chosen ones' account and come to their defense—He will not stand idly by—instead He will appear with His heavenly hosts.

³⁰He will lead the redeemed to victory and all heaven and earth will hear them rejoicing.

31The paths of the Lord are secure and those who trust in Him will walk steady.

32Listen closely as I speak words of truth unto you—let them uplift you and point to the better way I have selected.

33"My child—do not take the path of least resistance—that will not lead to the place I have in mind for you to go.

34The way I have chosen is not the easy one—but I will be by your side each step of the way when you trust in Me.

35Do not look at the cloud hanging overhead as a curse—I have sent it to bless and to protect you from the scorching heat of the sun.

36Praise Me through each incident that comes your way—whether good or bad—with this I am pleased.

37Look for the milepost markers I have placed along your journey—use each as a motive to rejoice in the distance you have come.

38I delight to see sweetness in your demeanor and hear the praises of your heart—then your manner will bring glory to My name.

39I will allow nothing to hinder My glory from being seen in all the earth and in the heavens above."

Psalm 218

The Marvels Of His Glory

1He has unearthed the treasures of my heart and stored them in His vault—He has mined them like the diamonds of the earth and placed them in His diadem.

2The treasures of my heart belong to Him—I will not lay claim to any of them—I relinquish all my rights to Him for His glory.

3He finds a resting place in the hearts of all who seek Him—the desires of His heart have become their treasure—and mine.

4Let Him use the songs of your heart to bring Him praise—do not cease to honor Him with your singing.

5Hang onto the Lord with the tenacity of a spider web clinging to a building—when the winds of adversity fiercely blow you will be unaffected and remain unflinchingly His.

⁶The glory of the Lord has appeared unto me—He has spread it out in front of me—and my eyes have witnessed it in the rising and the setting of His great sun.

⁷In the nighttime I have seen it as the numerous amount of stars that blanket the heavens—to man they are without number.

⁸I have beheld it through the eye of the Hubble telescope as it sends pictures of Your vast wonders back to earth.

⁹My mind's eye has been a spectator to Your glories through the insights You send my way—I am staggered by Your greatness—stunned by Your might.

¹⁰When I reflect upon Your glory I am reduced to silence—I get choked up with awe and I am made to hold my tongue.

¹¹He has stripped my pride away and ground it up as the Indians ground their grain with a pestle in a mortar.

¹²O that He would crush my pride like a broken heart after a failed puppy love or pulverize it into a fine powder so a cleansing stream might wash it away.

¹³All that is left is a humbled heart and a repentant spirit—I will now praise Him for His tender mercies—His favor floods me with forgiveness.

Psalm 219

True Worship Knows No Bounds

¹The Lord reigns over all—He abides in the heavens above and in the hearts of all who call upon His name in sincerity.

²Are there any who have breath who have not had the chance to praise and exalt Him?—No, not even one!

³Look inwardly and see if He sits on the throne of your heart and is in charge of all that consumes you.

⁴Let Him rule over all that moves you and give Him praise in the process.

⁵His love captures me like a trussed-up prisoner—only then can I be

Psalm 219 - True Worship Knows No Bounds

under His custody and willingly surrender all to Him.

⁶Daily I come before Him and ask Him to fill my openness so I can continue to draw upon His power each day.

⁷I pray He would be the choice of all mankind and the delight of the whole earth—of all who live and breathe.

⁸Who can deny the existence of his own soul and still speak the truth—if the words a person speaks are not true—then who does he belong to?

⁹As for me I rest in His faithfulness all day long.

¹⁰I grab every chance I have to think of God and His greatness—like someone grasping at straws—I am thankful for every opportunity.

¹¹The Lord has examined and scrutinized my soul and found it wanting—desperately wanting more of His presence.

¹²He will not question my sincerity of heart since He has probed its depth to know it fully.

¹³Each time I yield my weakness unto Him He carries me through in victory.

¹⁴His grace will not allow me to trust in my feelings—otherwise I would live in defeat on a daily basis.

¹⁵His presence is never farther than the skin that covers my bones—He is constantly with me and remains as close as each intake of air.

¹⁶Let the desire of your heart be to worship Him beyond the lifting of hands and uttered prayers—then your adoration will be pleasing unto Him.

¹⁷It must go higher than the smoke of a burnt offering—farther than a rocket to a distant planet—deeper than the deepest parts of the ocean.

¹⁸True worship has learned to conquer the might of distracted thoughts—it has slain worldly desires on the altar of sincerity.

¹⁹When honest praise is offered from a clean heart—He is honored above all.

²⁰I will crucify my weakness of spoken words and let the silence of my soul worship Him in purity—for He alone is Holy.

²¹God, my heart belongs to You—it is Yours and I have determined to rivet it on You all the days of this life.

²²I will let the last little bit of air I breathe praise Your majesty—it will bring honor and glory unto You, my Lord.

Psalm 220

Your Mercies Exceed My Needs

¹Today be snared by righteousness and roused by the Spirit of God so you can give heed to the needs of others.

²Those with a compassionate heart and a ready ear will surely have to face charges of living according to the Gospel.

³Let us stand convicted and plead guilty before His Majesty of these allegations.

⁴His name brings immediate relief to all who call on it—those who come to Him find comfort.

⁵In days gone by my soul was a rebel—now it worships my Creator with complete abandon—in that I find great peace.

⁶My soul will praise Him from the depths of the night until the dawning of the light.

⁷God—I have heard the power of Your might—my own ears have heard its crashing decibels in stereo.

⁸Your mercy has not allowed me to witness its true deafening power—but only sufficiently—so I could get an earful of Your glory.

⁹Yet my soul has heard Your holy whispers through the tumult surrounding me because You have accepted the pursuit of my worship.

¹⁰I will praise You as long as I have breath within me—and when that is no longer possible—my soul will rise to join You in never-ending praise.

¹¹You, my God, have stripped my independence as one removes the old varnish from a piece of wood.

¹²You have exposed me to the core of my being so that You might lacquer me with a fresh coat of dependence on You.

¹³Let the Lord be the splendor of your praise and the aroma of your offering—for this day belongs to Him.

¹⁴Let us eagerly find delight because He has allowed us to share the day with Him.

¹⁵The glory of the Lord has been my shadow all the days of this life—what else could I hope for?

¹⁶I will let my heart melt under the strength of Your Holy Spirit as the snow melts under the intensity of the sun.

17My heart longs to be a burning love that could never rest without You—an unquenchable fire of passion that burns eternal.

18Praises for His glory come bubbling up like a spring of water from the surface of the earth—let us praise His majesty and He will call us nearer than ever before.

19Those in the midst of brightness are unable to see its results—so let faith carry your light farther than you can see.

20His mercies have once again proven greater than my needs—when I awoke I cried unto Him and He was there.

21My strength had vanished—if He had not come to my rescue I would have gone down in a fiery crash—like a fighter pilot in a hail of bullets.

22The weariness of the season had taken its toll and risen against me like a venomous snake in the jungle—hopelessness had left me with only an empty canteen.

23But He poured into me the courage and the hope I was lacking and filled me with His power.

24I would surely have crumbled if He had not come to my aid—the provision He brought to my bedside was more welcome than that of an ambulance.

25He renewed my praise to Him when He came between me and my insufficiency—now I am spoiled by His abundance.

26O Lord—You are my strength and I will definitely praise Your name forever.

Psalm 221

I Will Praise You Beyond The Final Amen

1Time is in the palm of Your hand—yet You do not regard it as Your servant—instead You are head and master over it.

2Come, let us praise Him, everyone;—can any compare to our God or match His majesties?

3Why would He choose to reveal His glories to us mortals—why would He show us His wonders or unveil His secrets?

4So we might have all the more reason to praise Him—or perhaps even attempt to reach out and get

Psalm 221 - I Will Praise You Beyond The Final Amen

in touch with Him.

⁵How excellent are all of Your ways—they are incomparable and absolute—they are lofty and far superior to our knowledge and intellect.

⁶People have come up on the short end of the stick by trying to manipulate You in their minds—they have unwisely sought to contain You.

⁷O Lord, You have allowed their foolishness to lead some into the halls of insanity—those who desired to confine You became nuttier than a fruitcake.

⁸Release from this bondage can come only through praise unto Your great name.

⁹Have you noticed how extremely generous God is to you and given Him thanks for His many blessings—or have you been too preoccupied with hardships to notice them?

¹⁰When I think about His goodness I become aware that His generosities have exceeded my desires.

¹¹I yield myself to You this day, my God—I have no promise of any other.

¹²O God—by Your Holiness—take this weakened flesh and my yielded spirit and use it for Your glory.

¹³I freely admit and concede that in and of myself I have no power of my own.

¹⁴I will gladly surrender my praise to You—not only all the days of this life but all of time that remains, as well.

¹⁵The Lord brings deliverance by the strength of His Word and the power of His great name.

¹⁶My heart will lead me to the foot of His throne and be filled with His goodness.

¹⁷He has given me a heart that is more than glazed pottery—more than just a container to hold His precious Spirit;

¹⁸He has made it of a porous substance so it will absorb the fullness that He empties into it—like a cloth it becomes saturated by His anointing.

¹⁹When His indwelling soaks into the fabric of my being I am made whole.

²⁰And He—the Strong One—will make my life fruitful and it will shine like polished silver—He will permit my latter days to thrive more than the former ones.

21He will redeem my wasted days and require them to fall away—as chaff is blown away from the wheat.

22Will He hold against me forever the indiscretions of my youth? —no, He will make my final days more glorious than those past and I will find favor in His sight.

23Stir within me the song of Abraham—uplift me with the anthem of the redeemed so my spirit will be awakened with pure joy.

24Then I will want no more—all my desires will be fulfilled—in Your presence I will be satisfied as with the final amen.

Psalm 222

His Breath – Is Life

1When does the breath of life enter a man—is it not when he is delivered from the womb—does it not follow him all his appointed days on earth?

2The breath of God is more than the air a man inhales—it is the life of his journey—a delicate thread—merely a strand of hope illustrating our dependence on Him.

3God has placed a revelation of Himself deep within the hearts of all men—once they become aware of it they must act upon His stirrings from on high.

4He requires them to answer His calling from the depths of their souls—for He has planted His seed of love there.

5All matter must have a beginning and an end—even God's celestial bodies wear out.

6Yet when God breathed life into man and gave him an immortal soul—He permitted man to choose where his soul will spend eternity.

7God could not have given a more precious gift to a man—with it he can curse his Creator or he can bless and exalt His heavenly Father—the choice belongs to him.

8I made my choice long ago—God's Spirit has fashioned me—His breath gives me life.

9The wind of His Spirit gives me breath for my sail—I am moved by it in view of His promise.

Psalm 222 - His Breath - Is Life

¹⁰The very worship of my heart is God-breathed—my soul has unearthed a new song for the ages and taught it to my inner man.

¹¹It has translated the wind of my speech into praises for my King.

¹²It has caused my spirit to sing like never before—He smiles with gladness because the stirrings of His life within me bring praise.

¹³He has anointed me with power—with the breath of life I will praise Him all my earthly days.

¹⁴I will bring each thanksgiving unto Him and proclaim His splendor—until the spirit of this life returns to the One who sent it.

¹⁵With my dying gasp I will bear the last injustice of this life resolutely—until I am free in His presence forever.

¹⁶Then my soul will stand breathless before His Majesty and praise Him in a new home for all eternity.

¹⁷I will feel the breath of His kiss on my cheek and dance across the floor of heaven's ballroom.

¹⁸Join me in letting each involuntary breath be one of surrendered praise unto God—let it lift His greatness high.

¹⁹Bring righteous exaltations and the hallowed praises of your heart unto the One who sits on the throne.

²⁰Raise up a cause within my soul that is greater than the air I breathe.

²¹Enable me to be set free from the bonds of this life so I can praise You with winded liberation.

²²Accomplish Your will—O God—through the lives of Your saints—before they expire and breathe their last.

²³To those who have made Him their yearning—on the other side of their last breath stands unending praise and life everlasting.

²⁴Hail—The Almighty—Everlasting—Righteous—Bridegroom as victor over life and death—let your glad hosannas whisper His greatness until they are no more.

To order additional books visit ExaltedWorship.com

Books also available from Amazon.com

Ebooks available from Amazon - Barnes & Noble - iTunes

To contact the author - dwasmundt@exaltedworship.com